Mark

ONE JUMP AHEAD

THE TOP NH HORSES
TO FOLLOW FOR **2020/2021**

THE AUTHOR

Mark Howard is 45 and graduated from Manchester University with a BA Honours Degree in History. For the last 27 years, he has written the National Hunt horses to follow book *One Jump Ahead*. He also writes the Flat racing equivalent, *Ahead On The Flat*. In addition, he appears as a pundit on *Racing TV* (Sky Channel 426) and, prior to that, *Attheraces*. He is also a regular contributor to sportinglife.com and has written for *The Irish Field, Sports Advisor and Racing & Football Outlook (Borderer&Trainer File)*. He is Ambassador for the successful syndicate ValueRacingClub.co.uk

FRONT COVER: *Top 40 Prospects* entry, **FERNY HOLLOW** (Paul Townend) wins the Cheltenham Festival bumper by two and a half lengths in March.

BACK COVER: Another of last year's Top 40 **SHISHKIN** (Nico De Boinville) edges out Abacadabras in the *Skybet* Supreme Novices' Hurdle at Cheltenham.

Front & Back cover photographs supplied by GROSSICK RACING PHOTOGRAPHY. The Steadings, Rockhallhead, Collin, Dumfries DG1 4JW. Telephone: 01387 750 512.

**Published by *Mark Howard Publications Ltd*. 69, Fairgarth Drive, Kirkby Lonsdale, Carnforth, Lancashire. LA6 2FB.
Telephone: 015242 71826
Email: mark.howard@mhpublications.co.uk
Website: www.mhpublications.co.uk**

(Please note: If you are currently NOT on the *Mark Howard Publications* mailing list and you would like to be, and therefore receive all information about future publications then please post / email / phone your name and address to the above).

Printed by H&H REEDS. Southend Road, Penrith, Cumbria CA11 8JH. Telephone: 01768 864214. www.hhreeds.co.uk

All information correct at the time of going to press. Every care is taken with compilation of *One Jump Ahead*, but no responsibility is accepted by the publishers, for error or omissions or their consequences.

ISBN: 978-1-9161259-0-2

CONTENTS

INTRODUCTION

It has been a strange year to say the least – one we have never experienced before and hopefully something we don't endure again anytime soon. The Grand National meeting at Aintree never took place and neither did the Punchestown Festival, but the Cheltenham Festival was squeezed in before lockdown took over. There was nothing new there though with Willie Mullins and Gordon Elliott going hammer and tongs for four days. The pair emerged with seven winners apiece, but it was the former who became leading trainer at the meeting for a seventh time, thanks to his four seconds and six thirds. A four timer on the final afternoon swung it in Ireland's champion trainer's favour with his Festival tally now standing at 72 winners.

Congratulations to Brian Hughes for winning the jockeys' title for the first time. The 34 year old rode 141 winners and was 19 clear of former champion Richard Johnson when racing came to a premature halt in mid March. The northern Irishman became the first northern based rider to win the title since Jonjo O'Neill in 1979/80 and his success was richly deserved. There hasn't been a great deal to shout about as far as northern jump racing is concerned in recent times, so it is a significant boost.

Barry Geraghty announced his retirement from the saddle in July. Aged 40, he is the second most successful jockey of all time at the Cheltenham Festival with 43 winners – only Ruby Walsh has ridden more (59) – and he partnered five of those winners in March, including aboard Epatante in the Champion Hurdle. The Irishman rode 1,920 winners, including a Grand National, two Cheltenham Gold Cups and five Champion Chase winners. Twice champion jockey in Ireland, he was associated with some magnificent horses, including Moscow Flyer and Sprinter Sacre. Geraghty and Nicky Henderson were a potent combination together and it was no surprise when the latter won his first trainer's title for 26 years during the 2012/2013 campaign. That season the likes of Sprinter Sacre, Bobs Worth, Simonsig and Captain Conan were winning Grade 1 races like they were going out of fashion and the fact Geraghty was doing the steering wasn't a coincidence. He was a big race jockey with nerves of steel. The weighing rooms in England and Ireland without messrs Carberry, Fehily, Geraghty, McCoy and Walsh are very different to what they used to be, with only Robbie Power and Davy Russell left from that golden era of top-class Irish National Hunt riders.

Henrietta Knight handed in her licence in 2012 following a very successful training career, which included three Cheltenham Gold Cup wins, a Champion Chase and seven Festival winners in total. Based at West Lockinge Farm near Wantage, Hen is as busy now as she ever was pre training and schooling horses, plus buying and recommending horses for clients. It was announced last year that she has joined forces with North West owner Mike Grech and purchased some exciting young horses, who will be running in his colours this winter. These include high profile acquisitions Gallyhill and Keskonrisk amongst others. I am therefore delighted to include an interview with Hen, who I spoke to during her busy schedule in early September.

Since the last edition of *One Jump Ahead*, we have sadly lost Ferdy Murphy who passed away in September last year. Aged 70, he trained a dozen Cheltenham Festival winners, including the brilliant French Holly, who tragically broke his neck in a schooling fall in November 1999 having won on his chasing debut at Wetherby the previous month. Gold Cup winning trainers Peter Beaumont and Robert Alner also died earlier this year. The former, who will forever be associated with Jodami and other wonderful staying chasers such as Hussard Collonges, Island Chief and Young Kenny, was a true gentleman. Aged 85, he died at the end of March. In many respects, Alner was a similar type of trainer as he, too, excelled with staying chasers, in particular, Cool Ground and Sir Rembrandt.

The coronavirus has meant it has been a tough time for so many within the sport, including owners. Paul and Clare Rooney are now concentrating solely on Flat racing, while Trevor Hemmings has scaled down his string significantly. For different reasons, we will be no longer seeing the brown and beige silks of Andrea and Graham Wylie on our racecourses following their decision to sell their remaining horses. Responsible for 13 Cheltenham Festival winners, six of which were trained by both Howard Johnson and Willie Mullins, plus one for Paul Nicholls, they suffered a wretched time of things during the spring of last year when Ballyward, Invitation Only and Up For Review all lost their lives. That's enough to put anyone off. Horse racing is a fantastic game but a cruel one at times. The memory of Tidal Bay winning the Arkle Trophy under Denis O'Regan in 2008 will never fade though.

Listing the good things that have happened during lockdown can be written on the back of a postage stamp, but it did ensure I watched more French racing than I have ever done in my life during the summer. I have therefore extended the *French Revolution* section in this year's *One Jump Ahead*. With the assistance of former French champion jockey James Reveley, it is hoped there are some exciting prospects amongst the horses covered, especially in the juvenile hurdles department.

The *Talking Trainers* section includes Chris Gordon for the first time. Based at Morestead near Winchester, Chris enjoyed a personal best season last winter with 30 winners and total prize-money just shy of £300,000. Highway One O Two provided the yard with their first Graded winner when taking the Grade 2 Dovecote Novices' Hurdle at Kempton in February. Interviewing Chris was certainly entertaining and he has put together a decent team of horses for the new season.

Thank you once again to Rich Ricci and his racing manager Joe Chambers, who kindly ran through the 'pink and green' stars for the season. Min and Monkfish provided more Festival success last spring and remember the name **HUBRISKO**. Only three, he may not even race this season but is most definitely one for the future.

Finally, thank you to all those who have helped with the production of *One Jump Ahead* – from owners, trainers, jockeys, bloodstock agents, secretaries, photographers, proof readers etc – and subscribers for your continued support, it is much appreciated.

Enjoy the winter.

Mark Howard

FOREWORD
by Nick Luck
Broadcaster of the Year 2007, 2008, 2009, 2011, 2013, 2014 & 2016

To all Jumps fans who would regularly call for a summer break between seasons, 2020 has surely cautioned you to be careful what you wish for. If it seems an age since the last meaningful competition over obstacles, that's because it is. At the time of writing, no National Hunt racing of any consequence has taken place since the well named Indefatigable flew up the hill to land the final race of what will now and forever be known as the most controversial Cheltenham Festival ever to take place.

So much, yet so little, has happened in the interim that when I was presenting (via Zoom, naturally) the Thoroughbred Breeders' Association Jumps awards the other day, I momentarily forgot the name of the Gold Cup winner. The fact that he has won the race twice makes this even less forgivable, although I will maintain that Al Boum Photo is one of the worst names ever dished out to a top class racehorse. I know this is a complete folly of a sidetrack of a complete irrelevance, but I actually believe this ignominy has unfairly diminished his reputation - well, that combined with the fact that he is seen about as often as Halley's Comet.

Happily, there is zero danger of Mark Howard forgetting anything about the winter game, and what lies between the covers of this ever reliable guide will give succour to anyone suffering a bout of amnesia that prevents them recalling the Welsh National winner trained by Christian Williams or the 'good thing' of Willie Mullins that romped in the County Hurdle for J.P. or the forgotten mare who did much the same in the Coral Cup. (They were Potters Corner, Saint Roi and Dame de Compagnie, by the way, and were tipped in Mark's regular *Updates* at odds of 9/1, 20/1 and 10/1).

If there is one less heralded horse that I do remember, however, it is On The Slopes. I had it in my mind quite firmly towards the end of last season that this six year old would continue to make progress, and might even make it to Graded company, and I am really pleased to see an interview with his trainer Chris Gordon make it into *One Jump Ahead* for the first time. Beneath the wisecracking self-deprecation lurks one of the sharpest minds in the game. Joining him among the first timers is Anthony Honeyball, who continues a fairly relentless rise to somewhere near the top.

Of course, we are all looking forward to seeing Envoi Allen, who might be one of the best jumpers we have seen, and I'm particularly excited to see what Albert Bartlett winner Monkfish might do as he continues to furnish - no doubt you'll find out more in Mark's exclusive interview with Rich Ricci.

It has been a tough year for everyone, some more than others, but a positive is that racing has shown it can be a viable sport even in the most taxing of circumstances. We know that nothing will quite be the same; that Cheltenham next March may only be able to provide half the roar. But the quality of the sport will not be diminished and, if this book reminds you of anything, it's that it will be worth the wait.

TYPE OF TRACK

AINTREE	National Course	Left-Handed, Galloping
	Mildmay Course	Left-Handed, Tight
ASCOT		Right-Handed, Galloping
AYR		Left-Handed, Galloping
BANGOR-ON-DEE		Left-Handed, Tight
CARLISLE		Right-Handed, Stiff / Undulating
CARTMEL		Left-Handed, Tight
CATTERICK BRIDGE		Left-Handed, Tight / Undulating
CHELTENHAM		Left-Handed, Stiff / Undulating
CHEPSTOW		Left-Handed, Stiff / Undulating
DONCASTER		Left-Handed, Galloping
EXETER		Right-Handed, Stiff / Undulating
FAKENHAM		Left-Handed, Tight / Undulating
FFOS LAS		Left-Handed, Galloping
FONTWELL PARK	Chase Course	Figure of Eight, Tight
	Hurdle Course	Left-Handed, Tight
HAYDOCK PARK	Chase Course	Left-Handed, Galloping
	Hurdle Course	Left-Handed, Tight
HEREFORD		Right-Handed, Tight
HEXHAM		Left-Handed, Stiff / Undulating
HUNTINGDON		Right-Handed, Galloping
KELSO		Left-Handed, Tight / Undulating
KEMPTON PARK		Right-Handed, Tight
LEICESTER		Right-Handed, Stiff / Undulating
LINGFIELD PARK		Left-Handed, Tight / Undulating
LUDLOW		Right-Handed, Tight
MARKET RASEN		Right-Handed, Tight /Undulating
MUSSELBURGH		Right-Handed, Tight
NEWBURY		Left-Handed, Galloping
NEWCASTLE		Left-Handed, Galloping
NEWTON ABBOT		Left-Handed, Tight
PERTH		Right-Handed, Tight
PLUMPTON		Left-Handed, Tight / Undulating
SANDOWN PARK		Right-Handed, Galloping
SEDGEFIELD		Left-Handed, Tight / Undulating
SOUTHWELL		Left-Handed, Tight
STRATFORD-UPON-AVON		Left-Handed, Tight
TAUNTON		Right-Handed, Tight
TOWCESTER		Right-Handed, Stiff / Undulating
UTTOXETER		Left-Handed, Tight / Undulating
WARWICK		Left-Handed, Tight / Undulating
WETHERBY		Left-Handed, Galloping
WINCANTON		Right-Handed, Galloping
WORCESTER		Left-Handed, Galloping

IRELAND

BALLINROBE	Right-Handed, Tight
BELLEWSTOWN	Left-Handed, Tight / Undulating
CLONMEL	Right-Handed, Tight / Undulating
CORK	Right-Handed, Galloping
DOWNPATRICK	Right-Handed, Tight / Undulating
DOWN ROYAL	Right-Handed, Tight / Undulating
FAIRYHOUSE	Right-Handed, Galloping
GALWAY	Right-Handed, Tight / Undulating
GOWRAN PARK	Right-Handed, Tight / Undulating
KILBEGGAN	Right-Handed, Tight / Undulating
KILLARNEY	Left-Handed, Tight
LEOPARDSTOWN	Left-Handed, Galloping
LIMERICK	Right-Handed, Galloping
LISTOWEL	Left-Handed, Tight
NAAS	Left-Handed, Galloping
NAVAN	Left-Handed, Galloping
PUNCHESTOWN	Right-Handed, Galloping
ROSCOMMON	Right-Handed, Tight
SLIGO	Right-Handed, Tight / Undulating
THURLES	Right-Handed, Tight / Undulating
TIPPERARY	Left-Handed, Tight
TRAMORE	Right-Handed, Tight
WEXFORD	Left-Handed, Tight

ACKNOWLEDGEMENTS

I would like to thank all the following Trainers who have given up their time, during the summer, to answer my inquiries:

Talking Trainers: Kim Bailey, Harry Fry, Chris Gordon, Philip Hobbs, Anthony Honeyball, Alan King, Tom Lacey, Olly Murphy, Paul Nicholls, Jonjo O'Neill (and Joe O'Neill), David Pipe, Nicky Richards, Brian Ellison. Thank you also to the following secretaries for organising the appointments/answering queries: Sarah (Paul Nicholls), James (David Pipe), Carolyn Harty (Nicky Henderson), Antonia Reid (Nicky Richards), Dawn (Henrietta Knight).

Thank you also to Anthony Bromley, David Minton & Bernice Emanuel (Highflyer Bloodstock), Nick Luck (Foreword), Declan Phelan (Ireland), Jared Sullivan, James Reveley, Henrietta Knight, Mags O'Toole, Bobby O'Ryan, Rich Ricci, Joe Chambers (Racing Manager), Michael Shinners & Oliver Gray *(Skybet)*, Fran Berry, Jonathan Neesom *(Racing TV)*, Scott Salkeld, Kevin Blake, James Couldwell (ValueRacingclub. co.uk).

The TOP 40 PROSPECTS FOR 2020/2021

ADRIMEL (FR)

5 bb g Tirwanako (FR) – Irise De Gene (FR) (Blushing Flame (USA))
OWNER: Lady BAMFORD & ALICE BAMFORD
TRAINER: T.LACEY. Woolhope, Herefordshire.
CAREER FORM FIGURES: 1 - 110
CAREER WINS: 2019: Mar BALLYARTHUR Soft/Heavy 4YO PTP 3m; Dec UTTOXETER
Heavy NHF 2m: 2020: Feb DONCASTER Soft NHF 2m

Owner Lady Bamford made two expensive purchases during the spring of last year. Winning Irish pointer Adrimel was acquired for £280,000 at the Goffs UK Aintree Sale, then over a month later she wrote out a cheque for £340,000 for Huntingdon bumper winner Mister Coffey at the Goffs UK Spring Sale at Doncaster. The pair are both featured in this season's *Top 40 Prospects.*

Regular readers will be aware that the former was one of Declan Phelan's *Irish Pointers* in last year's *One Jump Ahead*and he wrote: **"The point to point track of Ballyarthur, which lies within a mile of the town of Fermoy, is one which places an emphasis on stamina: it can be punishing for younger horses and the two maidens it staged for four year olds in 2019 (one for mares, the other for geldings) clocked the two slowest recorded times for races in the four year old class of 2019: 7.38 and 7.26, the latter for the geldings race, which was won by Adrimel. With the ground riding on the soft to heavy side, the ability to stay the trip was of paramount importance. Adrimel is a tall bay gelding with four white socks around his hooves.He had been brought to Ireland from his native France by bloodstock agent J.D. Moore and purchased for less than ten grand by the Ryans from Clare. Joe Ryan and his son Josh (works as a pilot with Ryanair), have a healthy win strike-rate with their small squad and their charges are inevitably ready to roll on debuts. With James Hannon in the saddle, Adrimel led from the start, jumping fluently: he increased the pace on the climb to the third last and all but one of his rivals had surrendered as he raced towards the final fence, he popped it safely to score by an easy eight lengths. He is a son of a little-known French sire and there is one familiar name on his page, that of Halcon Genelardais...he was a proper mudlark, who won the 2006 Welsh Grand National. Another link to the same Welsh National, is that the 2018 runner up, Ramses De Teillee happened to win his maiden point at Ballyarthur, the 2016 version. The signs are that Adrimel could be destined one day to play a leading role in a soft/ground staying marathon over fences."**

The Tirwanako gelding joined Tom Lacey last season and developed into a useful bumper performer winning two out of three. Fitted with a tongue tie for his Rules debut at Uttoxeter shortly before Christmas, Adrimel ploughed through the heavy ground making all and winning by twenty six lengths. Ironically, another former Lacey inmate King Roland had won the same event twelve months earlier by twenty two lengths. Withdrawn from a Listed bumper at Newbury in February, due to the drying ground, he successfully carried his penalty to victory later the same month at Doncaster. Racing prominently, he got the better of a protracted duel with the highly regarded The Edgar Wallace (won easily since) conceding seven pounds to Kim Bailey's runner-up. The pair pulled over twenty lengths clear of the third in a race which has been contested by the likes of Black Op, Claimantakinforgan, Rather Be and Two For Gold in recent years. Well held in the Festival bumper at Cheltenham in March, he raced handily and was wide approaching the home straight but lacked the acceleration thereafter. Champion jockey Richard Johnson said beforehand: **"Adrimel is an extremely nice horse who loves very soft ground. He almost finds heavy ground as easy to get over as good ground."**

Two and a half miles plus novice hurdles on easy ground will be the order of the day this season for Adrimel. Reported to have thrived during the summer, Tom Lacey is understandably excited about the winter ahead.

POINTS TO NOTE:

Probable Best Distance	-	2m 4f - 3 miles
Preferred Going	-	Soft/Heavy

Connection's Comments: "We're very fortunate to have a lovely horse in Adrimel." Tom LACEY at Doncaster (19/2/20)

GOING:	R	W	P	TRACK:	R	W	P
Heavy	1	1	0	Left Handed	4	3	0
Soft/Heavy	1	1	0	Galloping	1	1	0
Soft	2	1	0	Stiff/Undul.	1	0	0
				Tight/Undul.	1	1	0

TRIP:	R	W	P	JOCKEY:	R	W	P
2m	3	2	0	R.Johnson	2	1	0
3m	1	1	0	N.De Boinville	1	1	0
				J.Hannon	1	1	0

AMARILLO SKY (IRE)

4 b g Westerner – Bag of Tricks (IRE) (Flemensfirth (USA))
OWNER: J.P.ROMANS & TAYLOR, O'DWYER
TRAINER: C.TIZZARD. Milborne Port, Dorset.
CAREER FORM FIGURES: 1
CAREER WIN: 2020: Mar BORRIS HOUSE Yielding/Soft 4YO PTP 3m

Despite a disappointing few days at the Cheltenham Festival – the stable's seventeen runners produced form figures of 0P734P6FP0P00PP30 – Colin Tizzard had another very good campaign with 61 winners and total prize-money of £1,216,570. Lostintranslation (*Betfair Chase*), Slate House (Kauto Star Novices' Chase) and Fiddlerontheroof (Tolworth Novices' Hurdle) were Grade 1 winners, while the first named ran a cracker to finish third in the Cheltenham Gold Cup.

An already powerful team of horses has been bolstered during the spring/summer with some exciting new additions. The Irish pointing field has been a rich source of success for the Tizzard outfit and they have recruited Shirocco's Dream (£260,000), Killer Kane (£300,000) and this unbeaten Westerner gelding for £280,000.

Irish point expert Declan Phelan takes up the story: **"With former Gold Cup winner Native River, leading current chaser Lostintranslation and budding starlet The Big Breakaway amongst past horses sourced from Irish pointing ranks, the Tizzard yard continues to trust and invest heavily in such stock. At the Cheltenham March sales, they shelled out £280,000 to add this youngster to their string. A powerfully built bay son of Westerner, who sports a white blaze on his face, he recorded the fastest time on the Borris (Yielding/ Soft) card in March. Representing Colin Bowe in that point, he was confidently handled by Barry O'Neill, sited close to the pace until taking the pole position entering the final mile. From the third last, the race whittled down to a match between himself and Tag Man. In the end, Amarillo Sky kept his rival at bay, scoring by three parts of a length, perhaps with something left in reserve. A feature of his win was his accurate slick jumping and, although this point win was registered over the three mile distance, this** four year old could be even more effective over shorter trips. He displayed a smooth action and may be able to handle soft and good ground. His pedigree traces to the "Trix" line with Atone a prominent name in the family tree. Capable of figuring up to Grade 3 level over hurdles in his novice season, he may upgrade to a higher class when he switches to chasing in a few years down the line."

POINTS TO NOTE:
Probable Best Distance	-	2m 4f –3 miles	
Preferred Going	-	Soft	

GOING:	R	W	P	TRACK:	R	W	P
Yielding/Soft	1	1	0	Left Handed	1	1	0

TRIP:	R	W	P	JOCKEY:	R	W	P
3m	1	1	0	B.O'Neill	1	1	0

BALLYADAM (IRE)

5 b g Fame And Glory – Grass Tips (IRE) (Bob Back (USA))
OWNER: CHEVELEY PARK STUD
TRAINER: G.ELLIOTT. Longwood, Co.Meath.
CAREER FORM FIGURES: 131
CAREER WINS: 2019: Oct PORTRUSH Yielding/Soft 4YO Mdn PTP 3m: 2020: Mar DOWNPATRICK Yielding NHF 2m 1f

It was another tremendous season for Cheveley Park Stud with a dozen winners in Ireland (a trio of Grade 1 wins) and a further three in the UK. Two of those successes came at the Cheltenham Festival with Envoi Allen maintaining his unbeaten record in the Ballymore Novices' Hurdle, while Ferny Hollow provided the Newmarket based team with their second consecutive win in the Festival bumper.

That pair were recruited from the Irish pointing field and their famous red, white and blue silks will be sported by three more ex-pointers this season, namely Ballyadam (£330,000), Rose of Arcadia (£170,000) and Sir Gerhard (£400,000). The trio look horses of huge potential with their owners set for another productive campaign.

Ballyadam, a gelding by Fame And Glory, began his career with Colin McKeever in Ireland, as expert Declan Phelan explains: **"One of the most impressive four year maiden winners from the pre-Christmas autumn session. In a strongly run race at Portrush (Yielding/ Soft), he was stationed in midfield until asked to improve on the downhill sweep to the second last. Charging home with intent, he jumped to the front at the final fence and kicked clear to win by four lengths. In winning, he clocked a time of 6m 30seconds, which was 17 seconds faster than the next best that afternoon: a noteworthy comparison is with Finian's Oscar who won the 2016 version of this race: on much faster ground, Finian's posted a time of 6.25, so all told, in terms of times, the 2019 victory of Ballyadam stood out as an excellent performance. Naturally, he became a much soughtafter commodity and owner Wilson Dennison elected to sell this tall elegant bay gelding at Cheltenham November Sales and he netted a price of £330,000 with Gordon Elliott purchasing him on behalf of Cheveley Park Stud. He raced on the track proper twice in 2020, in a pair of bumpers. He suffered a setback when beaten at cramped odds on his track debut at Navan: the slow early pace through the first mile compromised him as he raced too freely and, at the business end, he paid for the wasted energy out the country, as he had to accept a close third. At Downpatrick in**

March, he routed modest rivals as he posted a runaway 18 lengths bumper success. A sibling of Legal Eyes (current 137 chaser), the family tree traces back to Commerical Artist and Mass Appeal, above average chasers who were effective at a variety of distances. Ballyadam will be happiest when encountering true run races and therefore he may develop into a Grade 2 or 3 novice hurdler, and perhaps more as a chaser in time. That defeat at Navan would tend to suggest that, whilst he may be a high class jumper in the making, he may lack the star quality to reach the top of the tree."

Well supported for the Cheltenham Festival bumper, prior to his Rules debut at Navan in February, he was beaten two and a quarter lengths behind Julies Stowaway with Gordon Elliott commenting: **"I was disappointed with Ballyadam at Navan on Sunday – he was too keen. I still think he's a nice horse."** Reappearing a month later, the five year old was sent off 1/6 favourite for a similar event at Downpatrick and easily beat a dozen rivals by upwards of eighteen lengths. **"It was very heavy ground he got beaten on at Navan and he was a bit raw, but he couldn't do any more today and Jamie (Codd) was very impressed with him. He has a big future,"** remarked his trainer afterwards. Given the fact Ballyadam appreciates a strongly run race, the *Skybet* Supreme or Ballymore Novices' Hurdle are his most likely targets at the Festival in March.

POINTS TO NOTE:
Probable Best Distance   -   2m 4f
Preferred Going   -   Good/Soft
Connection's Comments: "We gave him a little tip around in a schooling race last Tuesday at Moira. Stephen (Connor) rode him and thought he was a little free, but I said he won't be free in a four year old maiden. He has always worked like he would go and do something like that. He is just a lovely horse and is the makings of a Grade 1 performer." Former trainer Colin McKEEVER speaking after his point-to-point win at Portrush (19/3/20)

GOING:	R	W	P	TRACK	R	W	P
Heavy	1	0	1	Left Handed	2	1	1
Yielding/Soft	1	1	0	Right	1	1	0
Yielding	1	1	0	Galloping	1	0	1
				Tight/Undul.	1	1	0

TRIP:	R	W	P	JOCKEY:	R	W	P
2m	1	0	1	J.J.Codd	2	1	1
2m 1f	1	1	0	S.Connor	1	1	0
3m	1	1	0				

BOB OLINGER (IRE)
5 b g Sholokhov (IRE) – Zenaide (IRE) (Zaffaran (USA))
OWNER: ROBCOUR
TRAINER: H.DE BROMHEAD. Knockeen, Co.Waterford.
CAREER FORM FIGURES: 11
CAREER WINS: 2019: Nov TURTULLA Yielding 4YO Mdn PTP 3m: 2020: Mar GOWRAN PARK Soft/Heavy NHF 2m 2f

"Bred by the Parkhill family (producers of Granville Again/Morley Street), this well proportioned bay gelding debuted at Turtulla (Yielding) in November and blew away his rivals over the final mile to post a fifteen lengths success. I noted he got a little low at some fences, though it did not hinder his momentum. A private sale mid-winter resulted

in a move to Henry de Bromhead and he maintained a pristine record as he made all for an untroubled success in the 2m2f pointers bumper at Gowran (Soft/Heavy) in March. Judged on these two performances, he deserves to be rated amongst the top three in the five year old age bracket from the 2019/20 point campaign. His half brother, Feel The Pulse, commanded a price of £330,000 following his point win and another sibling, Myska was a 140 rated listed winner over hurdles. Another half sister, Daring Carlotta was a three times bumper winner on fast ground. He is a relaxed mover and could be versatile in terms of terrain preference. He has led for the majority of his two starts to date and is an uncomplicated ride. One can reason he has not been tested, however he possesses a touch of class and I suspect that when competing over hurdles and fences, he can maintain a positive win strike rate. Facing into a season of novice hurdling, he will figure in the two and a half miles and upwards Graded events, and for now it is difficult to predict if he will develop into a Ballymore or Albert Bartlett contender. He is more than capable of bagging at the very least a Grade 3 novice hurdle and more this winter and, in due course, he will be an exciting chaser in the Robcour silks," believes point expert Declan Phelan.

A ten lengths winner of a point-to-point bumper at Gowran Park in March, that contest has been won by subsequent Cheltenham Festival winners First Lieutenant (2010) and Yorkhill (2015), plus Bob Olinger's new stablemate Minella Melody (2019). Having made all under Patrick Mullins, his trainer Henry De Bromhead commented: "Bob Olinger is an exciting horse. I was concerned about the ground being a bit too soft. He has worked well on good ground and up the sand at the Curragh, so better ground shouldn't be a problem."

Regular readers of One Jump Ahead will be aware that the same owner's GIN ON LIME was featured in last year's Top 40 Prospects. A winner over hurdles in France when trained by Guillaume Macaire, the daughter of Doctor Dino finished fourth and third at Fairyhouse and Naas respectively in two starts for Jessica Harrington. Rated 131, the four year old filly has been transferred to Henry De Bromhead and it will be interesting to see how she progresses this winter.

POINTS TO NOTE:
Probable Best Distance   -   2m 4f +
Preferred Going   -   Good/Soft
Connection's Comments: "He's a smashing horse and I thought the world of him all year and we just weren't having a lot of luck." His former trainer Pat DOYLE speaking at Turtulla (17/11/19)

GOING:	R	W	P	TRACK	R	W	P
Soft/Heavy	1	1	0	Right	2	2	0
Yielding	1	1	0	Tight/Undul.	1	1	0

TRIP:	R	W	P	JOCKEY:	R	W	P
2m 2f	1	1	0	P.W.Mullins	1	1	0
3m	1	1	0	B.W.Harvey	1	1	0

BRANDY LOVE (IRE)

4 b f Jet Away – Bambootcha (IRE) (Saddlers' Hall (IRE))
TRAINER: W.P.MULLINS. Bagenalstown, Co.Carlow.
CAREER FORM FIGURES: 1
CAREER WIN: 2020: Feb CRAGMORE Heavy 4YO Mdn PTP 3m

Willie Mullins has trained some exceptional mares over the years, including Champion Hurdle winner Annie Power and French champion hurdle winner Benie Des Dieux. The Closutton team is once again responsible for a strong team of fillies and mares and it was further strengthened in February when the once raced Brandy Love was purchased for £200,000 at the Cheltenham Sale. The daughter of Jet Away was an eight lengths winner of her only point-to-point in Ireland when handled by Colin Bowe six days earlier. Agent Harold Kirk was delighted to have bought the four year old saying: **"We always buy fillies as there's a great programme for them in England and Ireland now. She's a brilliant jumper, a fabulous jumper, so hopefully she'll jump fences one day. She showed a lot of class against the geldings. I didn't think we'd have to give that much for her, but to me, she's the best racehorse here today. Hopefully she'll be back here running in the fillies' chase."**

Point expert Declan Phelan also feels Brandy Love is a filly with a bright future saying: **"Medium sized bay lady with a white blaze on her face: the sole mare to defeat a field of geldings in a mixed four year old maiden in the spring. In that race over 2m4f at Cragmore (Heavy) in February, she was to the fore throughout and accelerated clear from her five rivals from the second last to register an eight lengths success for the Colin Bowe team. On the back of this performance, Willie Mullins paid a price of £200,000 to acquire her via the February Cheltenham sales. In recent years, the winners of the Cragmore four year old maiden have failed to live up to initial expectations: the 2019 victor, Wide Receiver, a prime example. He recorded a time nearly twenty seconds faster than Brandy Love in the 2020 edition (albeit on less testing ground). This mare is a half-sister to the 140 rated chaser Topofthecotswolds and her dam, a three times winner for Colm Murphy won a race at the 2008 Punchestown Festival. In general, most of the family produce their premium efforts on a sound surface, so Brandy Love having posted a win on heavy, could be more lethal on a better surface. She has gears and I rate her the top four year pointing mare of the shortened spring season in 2020. Winning a bumper will be a formality and she will be a factor in the premier mares' bumpers this winter."**

In other news from the stable, another four year old filly who has created a good impression since joining Mullins is the dual winner **FINEST EVERMORE**. A daughter of Yeats who finished runner-up in a junior bumper at Exeter last Autumn when trained by Harry Kelly, she won by five and a half lengths on her first run for her new yard at Cork in July when scoring by twenty three lengths on her hurdles bow at Tipperary (2m 4f : Soft) the following month. She has subsequently been bought by **John Turner**, who is also responsible for stablemate Buildmeupbuttercup.

POINTS TO NOTE:
Probable Best Distance   -   2 miles
Preferred Going   -   Soft
Connection's Comments: **"She is smart and Barry (O'Neill) said that she would have gone around again." Colin BOWE speaking after her point-to-point win at Cragmore (15/2/20)**

GOING:	R	W	P	TRACK:	R	W	P
Heavy	1	1	0	Left-Handed	1	1	0

TRIP:	R	W	P	JOCKEY:	R	W	P
2m 4f	1	1	0	B.O'Neill	1	1	0

BRING ON THE NIGHT

3 ch g Gleneagles (IRE) – Brasileira (Dubai Destination (USA))
OWNER: Mrs J.DONNELLY
TRAINER: W.P.MULLINS. Bagenalstown, Co.Carlow.
CAREER FLAT FORM FIGURES: 811
CAREER FLAT WINS: 2020: Mar COMPIEGNE Heavy Mdn 1m 4f; May DEAUVILLE Standard Conditions 1m 4f

Bookmaker turned investor and increasingly high profile owner Joe Donnelly enjoyed a memorable Festival in March. Al Boum Photo won the Cheltenham Gold Cup for a second successive year, while Shishkin got the better of Abacadabras in an epic duel in the *Skybet Supreme Novices' Hurdle*. Melon was denied by a nose in the JLT Novices' Chase and Asterion Forlonge wasn't disgraced in fourth in the Festival opener either.

With Asterion Forlonge, Shishkin and The Big Getaway set to go chasing, plus Melon could tackle three miles for the first time this winter, Donnolly has a huge amount to look forward to. His familiar yellow and black silks will also be sported by exciting Flat recruit Bring On The Night. A half-brother to Joseph O'Brien's Listed winner and Group 1 fifth Bolleville, he won two of his three starts for Andre Fabre earlier this year. Unraced at two, the chestnut was slowly away on his debut on the all-weather at Chantilly in early March before staying on in eighth over an inadequate nine furlongs. Reappearing thirteen days later and switching to turf at Compiegne, the son of Gleneagles relished the step up to a mile and a half and ran out an easy three and a half lengths winner. Held up, he made good headway under Pierre-Charles Boudot before pulling clear in the homestraight. Back in action a couple of months later, he beat six rivals in a twelve furlongs conditions event at Deauville in May. A three parts of a length winner, the third and fourth have scored since.

Purchased soon afterwards, Bring On The Night has been gelded since joining Willie Mullins. Proven in testing ground, he stays well and is lightly raced. Ireland's champion trainer won the Triumph Hurdle in March with a similar type, namely Burning Victory, who was a twelve furlongs winner on the Flat in France. He may have recruited a leading contender for the 2021 version.

POINTS TO NOTE:
Probable Best Distance	-	2 miles	
Preferred Going	-	Good/Soft	

GOING:	R	W	P	TRACK:	R	W	P
Standard	2	1	0	Left Handed	1	1	0
Heavy	1	1	0	Right	2	1	0
				Galloping	3	2	0

TRIP:	R	W	P	JOCKEY:	R	W	P
1m 1f	1	0	0	P.Boudot	3	2	0
1m 4f	2	2	0				

CAMPROND (FR)

4 b g Lope De Vega (IRE) – Bernieres (IRE) (Montjeu (IRE))
OWNER: J.P.McMANUS
TRAINER: P.J.HOBBS. Minehead, Somerset.
CAREER FLAT FORM FIGURES: 4 - 54181621
CAREER FLAT WINS: 2019: Mar PORNICHET Standard Mdn 1m 4f; Jun SAINT-CLOUD
Soft Hcap 1m 2f; Sept SAINT-CLOUD Very Soft Hcap 1m 4f

Philip Hobbs has taken charge of this three times Flat winner in France and the Lope De
Vega gelding appears to have all the ingredients to make a smart novice hurdler this season.
A half-brother to compatriot Berjou, who is a Listed hurdle and chase winner and third
behind Benie Des Dieux in the French champion Hurdle at Auteuil during the same year, he
was bought by J.P.McManus during the Autumn of 2019 and has been given plenty of time
to mature.

Trained across the English Channel by Pia Brandt, Camprond only raced once as a two year
old but won three of his eight races the following season. He is a horse who liked to race
prominently on the Flat and wore a hood. He appreciated the step up to a mile and a half for
the first time at Pornichet in March winning his maiden at the fourth time of asking by seven
and a half lengths. Taking over approaching the home turn, he powered clear before being
eased down close home by Cristian Demuro. A short neck winner of a ten furlongs handicap
at Saint-Cloud in June, he was sixth in Listed company at Deauville (1m 6f : Good) next time
Half a length runner-up in another handicap at Chantilly in late August, he then made all in a
twelve furlongs handicap at Saint-Cloud in September. Given a positive ride by Demuro, he
made all and ploughed through the testing ground to win by nine lengths.

Camprond is effective on slow ground, he stays well and the time off since his last run on
the Flat won't have done him any harm. The four year old has reportedly settled in well to his
new surroundings at Minehead and Philip Hobbs and J.P.McManus may have another classy
hurdler on their hands.

POINTS TO NOTE:

Probable Best Distance	-	2 miles
Preferred Going	-	Good/Soft

GOING:	R	W	P	TRACK:	R	W	P
Standard	4	1	0	Left-Handed	3	3	0
Very Soft	1	1	0	Right	6	0	1
Soft	1	1	0	Galloping	9	3	1
Good/Soft	2	0	1				
Good	1	0	0				

TRIP:	R	W	P	JOCKEY:	R	W	P
1m 1f	3	0	0	C.Demuro	6	3	1
1m 2f	2	1	0	M.Demuro	1	0	0
1m 4f	3	2	1	J.Monteiro	2	0	0
1m 6f	1	0	0				

CAP DU MATHAN (FR)

5 b g Kapgarde (FR) – Nounjya Du Mathan (FR) (Antarctique (IRE))
OWNER: The STEWART FAMILY
TRAINER: P.F.NICHOLLS. Ditcheat, Somerset.
CAREER FORM FIGURES: 42 - 6331
CAREER WIN: 2020: Jan PLUMPTON Heavy MH 2m

The ex-French trained gelding is included in the *Top 40 Prospects* for a second successive year (one of eight horses who featured in the same section last season) following an educational season over hurdles last winter. Rated 128, the five year old may have another run over the smaller obstacles, but it won't be long before Cap Du Mathan embarks on his chasing career and takes advantage of a lenient looking mark.

Twice raced in his native France under the tutelage of Arnaud Chaille-Chaille, he was subsequently bought by Anthony Bromley on behalf of Andy Stewart and joined Paul Nicholls. Reportedly in need of the outing on his British debut at Cheltenham's showcase meeting in October, Cap Du Mathan finished sixth behind subsequent winners Master Debonair (rated 149) and Fred (144). Third on his next two starts at Chepstow over two miles and two miles three, he ran particularly well on the latter occasion on Welsh National day. Despite being fitted with a hood for the first time, Bryony Frost's mount tanked through the race but was still in front between the final two flights. Beaten less than six lengths by Harry Senior (won a Grade 2 next time), it was a very good run considering the Kapgarde gelding had raced keenly throughout on heavy ground at one of the stiffest tracks in the country. A month later, Paul Nicholls' charge dropped back to the minimum trip at Plumpton and scored with the minimum of fuss. With the headgear discarded and Harry Cobden back in the saddle, Cap Du Mathan made all and strolled to a twelve lengths win.

Only raised a pound since, the five year old will appreciate stepping in distance as he learns to settle. A very good jumper, he will come into his own over fences and will be hard to beat in a novices' handicap chase off his current rating. Indeed, one envisages Cap Du Mathan reaching a much higher mark over the larger obstacles. The former champion trainer has purposely given him time to mature and that kindness is set to be rewarded.

POINTS TO NOTE:
Probable Best Distance   -   2m 4f – 3 miles
Preferred Going   -   Soft
Connection's Comments: "He's improving all the time, he's a beautiful model of a horse and he'll be a serious chaser one day. He's actually not a two miler as he's quite slow – he'll be running over three miles one day. We've got a lot to look forward to with him." Harry COBDEN at Plumpton (27/1/20)

GOING:	R	W	P	TRACK:	R	W	P
Heavy	3	1	2	Left Handed	6	1	3
Very Soft	1	0	0	Galloping	2	0	1
Soft	1	0	1	Stiff/Undul.	3	0	2
Good/Soft	1	0	0	Tight/Undul.	1	1	0

TRIP:	R	W	P	JOCKEY:	R	W	P
2m	3	1	1	H.Cobden	3	1	1
2m 1f	1	0	1	B.Frost	1	0	1
2m 2f	1	0	0	P.Dubourg	2	0	1
2m 3f	1	0	1				

CHANTRY HOUSE (IRE)

6 br g Yeats (IRE) – The Last Bank (IRE) (Phardante (FR))
OWNER: J.P.McMANUS
TRAINER: N.J.HENDERSON. Lambourn, Berkshire.
CAREER FORM FIGURES: U11 - 113
CAREER WINS: 2018: Dec TATTERSALLS FARM Yielding/Soft 4YO Mdn PTP 3m: 2019:
Mar WARWICK Soft NHF 2m; Dec CHELTENHAM Good/Soft NH 2m 1f: 2020: Feb
NEWBURY Good NH 2m

Another from last year's *Top 40* who features once again, the former Irish pointer Chantry House goes chasing for the first time and looks a prime candidate for races such as the Scilly Isles Novices' Chase at Sandown – a race his trainer has won six times – and the JLT Novices' Chase at the Cheltenham Festival, a prize which has thus far eluded Nicky Henderson.

Trained in Ireland by Cian Hughes, the Yeats gelding won the second of his two points before being bought for £295,000 at the Cheltenham December Sale in 2018. A bumper winner at Warwick the following March, the six year old made his hurdles debut at Cheltenham in December and ran out a comfortable one and three quarters of a lengths victor from subsequent Grade 2 winner Stolen Silver. The fourth Pileon won his next two outings before being beaten a short head in the Martin Pipe Conditional Jockeys' Handicap Hurdle at the same track in March. Denied an outing at Newbury in mid January, due to 'a nick on one of his legs which blew up,' the half-brother to The Last Day successfully carried his penalty to victory at the Berkshire track the following month. Barry Geraghty's mount moved smoothly throughout and, once hitting the front at the last, he pulled away for a four and a half lengths win. With the same owner's Sporting John lining up in the Ballymore Novices' Hurdle at Cheltenham, J.P.McMANUS and Henderson elected to run Chantry House in the *Skybet* Supreme Novices' Hurdle. While he ran well in third, he couldn't match either stablemate Shishkin or Abacadabras for speed and was readily left behind on the hometurn. **"It was a great run and Chantry House kept going really well, but the winner was really good. I missed the flight at the top of the hill, but it didn't really make a difference,"** commented Geraghty afterwards.

Yet to race beyond two miles under Rules, Chantry House will come into his own over longer trips over fences. A tall bay gelding, he reportedly jumped cleanly and accurately in his points and should develop into a top-class novice this winter.

POINTS TO NOTE:
Probable Best Distance   -   2m 4f - 3 miles
Preferred Going   -   Good/Soft
Connection's Comments: **"He's a smart horse and was very green when he won at Cheltenham last time. We know he stays and he's got speed. I'd be surprised if he didn't want another half a mile, but Barry (Geraghty) said he races very sweetly, you just press a button and it works." Nicky HENDERSON at Newbury (8/2/20)**

GOING:	R	W	P	TRACK:	R	W	P
Soft	2	1	1	Left-Handed	4	3	1
Good/Soft	1	1	0	Right	2	1	0
Yielding	2	1	0	Galloping	1	1	0
Good	1	1	0	Stiff/Undul.	2	1	1
				Tight/Undul.	1	1	0

TRIP:	R	W	P	JOCKEY:	R	W	P
2m	3	2	1	B.Geraghty	4	3	1
2m 1f	1	1	0	J.Codd	1	1	0
3m	2	1	0	A.J.Fox	1	0	0

EASY AS THAT (IRE)
5 b g Sans Frontieres (IRE) – Bell Storm (IRE) (Glacial Storm (USA))
OWNER: KATE & ANDREW BROOKS
TRAINER: Miss V.WILLIAMS. Kings Caple, Herefordshire.
CAREER FORM FIGURES: 11
CAREER WIN: 2019: Dec FFOS LAS Heavy NHF 2m: 2020: Feb MUSSELBURGH Soft
NHF 2m

It was announced earlier this year that stallion and former Irish St Leger winner Sans Frontieres had been relocated from Beeches Stud to Vauterhill Stud in North Devon. The son of Galileo produced his first Graded winner when Jason The Militant landed a Grade 2 novice hurdle at Naas in February. Hopes are high that the unbeaten bumper horse Easy As That may follow suit this winter having looked an above average type in both his wins last season.

From the family of Stayers' Hurdle runner-up Time For Rupert, he was bought for €18,000 at the Tattersalls Ireland May Store Sales in 2018. Trained by Venetia Williams, Easy As That made his racecourse debut in a six runner bumper at Ffos Las in bottomless ground in December. Sent off 5/4 second favourite, he ploughed through the conditions and won comfortably by four lengths from market rival Fanfaron Dino. Back in action a couple of months later and carrying a penalty, Gavin Sheehan's mount was even more emphatic in victory at Musselburgh. Making all, he galloped his ten opponents into submission to win easily by thirteen lengths. The winning margin could have been substantially more had his rider wished. The runner-up Onward Route was narrowly beaten next time at Newcastle.

Owners Kate and Andrew Brooks tasted Cheltenham Festival glory for the first time last March when Simply The Betts landed the Brown Advisory & Merriebelle Stable Plate Handicap Chase. They also have high quality chasers Itchy Feet, Rouge Vif and Saint Calvados to look forward to this season, plus this unbeaten gelding by Sans Frontieres. A step up to two and a half miles over timber ought to suit Easy As That, who has only raced on testing ground.

POINTS TO NOTE:
Probable Best Distance	-	2m 4f
Preferred Going	-	Soft

GOING:	R	W	P	TRACK:	R	W	P
Heavy	1	1	0	Left Handed	1	1	0
Soft	1	1	0	Right	1	1	0
				Galloping	1	1	0
				Tight	1	1	0

TRIP:	R	W	P	JOCKEY:	R	W	P
2m	2	2	0	G.Sheehan	2	2	0

ENVOI ALLEN (FR)

6 b g Muhtathir – Reaction (FR) (Saint Des Saints (FR))
OWNER: CHEVELEY PARK STUD
TRAINER: G.ELLIOTT. Longwood, Co.Meath.
CAREER FORM FIGURES: 1 – 1111 - 1111
CAREER WIN: 2018: Feb BALLINABOOLA Yielding/Soft 4YO Mdn PTP 2m 4f; Dec
FAIRYHOUSE Good NHF 2m, NAVAN Yielding Lstd NHF 2m: 2019: Feb LEOPARDSTOWN
Good/Yielding Grade 2 NHF 2m; Mar CHELTENHAM Soft Grade 1 NHF 2m; Nov DOWN
ROYAL Soft MH 2m; Dec FAIRYHOUSE Yielding/Soft Grade 1 NH 2m: 2020: Jan NAAS
Good/Yielding Grade 1 2m 4f; Mar CHELTENHAM Soft Grade 1 NH 2m 5f

I don't think there is much doubt Envoi Allen is the hottest property in National Hunt racing at present and the six year old therefore retains his position in the *Top 40 Prospects* for a third consecutive season. Bought for £400,000 at the Cheltenham February Sale in 2018, the Muhtathir gelding is a dual Cheltenham Festival winner andalready has four Grade 1 wins on his CV. From the family of Paddy Power Chase and La Touche Cup winner Auvergnat, and a ten lengths winner of his only point-to-point for Colin Bowe, he promises to make an even better chaser.

Having won the Festival bumper at Cheltenham in 2019, Gordon Elliott's charge switched to hurdling last Autumn and was a ready six and a half lengths winner at Down Royal in November. Partnered by Davy Russell for the first time in public, he jumped fluently before pulling clear between the final two flights. A month later, Envoi Allen provided his trainer with his second win in the Grade 1 Royal Bond Novice Hurdle at Fairyhouse when outstaying his stablemate and subsequent *Skybet* Supreme Novices' Hurdle runner-up Abacadabras by a length and a half. **"Envoi Allen I think is the real thing. If you look at all his races – Leopardstown and Cheltenham as well – the one thing he does is, he picks up,"** remarked Elliott afterwards. Stepped up to two and a half miles for the first time in the Grade 1 Lawlor's of Naas Novice Hurdle in early January, he stayed on strongly after the second last to beat Elixir D'Ainay by three and a half lengths. Given a break before the Festival (66 days), he was touted as a possible Champion Hurdle candidate but Gordon Elliott was always keen to keep Envoi Allen to novice events and he lined up as the 4/7 favourite for the Ballymore Novices' Hurdle at Cheltenham. Once again, the Cheveley Park Stud owned gelding produced an electric performance to beat his stablemate Easywork by over four lengths. Davy Russell's mount momentarily looked in trouble rounding the hometurn, but he picked up in the manner of a top-class horse to win going away with some high-class novices trailing in his wake.

There is little doubt Envoi Allen could make a major impact in the top two mile division over hurdles, but he was bought to be a chaser and his connections will be harbouring hopes the Cheltenham Gold Cup will be on his agenda next season. Therefore he is expected to go chasing this winter with either the JLT or RSA Chases his ultimate target in March, as he bids to win at the Festival for a third successive year. He is an outstanding horse.

POINTS TO NOTE:
Probable Best Distance   -   2m 4f – 3 miles
Preferred Going   -   Good/Soft
Connection's Comments: "He did everything he needed to do. He jumped, he stayed and when he got to the front, he just did what he had to do, he doesn't do a stroke when he gets to the front. Davy (Russell) said they went a proper gallop, and he showed how good he is." Gordon ELLIOTT at Cheltenham (11/3/20)

GOING:	R	W	P		TRACK	R	W	P
Soft	3	3	0		Left Handed	6	6	0
Yielding/Soft	2	2	0		Right	3	3	0
Yielding	1	1	0		Galloping	5	5	0
Good/Yielding	2	2	0		Stiff/Undul.	2	2	0
Good	1	1	0		Tight/Undul.	1	1	0

TRIP:	R	W	P		JOCKEY:	R	W	P
2m	6	6	0		D.Russell	4	4	0
2m 4f	2	2	0		J.J.Codd	4	4	0
2m 5f	1	1	0		B.O'Neill	1	1	0

EVERGLOW
5 br g Presenting – Cent Prime (Hernando (FR))
OWNER: PHIL MUNNELLY
TRAINER: P.J.HOBBS. Minehead, Somerset.
CAREER FORM FIGURES: 23

Bought for £35,000 at the Goffs UK Doncaster Spring Sale as an unraced store a couple of years ago, Everglow showed an abundance of promise in his two starts in bumpers last season and looks a fine prospect for staying novice hurdles this winter.

Beaten a neck on his debut at Chepstow's opening meeting in October, Philip Hobbs' gelding raced close to the pace throughout before making his challenge approaching the final furlong. Edged out by David Pipe's former Irish pointer Make Me A Believer, he had subsequently hurdle winners Oscar Robertson, Buckhorn George and Skylanna Breeze in behind. A month later, Everglow took his chance in the Listed bumper at Cheltenham's November meeting – a race his stablemate Crooks Peak won two years earlier. The race was won by another Pond House inmate, namely Israel Champ, who made all the running with the Hobbs runner finishing third. Only beaten four lengths, he stayed on well in the closing stages and will benefit from stepping up in trip once sent jumping.

The plan was for the five year old to contest the Goffs UK Spring Bumper at Newbury in March but, unfortunately, that never took place. Speaking to his trainer earlier that month, he said Everglow had benefited from the time off and is a horse who will get better with age. All set to go hurdling, it will be interesting to see if he makes his jumping bow in the Grade 2 Persian War Novices' Hurdle at Chepstow (9th October). Philip Hobbs has won the extended two miles three event on five occasions (Bonanza Boy (1987), One Knight (2001), Supreme Prince (2002), Fingal Bay (2011) and Thyme Hill (2019)). The last two named were both having their first runs over obstacles at the Welsh track.

POINTS TO NOTE:
Probable Best Distance   -   2m 4f - 3 miles
Preferred Going   -   Good/Soft
Connection's Comments: "He is a lovely individual who has pleased me since day one, so it wasn't a surprise he ran so well on his debut at Chepstow." Philip HOBBS speaking in early November 2019

GOING:	R	W	P	TRACK:	R	W	P
Soft	2	0	2	Left-Handed	2	0	2
				Stiff/Undul.	2	0	2

TRIP:	R	W	P	JOCKEY:	R	W	P
2m	2	0	2	R.Johnson	2	0	2

FAROUK D'ALENE (FR)

5 b g Racinger (FR) – Mascotte D'Alene (FR) (Ragmar (FR))
OWNER: GIGGINSTOWN HOUSE STUD
TRAINER: G.ELLIOTT. Longwood, Co.Meath.
CAREER FORM FIGURES: 1 - 11
CAREER WINS: 2019: Mar BELCLARE Soft 4YO Mdn PTP 3m; Dec DOWN ROYAL Soft/
Heavy NHF 2m 1f: 2020: Feb NAAS Soft/Heavy NHF 2m

Unbeaten in three career starts, Farouk D'Alene was an eighteen lengths winner of his only point-to-point at Belclare in March 2019 for Donnchadh Doyle. Purchased four days later at the Cheltenham Festival Sale for £260,000 on behalf of Gigginstown House Stud, the five year old won both his outings in bumpers for Gordon Elliott last term and looks a first class prospect for novice hurdles this time around.

Declan Phelan commented in last year's edition of *OJA*: **"Bulky bay French bred gelding with a white blaze on his face. He dominated the fiverunner maiden at Belclare (Soft) in March, jumping boldly and proving too classy for his rivals, posting an emphatic eighteen lengths win. He appears to possess a high cruising speed. He is one of the more exciting prospects to emerge from the spring 2019 crop of four year olds. Aspirations for Graded success over hurdles and fences are justifiable in his case and he can be viewed as future Cheltenham Festival material. His strong galloping style leads one to regard him as likely to excel when racing at two and a half miles and upwards rather than shorter trips."**

A seventeen lengths winner on his Rules debut in a bumper at Down Royal on Boxing Day, the heavily supported favourite never gave his supporters an anxious moment, making all under Jamie Codd and extending his advantage inside the final quarter of a mile. Back in action a couple of months later at Naas, he beat the same owner's Limerick winner Fire Attack by a head in a driving finish (three previous winners finished behind him). Headed with a furlong to run, Jamie Codd's mount rallied well to regain the advantage close home. **"He's a raw horse and one for the future. He's a fair horse and two and a half miles will be right up his street. Jamie said he gave the rail away to let the other horse come through and give him something to go at. He straightened up when he had something to go at,"** remarked Elliott afterwards. It was Gigginstown's seventh victory in the race during the last ten years and it is a contest which has produced the likes of Outlander (2013), Killultagh Vic (2014), Carefully Selected (2018) and Easywork (2019).

Back in training following his summer break, Farouk D'Alene is described as a gorgeous looking horse who loves soft ground. All set to go novice hurdling over two and a half miles plus, he looks a strong stayer and he could develop into a major contender for the Albert Bartlett Novices' Hurdle next spring.

POINTS TO NOTE:

Probable Best Distance - 2m 4f – 3 miles
Preferred Going - Soft
Connection's Comments: "His work has been incredible at home. We expected him to win and he's done that. He's another monster for the Gigginstown machine." Jamie CODD at Down Royal (26/12/19)

GOING:	R	W	P	TRACK	R	W	P
Soft/Heavy	2	2	0	Left-Handed	1	1	0
Soft	1	1	0	Right	2	2	0

TRIP:	R	W	P	JOCKEY:	R	W	P
2m	1	1	0	J.J.Codd	2	2	0
2m 1f	1	1	0	J.P.O'Rourke	1	1	0
3m	1	1	0				

FERNY HOLLOW (IRE)

5 bb g Westerner – Mirazur (IRE) (Good Thyne (USA))
OWNER: CHEVELEY PARK STUD
TRAINER: W.P.MULLINS. Bagenalstown, Co.Carlow.
CAREER FORM FIGURES: 1 - 2211
CAREER WINS: 2019: Feb KNOCKANARD Soft 4YO Mdn PTP 2m 4f: 2020: Feb FAIRYHOUSE Heavy NHF 2m; Mar CHELTENHAM Soft Grade 1 NHF 2m

As discussed, Willie Mullins was crowned the leading trainer at the Cheltenham Festival in March for a seventh time. The Closutton handler was responsible for 7 winners, 4 seconds and 6 thirds over the course of the four days, with the highlight being provided on the final day with a 2,196/1 four timer. The stable won the Festival bumper for a record tenth time with Ferny Hollow beating stablemate Appreciate It by two and a half lengths.

Featured in last year's *Top 40 Prospects*, point expert Declan Phelan marked our card in advance saying: **"Ferny Hollow could be top class and, if tracing the Bumper route this season will be a leading player in that division. One of a handful of four year olds from the 2019 academy who I predict will have little trouble winning Graded track races, even to Grade 1 rank in time."** A fifteen lengths winner of his only point-to-point for Colin Bowe, the Westerner gelding was subsequently bought on behalf of Cheveley Park Stud for £300,000 at the Cheltenham February Sale four days later. Ferny Hollow made his Rules debut in the same bumper at Fairyhouse in early December which has been won by subsequent Grade 1 winners Al Ferof (2009), Outlander (2012), Identity Thief (2014) and Envoi Allen (2018). Sent off 8/11 favourite, Patrick Mullins' mount spoilt his chance by racing much too keenly. He therefore did well to finish second, in the circumstances, behind Joseph O'Brien's well regarded debutant Eric Bloodaxe. Beaten two and a half lengths, he was a further six lengths clear of the third. It was a similar story at Leopardstown over Christmas with Ferny Hollow attempting to make all, but failing to relax and running too freely. Once again, he was edged out by an O'Brien trained opponent, namely Forged In Fire, with the pair pulling seventeen lengths clear of the third. Given a break of nearly two months, the five year old returned at Fairyhouse in late February and a change of tactics worked the oracle. Fitted with a hood for the first time and held up by Patrick Mullins, he outclassed his ten rivals to win easily by four and a quarter lengths with his rider barely moving a muscle.

One of three runners for Mullins in the Festival bumper, he was partnered for the first time by Paul Townend, who gave the Westerner gelding a superb ride. Anchored at the back of the field, Ferny Hollow travelled strongly before making his move coming down the hill. Appreciate It struck the front turning for home but couldn't match his stablemate's turn of foot inside the final furlong. A two and a half lengths winner, he provided Cheveley Park Stud with their second consecutive win in the race following the success of Envoi Allen twelve months earlier.

Despite the fact he is bred to stay further, Ferny Hollow is likely to be kept to the minimum trip over hurdles because he doesn't lack speed. Once learning to relax, he has the ingredients to become a household name. He oozes classes and could provide Willie Mullins with his seventh win in the *Skybet* Supreme Novices' Hurdle next March.

POINTS TO NOTE:

Probable Best Distance	-	2 miles
Preferred Going	-	Good/Soft

GOING:	R	W	P	TRACK:	R	W	P
Heavy	1	1	0	Left Handed	2	1	1
Soft	3	2	1	Right	3	2	1
Yielding/Soft	1	0	1	Galloping	3	1	2
				Stiff/Undul.	1	1	0

TRIP:	R	W	P	JOCKEY:	R	W	P
2m	4	2	2	P.Townend	1	1	0
2m 4f	1	1	0	P.W.Mullins	3	1	2
				J.P.O'Rourke	1	1	0

FISHKHOV (FR)

5 ch g Sholokhov (IRE) – Kavalle (FR) (Video Rock (FR))
OWNER: MASTERSON HOLDINGS Limited
TRAINER: H.FRY. Corscombe, Dorset.
CAREER FORM FIGURES: 2

Having moved into a new yard at Higher Crockermoor in Corscombe near Dorchester, these are exciting times for Harry Fry. Paul Nicholls' former assistant is blessed with a strong team of youngsters, especially in the novice chase department with Grade 1 winner If The Cap Fits (now owned by Simon Munir & Isaac Souede), King Roland, Phoenix Way and Winningseverything set to embark on their fencing careers this Autumn. His team of novice hurdlers isn't bad either with Boothill, Get In The Queue, Metier and ex-Irish pointer Fishkov.

The last named was bought at the Goffs UK January Sale at Doncaster for £115,000. Beaten three parts of a length on his only start at Dromahane when trained by Robert Tyner, bloodstock agent Kevin Ross commented at the sales: **"I loved the way he went through the race – he did everything right and the first two really quickened up, in what I thought was a good maiden. I thought it was a really promising debut and he looks like a lovely type for the future. He's a lovely looking individual and the sire is doing well."**

Declan Phelan comments: **"Emerged from his one outing in the point ranks with credit: racing for Robert Tyner at Dromahane (Soft/Heavy) in December, in what has turned out to be an above average maiden, he received a hold up ride from Derek O'Connor. The partnership crept closer in the final mile, and when Derek gave him the office to** leap to the front at the last, it looked like job done. Unfortunately, the always prominent Vanillier fought back and scalped Fishkhov in the final strides. Three of those in behind have all won maidens easily in subsequent months, solidifying the impression that it was a decent race. A French bred chestnut and well toned individual, his dam won on the Flat and over jumps and his Gallic family includes notable names like Antonin and Mighty Man .Bought by Kevin Ross bloodstock at Doncaster January sales for £115,000, he rates a better than average maiden pointer and has the capacity and talent to entertain realistic ambitions of becoming a 125+ chaser. On the evidence from Dromahane, perhaps distances around the two and a half miles mark, rather than three mile slogs will play to his strengths, as a strong traveller during a race."

Owned by Masterson Holdings Limited, Fishkhov's new trainer has indicated that the five year old may contest a bumper before going hurdling. The same patron was responsible for the ill-fated Neon Wolf (2016) and King Roland (2018), who both won bumpers at Uttoxeter. Therefore don't be surprised if this gelded son of Sholokhov heads to the Midlands track for a similar event – there is one on Saturday 14ᵗʰ November.

POINTS TO NOTE:
Probable Best Distance   -   2m – 2m 4f
Preferred Going   -   Good/Soft
Connection's Comments: "I bought him as a yearling in France. He's a lovely horse for the future with a nice bit of a scope over a jump. I sold Harry (Fry) a nice horse called American and I think this is a similar type." His former trainer Robert TYNER at the Goffs UK Doncaster Sales in January (22/1/20)

GOING:	R	W	P	TRACK:	R	W	P
Soft/Heavy	1	0	1	Left Handed	1	0	1

TRIP:	R	W	P	JOCKEY:	R	W	P
3m	1	0	1	D.O'Connor	1	0	1

FISTON DES ISSARDS (FR)
5 bb g Buck's Boum (FR) – Saboum (FR) (Robin Des Champs (FR))
OWNER: NOEL MORAN / MRS VALERIE MORAN
TRAINER: G.ELLIOTT. Longwood, Co.Meath.
CAREER FORM FIGURES: 1
CAREER WIN: 2019: Oct LOUGHANMORE Yielding 4YO Mdn PTP 3m

Owners Noel and Valerie Moran were responsible for Queens Brook (third in the bumper) and The Bosses Oscar (fifth in the Martin Pipe Conditional Jockeys' Handicap Hurdle) at last March's Cheltenham Festival. That pair are trained by Gordon Elliott and the same patrons, who sponsor the three times winning Grand National trainer's yard in County Meath, have invested heavily in new stock during the spring/summer. Winning pointers Clondaw Secret (£135,000) Fiston Des Issards (£255,000) Glenglass (£155,000) and Hollow Games (£255,000) were acquired, and Nicky Henderson's unbeaten novice hurdler Grand Roi was purchased for £400,000 at the Goffs UK Summer Sale in July.

The once raced Fiston Des Issards plied his trade in Irish points for Colin Bowe, the same source as multiple Grade 1 winning stablemates Envoi Allen and Samcro. Expert Declan Phelan explains: **"First foal of a French jumps winning dam. A tall elegant almost black gelding. By virtue of winning a classy maiden at Loughanmore (Yielding) in November, he ranked one of the top five talents from the autumn crop of four year olds in 2019.**

Jumping as though on springs, he landed in front four out and when threatened at the final fence, he found generously and won by over three lengths. When you consider the second (Boothill) and fourth (Smurphy Enki) were wide margin bumper winners in the UK in February/March, the form does indeed look tasty. It took a sum of £255,000 for Gordon Elliott to gain the successful bid at Cheltenham November Sales, and in truth this horse has the hallmarks of a Graded jumper, and may prove his worth and vindicate the hefty price. Blessed with gears, he could become a leading player in the bumper division, if that is his selected route in 2020/21: as he will be a six year old in 2021, connections may prefer to win a bumper and then move over to novice hurdles and he could readily become a candidate for the likes of the Albert Bartlett. Hard to say if he will be a Grade 1 horse, whilst impressive, the wow factor was not present at Loughanmore. Gordon Elliott has a proven record of maximising stock he receives from the Colin Bowe academy, and Fiston Des Issards will make a fist of trying to emulate horses such as Envoi Allen and Samcro. He should be capable of coping with good ground and he was effective on the cushioned yielding surface at the County Antrim track last autumn."

POINTS TO NOTE:
Probable Best Distance	-	2m 4f – 3 miles
Preferred Going	-	Good/Soft

Connection's Comments: "He's a fine big horse that was bought from Walter Connors (Sluggara Farm) at the spring sale in Doncaster last year. He should improve plenty." Colin BOWE after his victory in his point-to-point at Loughanmore (26/10/19)

GOING:	R	W	P	TRACK	R	W	P
Yielding	1	1	0	Left Handed	1	1	0

TRIP:	R	W	P	JOCKEY:	R	W	P
3m	1	1	0	B.O'Neill	1	1	0

FIVE O'CLOCK (FR)
5 b g Cokoriko (FR) – Rodika (FR) (Kapgarde (FR))
OWNER: Mrs S.RICCI
TRAINER: W.P.MULLINS. Bagenalstown, Co.Carlow.
CAREER FORM FIGURES: 032 - 2117
CAREER WINS: 2020: Jan LIMERICK Soft/Heavy MH 2m; Feb THURLES Soft Grade 3 NH 2m 5f

As discussed, a 2,196/1 four timer on the final day capped another memorable Cheltenham Festival for Willie Mullins. Stable jockey Paul Townend emerged as the leading rider for the week, too, with five winners. The 29 year old partnered three winners on the final afternoon, including Al Boum Photo's second consecutive victory in the Cheltenham Gold Cup. He was also on board Monkfish in the Albert Bartlett Novices' Hurdle with the six year old prevailing by a neck and, in doing so, providing owners Rich and Susannah Ricci with their seventeenth Festival success.

The Stowaway gelding is viewed as a very smart chasing prospect for the winter ahead and that comment also applies to the same connections Five O'Clock. Trained in France by Patrice Lenogue, he was placed in two of his three starts over hurdles at Auteuil before being purchased on behalf of the Ricci's. Runner-up on his Irish debut at Tramore in desperate conditions in December, the son of Cokoriko won by a length next time at Limerick (inner track) over an inadequate two miles. Returning to a longer trip at Thurles in

February, he stayed on strongly to win the Grade 3 Michael Purcell Memorial Novice Hurdle by six lengths. He rounded off his hurdles career by finishing seventh in the Martin Pipe Conditional Jockeys' Handicap Hurdle at the Festival. Partnered by Conor McNamara, he was badly hampered with a circuit to run before storming home on the run-in. Beaten less than five lengths, Five O'Clock is crying out for a step up to three miles and is very much a chaser in the making.

Willie Mullins has won the Martin Pipe Handicap Hurdle three times and this five year old reminds me of Sir Des Champs and Don Poli, who both won the two and a half miles event before developing into Grade 1 winning chasers. He is a fine prospect for fences and very much one to follow.

POINTS TO NOTE:
Probable Best Distance   -   **2m 4f - 3 miles**
Preferred Going   -   **Soft**
Connection's Comments: "Five O'Clock is a horse I think a lot of. He wasn't impressive over 2m on the inside track at Limerick, he really wants a galloping track. He's an out-and-out three miles chaser down the line." Willie MULLINS at Thurles (20/2/20)

GOING:	R	W	P	TRACK:	R	W	P
Heavy	1	0	1	Left Handed	4	0	2
Very Soft	3	0	2	Right	3	2	1
Soft/Heavy	1	1	0	Galloping	4	1	2
Soft	2	1	0	Stiff/Undul.	1	0	0
				Tight/Undul.	1	1	0
				Tight	1	0	1

TRIP:	R	W	P	JOCKEY:	R	W	P
1m 7f	1	0	0	P.Townend	2	1	1
2m	1	1	0	D.E.Mullins	1	1	0
2m 1f	2	0	2	C.McNamara	1	0	0
2m 4f	1	0	0	A.Merienne	2	0	2
2m 5f	2	1	1	M.Lefebvre	1	0	0

FLINTEUR SACRE (FR)
5 b g Network (GER) – Fatima III (FR) (Bayolidaan (FR))
OWNER: J.P.McMANUS
TRAINER: N.J.HENDERSON. Lambourn, Berkshire
CAREER FORM FIGURES: 21
CAREER WIN: 2020: Feb KEMPTON Good/Soft NHF 2m

Champion trainer Nicky Henderson has handled some top-class two mile chasers during his career with names such as Altior, Finian's Rainbow, Remittance Man and Travado springing to mind. However, few would argue that the brilliant Sprinter Sacre is the best. Rated 175 over fences, the Network gelding won 18 of his 24 races earning £1,136,884 in prize-money. A nine times Grade 1 winner, he was a triple winner at the Cheltenham Festival, including the Queen Mother Champion Chase in 2013 and 2016. At his very best during the 2012/2013 campaign, Sprinter Sacre was unbeaten in five races and won at Cheltenham, Aintree and Punchestown during the spring of 2013 in the space of six weeks. He was a phenomenal horse with the looks to match.

Therefore his full-brother Flinteur Sacre has an awful lot to live up to but, if his two races last season are anything to go by, then he has certainly inherited some of his older sibling's ability. Bought for €125,000 at the Arqana Summer Sale in July 2017, he made his debut in a bumper at Newbury in mid January with his trainer commenting beforehand: **"He's a slightly smaller version of his brother, but he's a quality horse and very good looking. He goes well, he's done everything right at home and we like him a lot, but I would be nervous about him in very soft ground. He's a very active horse, so it might not suit him. It will be nice to see him out, he's a lovely horse."** Beaten three and a quarter lengths by the well regarded Your Darling, the gelded son of Network raced keenly during the first half of the race but made smooth headway in the home straight and looked likely to win approaching the final couple of furlongs. However, the combination of the testing ground and racing freely took its toll late on. It was still an encouraging start to his career though. Back in action around three weeks later, he sauntered to a four and three quarters of a length victory at Kempton. Conceding ten pounds to the Richard Hughes trained runner-up Le Bateau, Barry Geraghty's mount barely came off the bridle as he pulled readily clear to win with any amount in hand. Contesting the second division of the bumper, his winning time was 4m 1.10secs compared to the first division, which was won by Hoi Polloi in 4m 7.75secs. It was Henderson's fourth win in the race during the last nine years. The Grade 2 bumper at Aintree in April was reportedly his end of season target but that never materialised.

Similar to his brother, Flinteur Sacre looks all speed and one can envisage him making his jumping debut at either Newbury or Kempton. Don't be surprised if this exciting gelding returns to the latter track on Boxing day for the opening two miles novice hurdle. It is a race his trainer has won five times in the last nine years, including with the aforementioned Altior in 2015.

POINTS TO NOTE:

Probable Best Distance   -   2 miles
Preferred Going   -   Good/Soft
Connection's Comments: **"We brought him out quite quickly since his first run as he's been crazy wild at home. He had a nice time at Newbury, he wasn't allowed to have too hard a race there, so all in all, it's a good start."** Nicky HENDERSON at Kempton (7/2/20)

GOING:	R	W	P	TRACK:	R	W	P
Heavy	1	0	1	Left Handed	1	0	1
Good/Soft	1	1	0	Right	1	1	0
				Galloping	1	0	1
				Tight	1	1	0

TRIP:	R	W	P	JOCKEY:	R	W	P
2m	2	1	1	B.Geraghty	2	1	1

FURY ROAD (IRE)

6 b g Stowaway – Molly Duffy (IRE) (Oscar (IRE))
OWNER: GIGGINSTOWN HOUSE STUD
TRAINER: G.ELLIOTT. Longwood, Co.Meath.
CAREER FORM FIGURES: 41 – 51 - 311143
CAREER WINS: 2018: May DROMAHANE Good 4YO Mdn PTP 3m: 2019: Feb
FAIRYHOUSE Good/Yielding NHF 2m; Nov DOWN ROYAL Yielding/Soft MH 2m 6f,
NAVAN Soft Grade 3 NH 2m 4f; Dec LIMERICK Heavy Grade 2 NH 2m 7f

Featured in the *Top 40 Prospects* a couple of seasons ago, Fury Road was involved in one of the races of the Festival at Cheltenham in March. Denied by a neck and nose, the six year old finished third in the Grade 1 Albert Bartlett Novices' Hurdle behind compatriots Monkfish and Latest Exhibition in a thrilling finish. Rated 151 over hurdles, he was bought for €205,000 as a three year old and began his career in Irish points with Pat Doyle. Given his pedigree and physique, the Stowaway gelding promises to be top-class over fences.

Despite winning one of his three races in bumpers during the 2018/2019 campaign, Gordon Elliott's gelding wasn't at his best but proved a different proposition over hurdles last term (had a wind operation after his final bumper run). Appreciating a step up in distance, he destroyed thirteen rivals by upwards of eighteen lengths at Down Royal – his stable enjoyed a 17.5/1 five timer – in early November. Fury Road then made all to win the Grade 3 Monkfield Novice Hurdle at Navan by ten lengths without coming off the bridle. Overcoming a mistake at the last, he landed the hat-trick in a Grade 2 over nearly three miles at Limerick over Christmas. That contest has produced subsequent Festival winners Faugheen, Martello Tower, Penhill and Weapon's Amnesty in recent years. Tackling Grade 1 company for the first time at the Dublin Racing Festival at Leopardstown in early February, Davy Russell's mount reportedly found the ground too lively and was given a sympathetic ride once his chance had gone. Still only beaten five and a quarter lengths, Fury Road was primed for a big run at Cheltenham and so it proved. Having made good headway after the second last, he challenged at the final flight and hit the front on the run-in. The six year old couldn't fend off the challengers late on though suffering an agonising defeat in the process.

Provided that titanic tussle hasn't left its mark – it is a race which has claimed its fair share of casualties over the years – then Fury Road is an outstanding chasing prospect for Gigginstown House Stud and Gordon Elliott. The latter have won the RSA Chase twice (Weapon's Amnesty (2010) & Don Poli (2015)) and they have a major contender for the 2021 renewal. Here's what point expert Declan Phelan wrote in the 2018/2019 edition of *OJA*: **"A real professional racehorse who oozes quality on physical inspection, Pat Doyle was given the task of teaching him the ropes as a pointer. He debuted at Stowlin (Yielding) in April and finished a close up fourth: Derek O'Connor who was aboard, was not seen at his finest, because he got caught in a pocket away from the second last, and on a tight bend to the last was not able to extract himself to mount a challenge, in effect, an inconclusive outcome. Three weeks later Pat Doyle brought Fury Road to Dromahane (Good) and this time there were no mistakes. With John Barry in the plate, the instructions were to make use of the horse: assuming the lead from the start, he travelled like a dream machine, jumping slickly, and pouring on the pace in the final mile, he burned off all his rivals bar the closing El Barra. John Barry gave Fury Road a squeeze jumping the second last and with the horse hitting top gear, he accelerated and easily held El Barra by four lengths. A top class front running display, capped off by defeating a proper rival. His half brother Monbeg Worldwide is a mudlark requiring a trip, Fury Road is a different beast. He has a high cruising speed, a rapid fire jumping technique and star quality."**

Probable Best Distance   -   2m 4f – 3 miles
Preferred Going   -   Soft

GOING:	R	W	P	TRACK	R	W	P
Heavy	1	1	0	Left Handed	5	2	1
Soft	2	1	1	Right	5	3	0
Yielding/Soft	1	1	0	Galloping	6	3	0
Yielding	2	0	0	Stiff/Undul.	1	0	1
Good/Yielding	3	1	0	Tight/Undul.	1	1	0
Good	1	1	0				

TRIP:	R	W	P	JOCKEY:	R	W	P
2m	3	1	0	D.Russell	4	2	1
2m 4f	1	1	0	K.Donoghue	1	1	0
2m 6f	2	1	0	J.C.Barry	1	1	0
2m 7f	1	1	0	Lisa O'Neill	3	1	0
3m	3	1	1	D.O'Connor	1	0	0

GALLYHILL (IRE)
5 b g Getaway (GER) – Tanit (Xaar)
OWNER: CLAUDIO MICHAEL GRECH
TRAINER: N.J.HENDERSON. Lambourn, Berkshire
CAREER FORM FIGURES: 1
CAREER WIN: 2019: Nov KIRKISTOWN Soft/Heavy 4YO Mdn PTP 3m

Owner Mike Grech enjoyed Graded success with Claimantakinforgan, Constantine Bay, Mr Whipped and River Wylde when in partnership with Stuart Parkin a few years ago. The pair went their separate ways last year with a dispersal sale of their stock at Doncaster in May 2019. Interconnected proved the headline act when selling for £620,000 and making him the most expensive National Hunt horse ever sold at public auction. The six year old has still yet to run for his new connections having suffered an injury last season.

Grech is back in the game now though and has called upon the experience and skill of three times Cheltenham Gold Cup winning trainer Henrietta Knight. Together they made some high profile 'signings' earlier this year, most notably Gallyhill (£450,000) and Keskonrisk (£370,000). Declan Phelan comments: **"Mike Grech has availed of the services of Hen Knight as his advisor and tasked her with assembling a new select band of horses. The horse at the forefront of this new recruitment drive is Gallyhill. With Ulster handler Ian Ferguson retiring as a trainer, Jamie Sloan took up the baton to continue as a licenced handler from Ferguson's Ballymena base. Wilson Dennison, as an owner, develops his young horses on his home farm (Loughanmore) and Colin McKeever trains them. Dennison uses Ian Ferguson as an ally and wise owl when he travels the country in quest of National Hunt youngsters, and, over the years, as a result Ferguson always traineda few for Dennison. The Costello family in Clare are one of the main sources where Dennison privately buys foals, unbroken yearlings or older, and Gallyhill was secured as a young three year old by Ferguson on behalf of Dennison on one of his trips south. Hen Knight has a big connection with the Costellos, she did after all buy her superstar, Best Mate from them. Apparently in recent times, Hen frequently travels to the Costello farms to cast her eye over the young stock and, by all accounts, she had noted Gallyhill as one of her favourites before he was sold to Dennison. Off the back of lovely piece of schooling work the previous week at Moira gallops, Gallyhill was saddled by James Sloan for a division of the four year old maiden at Kirkistown**

(Soft/Heavy) in late November: in truth it was a rather ordinary selection of runners with the exception of Gallyhill. This powerfully built bay gelding with a white star on his forehead, relaxed through the race and for minimum urging on the part of jockey Noel McParlan, he took control jumping the final fence to win untaxed by over two lengths. Now the raw evidence of the form is weak....a very slow time of 7m 24 seconds for the three miles, twelve lengths covering the first six home....however, I spoke to Noel and he said the horse is not a flashy customer and will do the minimum required to win a race. He rode the horse in schooling races and he maintained, if the horse received a proper gallop to attack, then he would look like the real deal. Well Hen Knight believed in him, as it took a price of £450,000 to purchase him for Mike Grech at Tattersalls Cheltenham December Sales. On pedigree, deep down his page, one can find middle distance Flat horses such as Pentire but no elite jumper, so he may be endowed with more speed than first strikes. He jumped beautifully at Kirkistown and stayed the three miles: the fact that he is an easy horse to settle may open up different avenues in terms of trip. Fertile raw material for Henderson to work with, I would not be sure if this is a Ballymore or Albert Bartlett horse for 2021, though he will become a proper contender for the RSA when he enters the novice chasing ranks."

POINTS TO NOTE:
Probable Best Distance   -   2m 4f – 3 miles
Preferred Going   -   Good/Soft
Connection's Comments: "We gave this lad a good summer to mature and it has paid dividends. I was quietly confident coming here today and it all went to plan." Jamie SLOAN at Kirkistown (23/11/19)

GOING:	R	W	P	TRACK:	R	W	P
Soft/Heavy	1	1	0	Left Handed	1	1	0

TRIP:	R	W	P	JOCKEY:	R	W	P
3m	1	1	0	N.McParlan	1	1	0

GALOPIN DES CHAMPS (FR)
4 b g Timos (GER) – Manon Des Champs (FR) (Marchand De Sable (USA))
OWNER: Mrs AUDREY TURLEY
TRAINER: W.P.MULLINS. Bagenalstown, Co.Carlow.
CAREER FORM FIGURES: 1
CAREER WIN: 2020: May AUTEUIL Very Soft Hdle 2m 2f

Owner Audrey Turley is responsible for the 2020 Triumph Hurdle winner Burning Victory. A daughter of Nathaniel who won over a mile and a half on the Flat in France when trained by Stephane Wattel, she is unbeaten in two runs over hurdles for Willie Mullins having captured a Grade 3 event on her jumping bow at Fairyhouse less than a month before her Festival victory last March.

The same patron has reinvested and purchased the unbeaten once raced Galopin Des Champs. From the same source as the stable's dual Grade 1 winning chaser Djakadam, namely Arnaud Chaille-Chaille, the Timos gelding overcame his inexperience to win a sixteen runner conditions hurdle at Auteuil in May. Partnered by conditional jockey Thomas Coutant, he was held up early on in the two miles two furlongs event. Making good headway turning for home, he led after the final hurdle before stretching clear to win going away. Both the runner-up and third had raced beforehand and there were three previous winners within the field.

Bought soon afterwards on behalf of Willie Mullins, he can only improve and the fact he remains a novice hurdler for the whole season is a bonus. On the evidence of his win at Auteuil, Galopin Des Champs left the impression he will stay further but he could develop in a similar manner to the stable's former *Skybet* Supreme Novice Hurdle winners Vautour and Klassical Dream – they were both strong stayers over the minimum trip. Either way, he looks a first class prospect who will hopefully be competing at the Cheltenham Festival next March.

POINTS TO NOTE:

| Probable Best Distance | - | 2m - 2m 4f |
| Preferred Going | - | Good/Soft |

GOING:	R	W	P	TRACK:	R	W	P
Very Soft	1	1	0	Left Handed	1	1	0
				Galloping	1	1	0

TRIP:	R	W	P	JOCKEY:	R	W	P
2m 2f	1	1	0	T.Coutant	1	1	0

GENTLEMAN DE MEE (FR)

4 b g Saint Des Saints (FR) – Koeur De Mee (FR) (Video Rock (FR))
OWNER: J.P.McMANUS
TRAINER: W.P.MULLINS. Bagenalstown, Co.Carlow.
CAREER FORM FIGURES: 22

Willie Mullins and J.P.McManus combined with Saint Roi to win the County Hurdle at Cheltenham in March. The Coastal Path gelding had been placed in his two starts over hurdles as a three year old when trained in France by Guy Cherel.

Gentleman De Mee has a similar profile having purchased for €280,000 at the Arqana Sale in November. A half-brother to the EBF Final and Grand Sefton Chase winner As De Mee, he raced twice for Guillaume Macaire in France finishing runner-up on both occasions. Beaten two lengths on his debut at Senonnes in October behind Grand De Thaix (won again since), he was then a length and a half second to Magrudy at Compiegne the following month (rallied well after the last). The winner has won over fences subsequently and finished runner-up in a Grade 3 chase at Auteuil, while the third has also won over fences at Auteuil. The form is strong and he is a potentially high-class recruit to the Mullins yard. When Ireland's champion trainer buys a three year old, he invariably leaves them off until the following season with their novice status in tact.

It remains to been seen whether Gentleman De Mee possesses the speed of his new stablemate but he looks set to make a major impact in novice hurdles in Ireland this winter and one who has realistic claims of appearing at the Cheltenham Festival next spring.

POINTS TO NOTE:

| Probable Best Distance | - | 2m – 2m 4f |
| Preferred Going | - | Good/Soft |

Connection's Comments: "He's a lovely horse who looks like he'll make up into a nice staying chaser. He's a horse for next year, so we'll take him back to Ireland and speak to the boss." Charlie SWAN speaking at the Arqana sale (18/11/19)

GOING:	R	W	P	TRACK:	R	W	P
Heavy	1	0	1	Left-Handed	1	0	1
				Right	1	0	1
				Galloping	2	0	2

TRIP:	R	W	P	JOCKEY:	R	W	P
2m 1f	1	0	1	B.Lestrade	1	0	1
2m 2f	1	0	1	M.Romary	1	0	1

GIPSY DE CHOISEL (FR)

4 bl g Great Pretender (IRE) – Beautiful Choisel (Sageburg (IRE))
OWNER: Mr SIMON MUNIR & Mr ISAAC SOUEDE
TRAINER: N.J.HENDERSON. Lambourn, Berkshire.
CAREER FORM FIGURES: 1
CAREER WIN: 2020: May ANGERS Very Soft Hdle 2m 3f

The well known two shades of green silks of Simon Munir and Isaac Souede have tasted Cheltenham Festival glory with Soldatino and Peace And Co in the Triumph Hurdle, Concertista (Dawn Run Mares' Novices' Hurdle), Footpad (Arkle Trophy) and Une Artiste (Boodles Juvenile Hurdle) during the last ten years. All five of those winners began their careers in France and, with the assistance of racing manager Anthony Bromley, the pair have recruited some exciting prospects from the other side of The English Channel this spring/summer.

The once raced and unbeaten Gipsy De Choisel has joined Nicky Henderson and the gelded son of Great Pretender could be a very interesting novice hurdler this term. Previously trained by Jean-Philippe Dubois, he made his debut in a sixteen runners hurdle at Angers in mid May. Held up early on, he overcame a slight error at the first before a more serious mistake at the third. However, the four year old made good headway down the backstraight and, even though he was only eighth turning for home, he was a close third at the final flight before leading close home. A short head winner, both the second and fourth have won since.

Bought soon afterwards by the Highflyer Bloodstock supremo, he remains eligible for novice hurdles all season and looks a fine long-term prospect.

POINTS TO NOTE:
Probable Best Distance   -   2m – 2m 4f
Preferred Going   -   Good/Soft

GOING:	R	W	P	TRACK:	R	W	P
Very Soft	1	1	0	Right	1	1	0
				Galloping	1	1	0

TRIP:	R	W	P	JOCKEY:	R	W	P
2m 3f	1	1	0	M.Farcinade	1	1	0

HAPPYGOLUCKY (IRE)

6 br g Jeremy (USA) – Mydadsabishop (IRE) (Bishop of Cashel)
OWNER: Lady DULVERTON
TRAINER: K.C.BAILEY. Andoversford, Cheltenham.
CAREER FORM FIGURES: 2 - 1334
CAREER WIN: 2019: Oct STRATFORD Soft MH 2m 6f

Imperial Aura provided Kim Bailey with his fifth Cheltenham Festival winner when capturing the Listed novices' handicap chase in March. The Grand National, Cheltenham Gold Cup and Champion Hurdle winning trainer has enjoyed a resurgence in recent seasons. Thorndale Farm near Cheltenham has assembled a strong team of youngsters, especially in the novice chase department for the campaign ahead.

A six year old by Jeremy who was runner-up in his sole Irish point for Francis Flood, Happygolucky was acquired less than a month later at the Cheltenham December Sale 2018 for £55,000. Sent hurdling last winter, he returned from an absence of 328 days to win a two miles six maiden hurdle at Stratford by eleven lengths. Having chased the leaders, David Bass's mount led between the final two flight before pulling clear. Tackling Graded company for the first time at Cheltenham the following month, he acquitted himself well finishing third behind subsequent Grade 1 winner Thyne Hill. Beaten less than four lengths, he kept on without being able to match Philip Hobbs' winner. Despite filling third position once again in another Grade 2 novice hurdle at Sandown in December, he reportedly found the ground too soft behind Enrilo. Kim Bailey's lightly raced gelding wasn't seen again until the Festival in March when he ran a cracker in the Martin Pipe Conditional Jockeys' Handicap Hurdle off a mark of 137. Partnered by Sam Sheppard, he stayed on well in fourth behind Indefatigable. Beaten three and a half lengths, he would have been even closer had he not been hampered by the fall of Column of Fire at the final flight.

Happygolucky gives the impression he will make an even better chaser, especially when tackling three miles for the first time under Rules. Given the fact he appears to go well fresh, he is very much one to watch out for on his fencing bow.

POINTS TO NOTE:
Probable Best Distance   -   2m 4f - 3 miles
Preferred Going   -   Good/Soft
Connection's Comments: "Stepping up to three miles will definitely help him and, whatever he does over hurdles this season, he's going to be a cracking novice chaser next season." Kim BAILEY speaking in November 2019

GOING:	R	W	P	TRACK:	R	W	P
Soft	4	1	2	Left Handed	4	1	3
Good	1	0	1	Right	1	0	0
				Galloping	1	0	0
				Stiff/Undul.	2	0	2
				Tight	1	1	0

TRIP:	R	W	P	JOCKEY:	R	W	P
2m 4f	2	0	1	D.Bass	3	1	1
2m 5f	1	0	1	S.Sheppard	1	0	1
2m 6f	1	1	0	D.O'Connor	1	0	1
3m	1	0	1				

KESKONRISK (FR)

5 b g No Risk At All (FR) – La Courtille (FR) (Risk Seeker)
OWNER: CLAUDIO MICHAEL GRECH
TRAINER: J.P.O'BRIEN. Piltown, Co.Kilkenny.
CAREER FORM FIGURES: 1
CAREER WIN: 2020: Jan FAIRYHOUSE Yielding NHF 2m

"I love the stallion (No Risk At All) and I'd been to see the horse in Ireland – he's a real athlete, I've seen him jumping and I really like him as a type. He's not the big, old fashioned Irish chasing type, he's very French. The horse I bought at Cheltenham in December (Gallyhill) is very different – he's a big strapping chasing type whereas this horse is more of a hurdler – to start with at least," remarked Henrietta Knight after she had purchased Fairyhouse bumper winner Keskonrisk on behalf of owner Mike Grech for £370,000 at the Goffs UK January Sale at Doncaster.

A half-brother to Grade 2 winning hurdler Grand Sancy, the five year old was trained in Ireland by Timmy Hyde and was ridden by his sixteen year old grandson Daniel on his debut on New Year's day. Keskonrisk led the six runner field at halfway and maintained the gallop to win cosily by four and a half lengths. The runner-up Favori De Champdou won next time. His former handler explained at the sale: **"Timmy junior bought him in France as a two year old and he's been with us ever since. He always showed a lot of pace and has been very straightforward."**

By the same sire as Champion Hurdle winner Epatante, Keskonrisk joined Joseph O'Brien and was reportedly due to contest another bumper at the Punchestown Festival. An exciting prospect for novice hurdles this season, he may not want the ground too testing.

POINTS TO NOTE:
Probable Best Distance   -   2m – 2m 4f
Preferred Going   -   Good/Soft
Connection's Comments: "I think he is a good horse. He's got a lot of speed and is well bred. He's well schooled and jumped like a buck here one day over hurdles. He's a good looking individual and an easy mover." Timmy HYDE at Fairyhouse (1/1/20)

GOING:	R	W	P	TRACK:	R	W	P
Yielding	1	1	0	Right	1	1	0
				Galloping	1	1	0

TRIP:	R	W	P	JOCKEY:	R	W	P
2m	1	1	0	D.T.Hyde	1	1	0

KILLER KANE (IRE)
5 b g Oscar (IRE) – Native Idea (IRE) (Be My Native (USA))
OWNER: J.P.ROMANS & TAYLOR, O'DWYER
TRAINER: C.TIZZARD. Milborne Port, Dorset.
CAREER FORM FIGURES: 1
CAREER WIN: 2020: Mar BALLYCAHANE Yielding/Soft 4YO PTP 3m

As discussed, owners John Romans, Paul Taylor and Richard O'Dwyer paid £280,000 for winning pointer Amarillo Sky at the Cheltenham Festival Sale in March and the trio also parted with £300,000 for this gelded son of Oscar at the same sale.

Expert Declan Phelan comments: **"Don Doyle of the Monbeg team forked out €70,000 for this horse at the 2018 Derby Sale: as a half-brother to 2009 Supreme Novice winner, Go Native, he commanded a premium price at that store sale. It was a long haul to get a return on that risk investment, as this lanky bay gelding with a white nose, had to wait until March 2020 to make his debut in the five year old maiden at Ballycahane (Yieldng/Soft). With just the six runners, it was a middling contest, yet Killer Kane asserted rounding the home turn and, although posting a three lengths winning margin, he was never in any danger of defeat. He commanded a price of £300,0000 at Cheltenham March Sales, providing a profitable return in this instance for the Monbegs. Go Native never raced beyond two miles, so already this sibling is more versatile in terms of trip and has the stamina to cope with three miles. Another member of this equine clan is Galway Plate winner, General Idea, bred by Killer Kane's granny, and perhaps Go Native was the outlier in the family, specialising at two miles. As an expensive pointer, now stationed with Colin Tizzard, on the evidence of this one outing it is tricky to predict his future. A track spin against a higher spec of opponent may offer more clues. For now, he copes with soft/heavy, should be comfortable racing between two and a half and three miles and as a minimum will be capable of earning a track mark of 130+: should he progress in his new environs then he may become a short term player for the 2021 Albert Bartlett at the Festival next March."**

POINTS TO NOTE:
Probable Best Distance   -   2m 4f – 3 miles
Preferred Going   -   Soft
Connection's Comments: "This is a smashing big horse that's just taken a bit of time. He'll improve plenty for that and will be a fine chaser down the line." Donnchadh DOYLE at Ballycahane (7/3/20)

GOING:	R	W	P	TRACK:	R	W	P
Yielding/Soft	1	1	0	Left Handed	1	1	0

TRIP:	R	W	P	JOCKEY:	R	W	P
3m	1	1	0	R.James	1	1	0

MAROWN (IRE)

6 b g Milan – Rosie Suspect (IRE) (Presenting)
OWNER: Mr TREVOR HEMMINGS
TRAINER: N.G.RICHARDS. Greystoke, Cumbria.
CAREER FORM FIGURES: 1 - 11
CAREER WINS: 2019: Mar NEWCASTLE Heavy NHF 2m: 2020: Jan AYR Soft MH 2m 4f;
Mar AYR Soft NH 2m 4f

Triple Grand National winning owner Trevor Hemmings announced in August that he is reducing his string of around 75 horses to a third of that this season following the impact of the coronavirus. The eighty five year old, who tasted Aintree glory courtesy of Hedgehunter (2005), Ballabriggs (2011) and Many Clouds (2015), has been associated with some top-class horses, including Grade 1 winners Albertas Run and Trabolgan.

With approximately 25 horses remaining in training, arguably the most exciting youngster in his familiar green, yellow and white silks is the unbeaten Marown. Ironically, the six year old is from the family of another Grand National winner, Last Suspect, and he was acquired for €80,000 as a three year old at the Tattersalls Derby Sale in Ireland.

Given plenty of time to mature, the Nicky Richards' trained gelding didn't make his racecourse debut until March 2019. Contesting a six runner bumper at Newcastle, he overcame greenness to lead close home and win by a length. The field included subsequent hurdle winners Rock On Rocco (rated 117), Ask Himself (125) and Elf De Re (135). Marown made his hurdling debut last season over two and a half miles at Ayr in early January and wasn't hard pressed to beat Sirwilliamwallace (won next time) by two and a half lengths. Partnered by Brian Hughes, he jumped well and was always travelling strongly. Leading at the penultimate flight, the six year old only had to be shaken up to win cosily. Returning to the same course and distance a couple of months later, he readily carried his penalty to victory. Taking charge at the third last, he powered away on the run-in to easily beat the once useful chaser Aloomono by nine and a half lengths.

The plan thereafter was for Marown to run over three miles for the first time in the Grade 1 Sefton Novices' Hurdle at Aintree in April, but the season came to an end prematurely. Nicky Richards is hoping the BHA may put on some additional introductory hurdles this Autumn for horses who have only raced a couple of times over timber. Otherwise, the big strapping son of Milan will be schooled over fences with a view to going novice chasing. Rated 130 over the smaller obstacles, he is expected to reach a much loftier rating as a chaser. Owner Trevor Hemmings has another exciting youngster on his hands.

POINTS TO NOTE:
Probable Best Distance   -   2m 4f - 3 miles
Preferred Going   -   Soft
Connection's Comments: "That was a good performance first time over hurdles. He stays very well and will have learned a lot from that. He's a proper chaser in the making." Nicky RICHARDS at Ayr (2/1/20)

GOING:	R	W	P	TRACK:	R	W	P
Heavy	1	1	0	Left Handed	3	3	0
Soft	2	2	0	Galloping	3	3	0

TRIP:	R	W	P	JOCKEY:	R	W	P
2m	1	1	0	B.Hughes	3	3	0
2m 4f	2	2	0				

MISTER COFFEY (FR)

5 b g Authorized (IRE) – Mamitador (Anabaa)
OWNER: Lady BAMFORD & ALICE BAMFORD
TRAINER: N.J.HENDERSON. Lambourn, Berkshire.
CAREER FORM FIGURES: 1 - 12
CAREER WINS: 2019: Apr HUNTINGDON Good NHF 2m; Dec NEWBURY Soft Hurdle 2m

The 2007 Epsom Derby winner Authorized is responsible for the dual Grand National winner Tiger Roll, the ill-fated eight times Grade 1 winning hurdler Nichols Canyon and the hugely exciting Goshen, who was robbed of victory in the Triumph Hurdle when unseating Jamie Moore at the last.

The lightly raced Mister Coffey was also sired by the son of Montjeu and, while he has some way to go before he can be mentioned in the same breath as that trio, he is considered a potentially well treated young hurdler. Purchased as a yearling for €42,000 at the Arqana Autumn Sales in November 2016, he was trained at the start of his career by Harry Whittington and was all the rage for his racecourse debut in a bumper at Huntingdon in April 2019. Partnered by Gavin Sheehan, the 8/11 favourite was always in control and, having led with three quarters of a mile to run, he streaked clear to win by eight lengths. A month later, he was sold at the Goffs UK Spring Sale at Doncaster for £340,000 and joined Nicky Henderson. Purchased on behalf of Lady Bamford, his new trainer commented in September: **"He's a great big type who has done well and schooled absolutely brilliantly. Whether he's for this year – he's only four and huge."**

Sent off 11/8 favourite on his jumping bow in a seventeen runner Introductory hurdle at Newbury in late December, Mister Coffey made a striking impression and maintained his unbeaten record in the process. Quite keen early on, Nico De Boinville's mount travelled powerfully and jumped well before taking over on the run-in. Pushed out for a length and three quarters win, he beat the 127 rated Shakem Up'Arry in second and the useful On To Victory (rated 125) in third. Less than a month later, Nicky Henderson's gelding contested the same two miles novice hurdle at Huntingdon his stablemate and dual Champion Hurdle winner Buveur D'Air had won four years earlier. Unfortunately, the five year old spoilt his chance by racing too enthusiastically and, having attempted to make all, he was headed after the second last and well beaten by Dan Skelton's West Cork. Seven lengths in arrears, the winner subsequently finished runner-up in the Grade 2 Dovecote Novices' Hurdle at Kempton and is rated 139. Mister Coffey shaped like the most talented horse in the field at Huntingdon but failed to settle and ran himself into the ground.

Provided the Seven Barrows team can teach him to relax, the handicapper hasn't overburdened Mister Coffey with an official rating of 128. Champion Hurdle winner Epatante provided Nicky Henderson with his seventh win in the Listed Gerry Feilden Hurdle at Newbury (28th November) last season and the two miles event looks tailormade for this gelded son of Authorized.

POINTS TO NOTE:
Probable Best Distance	-	2miles
Preferred Going	-	Good/Soft

Connection's Comments: "Mister Coffey is a lovely horse. He is going to be a spectacular horse. Lady Bamford said there was no rush, to mind him, as you could see Nico was trying to do. He didn't know he'd been in a race and it was a lovely introduction. He's got there on the bridle and just had to be squeezed. A couple of weeks ago, I was saying I'd love to have him as a maiden for next season, but he's got to race. You could go chasing next season, but I don't want to do too much with him

this term. He's won his maiden so we can't put him to bed now. If anything he was too keen and he's got plenty of pace; you wouldn't want him going any further at the moment." Nicky HENDERSON at Newbury (28/12/19)

GOING:	R	W	P	TRACK:	R	W	P
Soft	2	1	1	Left Handed	1	1	0
Good	1	1	0	Right	2	1	1
				Galloping	3	2	1

TRIP:	R	W	P	JOCKEY:	R	W	P
2m	3	2	1	N.De Boinville	2	1	1
				G.Sheehan	1	1	0

PIC D'ORHY (FR)
5 b g Turgeon (USA) – Rose Candy (FR) (Roli Abi (FR))
OWNER: Mrs JOHNNY DE LA HEY
TRAINER: P.F.NICHOLLS. Ditcheat, Somerset.
CAREER FORM FIGURES: 11 – 21U220 – F61
CAREER WINS: 2018: Mar AUTEUIL Heavy Hdle 1m 7f; Apr AUTEUIL Very Soft Hdle 1m 7f; Sept AUTEUIL Very Soft Hdle 2m 2f: 2020: Feb NEWBURY Grade 3 HH 2m

Paul Nicholls has won the Arkle Trophy at Cheltenham twice with Flagship Uberalles (1999) and Azertyuiop (2003), but it is a number of years since he has had such a highly rated hurdler (151) going chasing for the first time as the ex-French trained Pic D'Orhy. Indeed, the five year old, who won three times over hurdles at Auteuil, was bought with fences in mind.

Successful in three of his seven races over hurdles in his home country when trained by Francois Nicolle, the Turgeon gelding finished runner-up in the Grade 1 Grand Course de Haies des 3 Ans at Auteuil in November 2018 on his final start for his previous connections. While he only finished tenth in the Triumph Hurdle on his first run for the former champion trainer in March last year, he travelled strongly until making a mistake at the second last and weakened thereafter. Reappearing in the Grade 2 Prix Renaud du Vivier at Auteuil in November – a race Team Ditcheat won in 2013 with Ptit Zig – he fell at the seventh. Back in action 69 days later at Ascot, Pic D'Orhy was fitted with a tongue tie for the first time but he pulled hard and didn't get home over the extended two miles three trip. Beaten nearly fifteen lengths in sixth, he then dropped back to the minimum distance in the *Betfair* Hurdle at Newbury in February. Racing off a mark of 146, Harry Cobden's mount belied his odds of 33/1 beating Ciel De Neige by three parts of a length. The five year old moved well throughout before being driven out to win the valuable prize for a second time for the Nicholls outfit. **"We bought him to go chasing and he's a big horse who will be a serious chaser. He doesn't lack speed. He's one for the future and we'll mind him,"** commented his trainer afterwards.

I like the fact Pic D'Orhy's connections elected to swerve the Cheltenham Festival – Nicholls has been crowned champion trainer on eleven occasions and it hasn't happened by accident. He protected the likes of Cyrname and Silviniaco Conti early in their careers and reaped the rewards later on. A lesser handler would have supplemented him for the Champion Hurdle and he would have endured a hard race so early in his career. There is every chance Pic D'Orhy will gain some experience of the Cheltenham fences in the Grade 2 event at the November meeting (15th) – his stable have won it ten times.

POINTS TO NOTE:
Probable Best Distance - 2 miles
Preferred Going - Good/Soft
Connection's Comments: "He's only a five year old but looks fantastic and what a smashing chaser he'll be next season. If you look at him as a model, you can see why I like him so much. He's every bit a chaser. He's a hugely exciting horse for chasing. He loved the decent ground at Newbury. He hated the mud at Ascot and was a different animal on good ground." Paul NICHOLLS speaking in February

GOING:	R	W	P		TRACK:	R	W	P
Heavy	3	1	0		Left Handed	10	4	3
Very Soft	6	2	3		Right	1	0	0
Good/Soft	1	0	0		Galloping	10	4	3
Good	1	1	0		Stiff/Undul.	1	0	0

TRIP:	R	W	P		JOCKEY:	R	W	P
1m 7f	2	2	0		H.Cobden	3	1	0
2m	1	1	0		S.T-Davies	1	0	0
2m 1f	3	0	1		T.Gueguen	6	3	2
2m 2f	3	1	2		G.Masure	1	0	1
2m 3f	2	0	0					

QUEENS BROOK (IRE)

5 b m Shirocco (GER) – Awesome Miracle (IRE) (Supreme Leader)
OWNER: NOEL MORAN / MRS VALERIE MORAN
TRAINER: G.ELLIOTT. Longwood, Co.Meath.
CAREER FORM FIGURES: 3 - 113
CAREER WINS: 2019: Nov DROMAHANE Yielding/Soft 4YO Mdn PTP 3m: 2020: Feb GOWRAN PARK Heavy NHF 2m 1f

Gordon Elliott won the Cheltenham Festival bumper for the first time in 2017 with the ill-fated mare Fayonagh and he nearly repeated the trick in March with another high-class filly, namely Queens Brook. The daughter of Shirocco held every chance in the homestraight before coming off third best behind the Willie Mullins trained pair Ferny Hollow and Appreciate It. Beaten less than six lengths, the former Irish pointer will be a major force in mares' novice hurdles this season with the Grade 2 Dawn Run Novices' Hurdle at Cheltenham her ultimate target – a race his trainer has never won.

"It is easy to describe her as the leading mare from the 2019/20 pointing season. Aidan Fitzgerald paid €25,000 for her at the 2018 Derby Store Sale: allowed time to develop, she was given a considerate introduction when a ten length third to Cill Anna at Monksgrange in March 2019. On her next start, at Dromahane (Yielding/Soft) in November, she mastered Hand In My Pocket in a fine shoot out over the final half mile: jumping crisply under the cosh and finding generously to take the win. A medium sized, muscular lady, a visit to Cheltenham Tattersalls Sales resulted in Gordon Elliott buying her for £160,000. On her track debut she coped with very testing heavy ground at Gowran when pulverising her rivals by 21 lengths and earned a crack at the Cheltenham Festival bumper. She ran a highly commendable third at the Festival, given that she was experiencing a massive hike in the class of rival she was facing, the bronze medal was more than acceptable and confirmed that she was continuing to improve with each start. To date she has won over two miles and three miles, left and right handed, on heavy and on yielding to soft, the versatility of this mare makes her exciting as she can take advantage of plenty of opportunities. Bound to win at Graded level over hurdles this winter, she could be capable of winning a Cheltenham Festival race, in due course."

POINTS TO NOTE:
Probable Best Distance   -   2m – 3 miles
Preferred Going   -   Good/Soft
Connection's Comments: "Queens Brook is a good mare we think. We were a bit worried today with the ground as heavy as it was. We think a lot of her. I think she'll go on most ground." Gordon ELLIOTT at Gowran (15/2/20)

GOING:	R	W	P	TRACK	R	W	P
Heavy	1	1	0	Left Handed	3	1	2
Soft	1	0	1	Right	1	1	0
Yielding/Soft	1	1	0	Stiff/Undul.	1	0	1
Good/Yielding	1	0	1	Tight/Undul.	1	1	0

TRIP:	R	W	P	JOCKEY:	R	W	P
2m	1	0	1	J.J.Codd	2	1	1
2m 1f	1	1	0	R.Deegan	2	1	1
3m	2	1	1				

ROSE OF ARCADIA (IRE)
5 b m Arcadio (GER) – Rosie Lea (IRE) (Supreme Leader)
OWNER: CHEVELEY PARK STUD
TRAINER: C.TIZZARD. Milborne Port, Dorset
CAREER FORM FIGURES: 11
CAREER WINS: 2019: Dec TATTERSALLS FARM Soft/Heavy 4YO Mdn PTP 3m: 2020: Mar TAUNTON Heavy NHF 2m

Colin Tizzard has trained 32 Grade 1 winners during his career, including top-class chasers Cue Card (9), Lostintranslation (2) and Native River (2). It is fair to say though the West Country handler has yet to have a high-class mare through his hands. That may be about to change though having taken charge of the unbeaten winning pointer Rose of Arcadia, who was acquired for £170,000 at the Cheltenham December Sale on behalf of Cheveley Park Stud.

"By virtue of winning her only point this lady made one of the highest prices for her sex amongst the crop of mares from the 2019/20 point campaign. She raced for Ulster handler Danny Fitzsimons at Tattersalls (Soft/Heavy) in December. Amateur jockey, Declan Lavery, gave her the freedom to move along at a slick pace and the partnership established a healthy lead. She commanded a fifteen lengths advantage at the third last. A couple of her pursuers got to within three or four lengths at the final fence: this mare merely had to be nudged out without any pressure applied to win by a snug two lengths. She then sold to Tizzard/Cheveley Park for £170,000 at Cheltenham December Sales. Her immediate pedigree does not offer encouragement: her dam was 0/12 on the track: you delve back a few blood lines to notice that the grand dam produced Hennessy winner / Aintree Grand National runner up, Suny Bay. Tizzard introduced her to track racing in a bumper at Taunton (Heavy) in March and she made all to pulverise weak opposition. In the two wins to date, she has yet to see a rival: she is a relaxed and controlled front runner: her jumping of point fences is precise and this trait will bring rewards. The Tizzard's signalled the esteem in which they hold her, as they paid £260,000 to capture Shirocco's Dream, the mare who finished second in the Tattersalls point. This "Rose" could be a leading light in the UK in the mares' novice hurdle division in 2020/21, as she has natural speed and a fine jumping technique," believes expert Declan Phelan.

A five and a half lengths winner of her bumper at Taunton, Rose of Arcadia has only raced right handed and on testing ground. A free going type, she will take some pegging back in mares' novice hurdles.

POINTS TO NOTE:

Probable Best Distance	-	2m 4f - 3 miles
Preferred Going	-	Soft

GOING:	R	W	P	TRACK:	R	W	P
Heavy	1	1	0	Right	2	2	0
Soft/Heavy	1	1	0	Tight	1	1	0

TRIP:	R	W	P	JOCKEY:	R	W	P
2m	1	1	0	J.J.O'Neill Jnr	1	1	0
3m	1	1	0	D.Lavery	1	1	0

SHISHKIN (IRE)

6 b g Sholokhov (IRE) – Labarynth (IRE) (Exit To Nowhere (USA))
OWNER: Mrs J.DONNELLY
TRAINER: N.J.HENDERSON. Lambourn, Berkshire.
CAREER FORM FIGURES: 3 – 11 – F111
CAREER WINS: 2018: Nov LINGSTOWN Good 4YO Mdn PTP 3m: 2019: Mar KEMPTON Good/Soft NHF 2m: Jan NEWBURY Heavy NH 2m; Feb HUNTINGDON Good/Soft Lstd NH 2m 3f; Mar CHELTENHAM Soft Grade 1 NH

There can be few, if any, more exciting two mile novice chase prospects in training than last season's *Skybet* Supreme Novices' Hurdle winner Shishkin. The current ante-post favourite for next March's Arkle Trophy, a race Nicky Henderson has won six times, including with Sprinter Sacre (2012) and Altior (2017), this winning Irish pointer looks to be cut from the same cloth.

The Sholokhov gelding contested two point-to-points for Virginia Considine winning by eight lengths on the second occasion in November 2018. Snapped up for £170,000 at the Cheltenham Sales the following month, he was an impressive winner by the same margin of a bumper at Kempton in March 2019 on his first start for the champion trainer. Things didn't go to plan on his hurdles debut at Newbury in December last year though when falling at the second flight. Back in action at his local track less than a month later, Shishkin oozed class as he powered clear on the run-in to beat Shakem Up'Arry by eleven lengths. Henderson remarked: **"He's smart. Not many horses quicken out of that ground, so you'd have to be impressed. It was unfortunate what happened the first time over hurdles, but Nico (De Boinville) said it was like he learned something that day. He was quite gassy that day because he's enthusiastic. Today, he was beautifully relaxed and never touched a hurdle."** Stepping up to an extended two miles three in the Listed Sidney Banks Memorial Novices' Hurdle at Huntingdon in February, he readily swept aside the 139 rated Shan Blue to win by eleven lengths. The six year old then provided Henderson with his fourth win in the Festival opener but not without a scare or two along the way. A big drifter beforehand, the 6/1 chance overcame a serious mistake at the third flight and was forced wide on the hometurn following the departures of Elixir D'Ainay and Captain Guinness. Challenging at the last, Nico De Boinville's partner edged out Abacadabras by a head with eleven lengths back to stablemate Chantry House. **"I thought that was a super run all things considered. That showed a bit of superstar quality. Everything conspired against him today but he managed to find a way to win and that's what champions tend to do. Going to the downhill hurdle, he had to grab it and landed on all fours. From then on down the back, it was really hard work. He's so talented this horse. He has tremendous gears and gets you out of an awful lot of trouble. Wherever he goes next season, it might be that we've found another really good one,"** stated his jockey afterwards.

Finally, leading amateur Rob James, who rode his first Cheltenham Festival winner in March aboard Milan Native in the Kim Muir, partnered Shishkin in his two point-to-points and the 27 year old commented in late March: **"He won on the bridle for me one day at Lingstown. Virginia Considine trained him and he's not slow at all, he showed me plenty of gears. He actually took a run – he was a backward type of horse and he finished third first time out – but he was a completely different proposition at Lingstown that day. He travelled and jumped, and he quickened up going to the last and then quickened up again going to the line. I'd say they'll probably go chasing with him next year, he's a great lepper and will go right to the top."** Shishkin is top-class and, granted luck with injuries, it will take a very good horse to deny him victory in next March's Arkle Trophy.

POINTS TO NOTE:
Probable Best Distance - **2 miles**
Preferred Going - **Good/Soft**
Connection's Comments: "He's a beautiful horse. He's a chaser in the making. I'm not saying he's another Altior, but he's an Altior type of horse. He has a lot of speed and a lot of scope." Nicky HENDERSON at Huntingdon (6/2/20)

GOING:	R	W	P	TRACK:	R	W	P
Heavy	1	1	0	Left-Handed	3	2	0
Soft	2	1	0	Right	4	3	0
Yielding/Soft	1	0	0	Galloping	3	2	0
Good/Soft	2	2	0	Stiff/Undul.	1	1	0
Good	1	1	0	Tight	1	1	0

TRIP:	R	W	P	JOCKEY:	R	W	P
2m	4	3	0	N.De Boinville	5	4	0
2m 3f	1	1	0	R.James	2	1	0
3m	2	1	0				

SIR GERHARD (IRE)

5 b g Jeremy (USA) – Faanan Aldaar (IRE) (Authorized (IRE))
OWNER: CHEVELEY PARK STUD
TRAINER: G.ELLIOTT. Longwood, Co.Meath.
CAREER FORM FIGURES: 1
CAREER WIN: 2019: Nov BOULTA Yielding/Soft 4YO Mdn PTP 3m

The Cheltenham Festival bumper has been dominated by Willie Mullins (10 wins) and Gordon Elliott (2 wins) in recent seasons with the pair sharing the honours during the last four years. Owners Cheveley Park Stud have been responsible for the last two winners, namely Envoi Allen (Elliott) and Ferny Hollow (Mullins). It is possible the same red, white and blues colours could be carried to glory next March in the same event by expensive purchase Sir Gerhard, who was acquitted for £400,000 at the Cheltenham December Sale. Yet to run for his new connections, he was a twelve lengths winner of his only Irish point the previous month.

"Derek O'Connor has linked up with Ellmarie Holden in the last two years, helping prepare and ride her pointers: the partnership has enjoyed some success, the highlight no doubt was the debut victory of this horse at Boulta (Yielding/Soft) in November. Derek was keen for the horse to get as much daylight at the fences as possible, and positioned his charge a close second/third until upping the ante heading to the second last and then accelerating away for minimum pressure to win by a handsome twelve lengths. The time compared to other races on the card was nothing out of the ordinary, yet the style of the win stood out like a sore thumb. A solid bay gelding with a broad white face, he cost Holden €72,000 as a store in 2018: his dam was rated 77 on the Flat and recorded one win in her stint of racing, a two mile maiden hurdle at Roscommon. The grand dam has an eye catching set of offspring, included amongst them Group 1 winner Zafeen (St James Palace Stakes 2003). On pedigree, this horse ought to have more speed than stamina. Gordon Elliott paid £400,000 to add him to his string at Cheltenham Sales in December and winning an ordinary bumper should be a formality, and he could be entertained as a possible for the 2020 Cheltenham Festival bumper (remains to be seen how he will handle an uphill finish). Over the years, Boulta has been a track which tends to unearth speedier chasing types rather than dour stayers. If Gordon can cultivate this five year old, then in time his career path could lead towards Arkle and Queen Mother races, and that natural speed he possesses will come in handy," believes expert Declan Phelan.

POINTS TO NOTE:
Probable Best Distance	-	2m – 2m 4f
Preferred Going	-	Good/Soft

GOING:	R	W	P	TRACK	R	W	P
Yielding/Soft	1	1	0	Left Handed	1	1	0

TRIP:	R	W	P	JOCKEY:	R	W	P
3m	1	1	0	D.O'Connor	1	1	0

SIZABLE SAM

5 ch g Black Sam Bellamy (IRE) – Halo Flora (Alflora (IRE))
OWNER: The HOPEFULS & KELVIN-HUGHES
TRAINER: J.SCOTT. Brompton Regis, Somerset.
CAREER FORM FIGURES: 21
CAREER WIN: 2020: Feb WARWICK Good/Soft NHF 2m

West country handler Jeremy Scott has tasted Graded success with Melodic Rendezvous (Grade 1 Tolworth Hurdle, plus triple Grade 2 winner) and Gone To Lunch. He was also responsible for a couple of useful novice chasers last winter, namely Champagne Court and Dashel Drasher (injured after his win at Haydock in December).

The stable are believed to be looking forward to sending the twice raced Sizable Sam over timber for the first time this season. Purchased for £18,000 at the Doncaster Spring Sales a couple of years ago, the Black Sam Bellamy gelding was denied by a short head on his debut in a bumper at Wincanton in November. Confirmation Bias provided Paul Nicholls with his fourth win in the race in the last eight years, but the runner-up was in the firing line from the outset only to be headed close home. The third Mont Segur, who hung left late on, won impressively next time. Given a break (91 days), the five year old returned in a similar event at Warwick in February and produced a smart performance. Sent off 6/1, Sizable Sam moved well throughout and only had to be nudged out to beat the well regarded Cadzand by a length and a quarter.

Previously owned by the trainer's wife Camilla, he has been bought by a syndicate headed by Richard Kelvin-Hughes, of Santini fame, since, which suggests Sizable Sam is a horse with a rosy future. Although bred to stay further, one would expect him to reappear over two miles over hurdles with a trip to somewhere like Exeter in the Autumn a distinct possibility. Provided he isn't overfaced, the chestnut should be in for a profitable campaign.

POINTS TO NOTE:

Probable Best Distance -	**2m – 2m 4f**
Preferred Going -	**Good/Soft**

GOING:	R	W	P	TRACK:	R	W	P
Good/Soft	2	1	1	Left Handed	1	1	0
				Right	1	0	1
				Galloping	1	0	1
				Tight/Undul.	1	1	0

TRIP:	R	W	P	JOCKEY:	R	W	P
2m	2	1	1	N.Scholfield	2	1	1

SOUTHFIELD HARVEST

6 b g Kayf Tara – Chamoss Royale (FR) (Garde Royale (IRE))
OWNER: Mrs ANGELA YEOMAN & PAUL K.BARBER
TRAINER: P.F.NICHOLLS. Ditcheat, Somerset.
CAREER FORM FIGURES: 31 - 21
CAREER WINS: 2019: Apr CHEPSTOW Good NHF 2m: 2020: Feb LUDLOW Soft MH 3m

From a family Paul Nicholls knows well, the lightly raced Southfield Harvest is a half-brother to former stablemates Southfield Theatre (won 9 times, including Grade 2 novice chase) and Southfield Vic. Indeed, the former champion trainer handled the dam Chamoss Royale to win four times.

There is a belief at Ditcheat the latest offspring is a potentially well handicapped young hurdler who will make an even better chaser in time. Southfield Harvest ran in two bumpers during the spring of last year and, having finished third behind the subsequent Cheltenham Festival runner-up Pileon on his debut, he won next time at Chepstow beating Stolen Silver (won a Grade 2 novice hurdle last season). Switched to hurdles last term, he didn't make his jumping bow until early January when a length and a half runner-up behind Hurricane Harvey at Wincanton over an extended two miles five. Bryony Frost's mount attempted to make all and, once headed between the final two flights, the Kayf Tara gelding rallied on the run-in. Four lengths clear of the third (St Barts), who won next time, he appreciated the step up to three miles at Ludlow over a month later. Ridden with more restraint, he reeled in Muckamore (won since) after the last to win going away by a length and a quarter.

Eligible for novice hurdles until the 1st December, the handicapper has granted Southfield Harvest a mark of 127, which appears favourable. There is a three miles Listed handicap hurdle at Cheltenham (14th November), which could be a first half of the season target before his connections decide whether to send him chasing thereafter. The aforementioned Southfield Theatre finished a narrow third in the race seven years ago. Either way, there are plenty more races to be won with this fine staying prospect.

POINTS TO NOTE:

Probable Best Distance	-	**3 miles**
Preferred Going	-	**Good/Soft**

GOING:	R	W	P	TRACK:	R	W	P
Soft	2	1	1	Left Handed	1	1	0
Good/Soft	1	0	0	Right	3	1	1
Good	1	1	0	Galloping	1	0	1
				Stiff/Undul.	2	1	0
				Tight	1	1	0

TRIP:	R	W	P	JOCKEY:	R	W	P
2m	1	1	0	H.Cobden	2	1	0
2m 1f	1	0	0	B.Frost	2	1	1
2m 5f	1	0	1				
3m	1	1	0				

SPORTING JOHN (IRE)

5 bb g Getaway (GER) – Wild Spell (IRE) (Oscar (IRE))
OWNER: J.P.McMANUS
TRAINER: P.J.HOBBS. Minehead, Somerset.
CAREER FORM FIGURES: 1 - 1117
CAREER WINS: 2019: Mar BORRIS HOUSE Soft 4YO Mdn PTP 3m; Nov EXETER Soft NH
2m 1f; Dec EXETER Soft NH 2m 1f: 2020: Feb ASCOT Soft NH 2m 3f

Philip Hobbs has 20 Cheltenham Festival winners on his CV, but the 2020 version won't be one he will look back on with fond memories. Stable star Defi Du Seuil was sent off 2/5 favourite for the Queen Mother Champion Chase but could only finish fourth of five, while Grade 1 winning novice Thyme Hill, who filled the same position, was mounting his challenge when meeting trouble in running in the Albert Bartlett Novices' Hurdle. The short head defeat of Pileon in the Martin Pipe Conditional Jockeys' Handicap Hurdle typified the Minehead trainer's week.

Aside from Defi Du Seuil, the other major disappointment for Hobbs over the four days was Sporting John's performance in the Ballymore Novices' Hurdle. The unbeaten Getaway gelding was sent off 5/1 second favourite behind Envoi Allen, but Barry Geraghty's mount looked out of sorts with a circuit to run. The five year old trailed in a well beaten seventh and was thirty lengths in arrears of Gordon Elliott's superstar. His trainer said afterwards: **"He was a bit odd behind after the race, as if something was amiss, but he's come right now."**

Prior to that, the winning Irish pointer (won the same maiden at Borris House which Andy Dufresne had scored in the year before),who was bought for £160,000 at the Cheltenham Festival Sale twelve months earlier, had looked a top-class novice hurdler winning twice at Exeter and Ascot. A length and three quarters winner at the former track on his Rules debut in November, he had subsequent scorers Harry Senior (Grade 2), Bullionaire, Kissesforkatie and Eritage in behind. The J.P.McManus owned gelding then beat Buckhorn George by eight lengths over the same course and distance a month later under a penalty with Barry Geraghty barely moving a muscle. Off the track for a couple of months, he produced an even more convincing display when beating Pipesmoker and Grade 2 winner Master Debonair by upwards of six and a half lengths at Ascot in February. Tackling two miles three for the first time, he led two out before treating his market rivals with disdain. Perhaps that performance left its mark on Sporting John because 25 days later at Cheltenham, he looked a shadow of his former self and never threatened.

Having spent the summer at his owner's Martinstown Stud in Ireland, Sporting John has had a long break and remains a tremendous chasing prospect. The now retired Barry Geraghty feels the gelding possesses enough speed for two miles, which brings the Arkle Trophy into consideration, otherwise the JLT Novices' Chase looks the obvious target next spring. McManus and Hobbs combined to win the latter event in 2019 with the aforementioned Defi Du Seuil. The Getaway gelding looked every inch a Grade 1 horse when winning at Ascot in February.

POINTS TO NOTE:
Probable Best Distance   -   2m 4f
Preferred Going   -   Soft
Connection's Comments: **"Barry (Geraghty) thinks he has enough pace for two miles but he obviously stays two and a half. He's probably going to be better over fences and that's something to look forward to." Philip HOBBS at Ascot (15/2/20)**

GOING:	R	W	P		TRACK:	R	W	P
Soft	5	4	0		Left Handed	2	1	0
					Right	3	3	0
					Galloping	1	1	0
					Stiff/Undul.	3	2	0

TRIP:	R	W	P		JOCKEY:	R	W	P
2m 1f	2	2	0		B.Geraghty	4	3	0
2m 3f	1	1	0		J.P.O'Rourke	1	1	0
2m 5f	1	0	0					
3m	1	1	0					

THE BIG BREAKAWAY (IRE)

5 ch g Getaway (GER) – Princess Mairead (IRE) (Blueprint (IRE))
OWNER: ERIC JONES, GEOFF NICHOLAS, JOHN ROMANS
TRAINER: C.TIZZARD. Milborne Port, Dorset.
CAREER FORM FIGURES: 1 - 114
CAREER WINS: 2019: Apr QUAKERSTOWN Good/Yielding 4YO Mdn PTP 3m; Nov CHEPSTOW Soft MH 2m 3f; Dec NEWBURY Soft NH 2m 4f

With a cast which could potentially include the first three home in last season's Albert Bartlett Novices' Hurdle, namely Monkfish, Latest Exhibition and Fury Road, plus the Ballymore Novices' Hurdle third The Big Getaway, next March's RSA Chase is already threatening to be one of the races of the 2021 Cheltenham Festival.

Even allowing for those possible top notch novices, the one who appeals most from an ante-post point of view is The Big Breakaway. Colin Tizzard's former Irish pointer is widely available at 33/1 and that represents tremendous value. The big strapping Getaway gelding is crying out for a step up to three miles and is expected to make an even better chaser. A ten lengths winner of his only point-to-point (Champagne Fever (2011), Next Destination (2016) and Brewin'upastorm (2017) won the same maiden at Quakerstown) when trained by Donnchadh Doyle, he was subsequently bought for €360,000 at the Goffs Punchestown Horses in Training Sale in May 2019.

A half-brother to Grade 3 winning chaser and Cheltenham Festival runner-up Kildisart, he was an eight lengths winner on his hurdles debut at Chepstow in November. Leading between the final two flights, he bounded clear from subsequent winner Blackjack Kentucky. Reappearing a month later, it was a similar story as Robbie Power's mount handed out a seven lengths beating to another expensive ex-pointer Papa Tango Charly at Newbury. Conceding six pounds to Jonjo O'Neill's runner-up, he sauntered clear on the approach to the final flight. His trainer commented afterwards: **"He is a beautiful young horse. He's as lovely a staying novice as we've had I'd say."** The five year old was then due to contest the Grade 2 novice hurdle at Cheltenham's Trials meeting in late January but banged his hock at home. Assistant trainer Joe Tizzard explained: **"We wanted to take him to Trials day but he was fighting with a horse next door when they got fed and he kicked the stable and his hock swelled up. He's a very talented horse and takes everything in his stride. He jumps for fun and has a lot of raw ability. Robbie (Power) is in love with him and he could be anything. He's as nice and exciting a young horse as we've ever had."**

The Big Breakaway therefore headed to the Cheltenham Festival in March with limited experience and hadn't been in action for 84 days. Still in contention approaching the second last in the Grade 1 Ballymore Novices' Hurdle, he was unable to muster the speed of the

Gordon Elliott trained pair Envoi Allen and Easywork but stayed on to finish fourth. Beaten less than fifteen lengths, he will be in his element tackling longer trips over fences and it will be a surprise if the 144 rated hurdler doesn't reach a considerably higher mark as a chaser.

POINTS TO NOTE:
Probable Best Distance   -   3 miles
Preferred Going   -   Good/Soft
Connection's Comments: "The Big Breakaway has excited us all the way through and has gone about that like a really nice horse, but we've got to remind ourselves he's only four. He's 17hh, so he's going to keep improving. He's a lovely actioned horse and I'm sure he'll be even better on better ground, but he can cope with easy ground with his size and raw ability. He's not short of pace and works well at home. He's one of our nicest young horses." Joe TIZZARD at Chepstow (20/11/19)

GOING:	R	W	P	TRACK:	R	W	P
Soft	3	2	0	Left Handed	4	3	0
Good/Yielding	1	1	0	Galloping	1	1	0
				Stiff/Undul.	2	1	0

TRIP:	R	W	P	JOCKEY:	R	W	P
2m 3f	1	1	0	R.M.Power	3	2	0
2m 4f	1	1	0	R.James	1	1	0
2m 5f	1	0	0				
3m	1	1	0				

THE BIG GETAWAY (IRE)
6 b g Getaway (GER) – Saddlers Dawn (IRE) (Saddlers' Hall (IRE))
OWNER: Mrs J.DONNELLY
TRAINER: W.P.MULLINS. Bagenalstown, Co.Carlow.
CAREER FORM FIGURES: 1 – 2 - 21413
CAREER WINS: 2018: Mar HORSE & JOCKEY Yielding/Soft 4YO Mdn PTP 3m: 2019: Nov PUNCHESTOWN Soft NHF 2m: 2020: Jan NAAS Yielding/Soft MH 2m 3f

The Big Breakaway's stiffest opposition in March may be provided by The Big Getaway. Willie Mullins' huge imposing gelding finished six and a half lengths in front of Colin Tizzard's five year old when the pair met in the Ballymore Novices' Hurdle last spring, filling the third and fourth positions respectively. Indeed, the pair have similar profiles. He, too, began his career by winning a point-to-point in Ireland for Donnchadh Doyle – a thirty lengths winner at Horse & Jockey in March 2018 before being sold to Ireland's champion trainer for £230,000 at the Cheltenham Festival Sale four days later.

Here is what point expert Declan Phelan wrote in the 2018/2019 edition of OJA: "As his name would hint, this is a powerfully built bay son of Getaway from the Dawn Run family line. He set out to make all at Horse & Jockey (Yielding/Soft) and his task was simplified when his main danger Diol Ker fell at the third last: thereafter he galloped clear from the rest winning by a wide margin. Despite his size, he is nimble and agile and he has the hallmarks of a horse capable of developing into a proper staying Graded chaser. I noted a knee action, and he may prefer some juice in the ground: he is a horse with an immense stride and covers ground easily."

Runner-up in a couple of bumpers at Navan (behind subsequent Grade 1 winning novice hurdler Fiddlerontheroof) and Punchestown, he returned to the latter track in November and scored at the third time of asking. Following The Big Getaway's seven lengths win, Mullins commented: **"He's as big a horse as I've ever had. He just gallops all day and probably wants softer ground."** Sent hurdling, he was unlucky not to win at the first time of asking at Leopardstown's Christmas meeting. Stepping up to two and a half miles, Paul Townend partnered him for the first time and, having gone to the front on the approach to the final hurdle, he made a mistake and lost his momentum. That proved costly and he crossed the line in fourth place behind Cobbler's Way. Back in action less than a month later at Naas, he was suited by a change of tactics and made all to win by seventeen lengths. It was a powerful display with his trainer saying: **"The more positive tactics we used today paid off handsomely. He really loves jumping and galloped all the way to the line."**Despite the fact The Big Getaway was beaten eight lengths at Cheltenham in March, he still ran well and appeared to have all his rivals in trouble rounding the final bend. Paul Townend's mount couldn't match the finishing burst of Envoi Allen though.

Rather like The Big Breakway, three miles and fences will bring out the best in The Big Getaway. The thought of the Getaway gelding bowling along in front in staying novice chases this winter and running his rivals ragged is something to look forward to. Owner Joe Donnelly may have another budding Al Boum Photo on his hands.

POINTS TO NOTE:
Probable Best Distance - **2m 4f - 3 miles**
Preferred Going - **Soft**
Connection's Comments: "He was beaten by a proper horse. Ours looks a real chasing type and I imagine we'll be looking towards the RSA Chase next season." Willie MULLINS speaking at Cheltenham (11/3/20)

GOING:	R	W	P	TRACK:	R	W	P
Soft	3	1	2	Left Handed	5	2	2
Yielding/Soft	2	2	0	Right	2	1	1
Yielding	1	0	0	Galloping	5	3	0
Good/Yielding	1	0	1	Stiff/Undul.	1	0	1

TRIP:	R	W	P	JOCKEY:	R	W	P
2m	3	1	2	P.Townend	3	1	1
2m 3f	1	1	0	P.W.Mullins	3	1	2
2m 4f	1	0	0	H.Dunne	1	1	0
2m 5f	1	0	1				
3m	1	1	0				

THE EDGAR WALLACE (IRE)
5 b g Flemensfirth (USA) – Annalecky (IRE) (Bob's Return (IRE))
OWNER: P.J.ANDREWS
TRAINER: K.C.BAILEY. Andoversford, Cheltenham.
CAREER FORM FIGURES: 321
CAREER WIN: 2020: Mar HEREFORD Soft NHF 2m

It was announced in August that dual champion National Hunt sire Flemensfirth has been retired from stallion duties at the age of 28. Based at The Beeches Stud, Coolmore's division in County Waterford, he was a dual Group 1 winner on the Flat for Sheikh Mohammed and John Gosden. Responsible for Cheltenham Gold Cup winner Imperial Commander, plus other Grade 1 winning chasers Flemenstar, Lostintranslation, Topofthegame, Waiting Patiently and one of my all-time favourites Tidal Bay, he has made a huge impression on the jumping scene this century.

The Edgar Wallace is another of his progeny and his trainer Kim Bailey is understandably looking forward to unleashing the five year old over timber this season. Bought for €140,000 as a three year old at the Goffs Landrover Sale in Ireland in June 2018, he is a half-brother to another Cheltenham Festival winner, Black Hercules. Sent off 3/1 joint favourite on his debut in a bumper at Exeter in December, he was prominent throughout and, having been headed with quarter of a mile to run, Ned Curtis' mount rallied well to finish third. Beaten less than two lengths, both the fourth and fifth have won since. A couple of months later, The Edgar Wallace had the misfortune to bump into the aforementioned Adrimel at Doncaster in mid February. Challenging strongly inside the final two furlongs, he failed by a length and a quarter to get passed Tom Lacey's former pointer, in receipt of seven pounds, but pulled twenty one lengths clear of the third. It was a case of third time lucky at Hereford the following month as he outclassed six opponents by upwards of eight lengths. Making all under David Bass, the Flemensfirth gelding looked a relentless galloper as he dominated throughout.

Speaking to Kim Bailey during the summer, one gets the impression he thinks The Edgar Wallace could be something special once jumping obstacles. Very much a stayer in the making, it will be disappointing if he doesn't develop into an above average two and a half miles plus novice hurdler this winter.

POINTS TO NOTE:

Probable Best Distance			-	**2m 4f - 3 miles**			
Preferred Going			-	**Good/Soft**			

GOING:	R	W	P	TRACK:	R	W	P
Soft	3	1	2	Left Handed	1	0	1
				Right	2	1	1
				Galloping	1	0	1
				Stiff/Undul.	1	0	1
				Tight	1	1	0

TRIP:	R	W	P	JOCKEY:	R	W	P
2m	2	1	1	D.Bass	2	1	1
2m 1f	1	0	1	N.Curtis	1	0	1

ZANAHIYR (IRE)
3 ch g Nathaniel (IRE) – Zariyna (IRE) (Marju (IRE))
OWNER: NOEL MORAN & Mrs VALERIE MORAN
TRAINER: G.ELLIOTT. Longwood, Co.Meath.
CAREER FLAT FORM FIGURES: 6 - 921
CAREER FLAT WIN: 2020: July FAIRYHOUSE Good/Yielding Mdn 1m 4f

Another of Noel and Valeire Moran's new recruits is the potential Triumph Hurdle contender Zanahiyr, who was bought privately following his win on the Flat at Fairyhouse this summer. Trained by Mick Halford, the former Aga Khan owned three year old has been gelded since joining Gordon Elliott with the view to going hurdling this Autumn. Sixth on his only run as a juvenile over seven furlongs at the Curragh in October last year, the son of Nathaniel may have found the ground a shade lively when ninth on his reappearance at the same track in June. Stepped up to a mile and five at Navan eleven days later, Zanahiyr appreciated the rain softened ground and finished a staying on second behind Hy Brasil. He then got off the mark at the fourth time of asking when running on strongly to beat Ciel D'Afrique (runner-up at Galway since and rated 79) by a length and a quarter in a twelve furlongs maiden at

Fairyhouse in early July. It was his third run in 23 days and he is seemingly thriving with racing.

Nathaniel produced two winners at the Cheltenham Festival this year, namely Burning Victory (Triumph Hurdle) and Concertista (mares' novice hurdle), plus Navajo Pass finished fourth in the former event, too. There is every chance he may repeat the trick in the 2021 renewal with this potentially high-class recruit. It is a race Gordon Elliott has won twice with Tiger Roll (2014) and Farclas (2018), plus Coeur Sublime (has joined Gearoid McLoughlin) finished runner-up in 2019.

POINTS TO NOTE:
Probable Best Distance	-	2 miles
Preferred Going	-	Good/Soft

Connection's Comments: "He's a lovely big horse. He was very babyish and, even in Navan, he really only got the hang of things up the hill. I knew he'd come on from it and he was a lot more on the ball today. I'll give him a bit of a chance now and we'll take it from there. He's a horse with a future. He stays well and has a great attitude. I'd say he's going to keep on improving and he has the scope to do it." Former trainer Mick HALFORD at Fairyhouse (5/7/20)

GOING:	R	W	P	TRACK:	R	W	P
Soft	2	0	1	Left Handed	1	0	1
Good/Yielding	1	1	0	Right	3	1	0
Good/Firm	1	0	0	Galloping	4	1	1

TRIP:	R	W	P	JOCKEY:	R	W	P
7f	1	0	0	S.Davis	1	1	0
1m 2f	1	0	0	R.P.Whelan	3	0	1
1m 4f	1	1	0				
1m 5f	1	0	1				

Please see pages 182-194
for details of the

One Jump Ahead Updates

RICH & SUSANNAH RICCI

CHELTENHAM FESTIVAL WINNERS: 17

Novice Hurdlers

EDEN FLIGHT raced twice over hurdles last season and, having disappointed first time out at Navan, he was runner-up at Fairyhouse on his latest start. Beaten six lengths by the 122 rated Braeside, he is a chaser in the making, but is capable of winning a staying novice hurdle before going over fences. **EL BARRA** is a six year old but has yet to run for us having had a minor injury the previous season. He was due to run last spring with the intention of giving him one run before heading to the Punchestown Festival. Unfortunately, it never happened but he remains a promising horse who finished second behind Fury Road in his only point-to-point. It is possible he will run in a bumper before going novice hurdling. **ELEONORE D'APSIS** was bought at the Arqana May sale a couple of years ago, but hasn't run for us yet. A nice mare by Apsis, she won her only AQPS Flat race in France by three and a half lengths. She looks a staying type and will be aimed at mares' novice hurdles. **FEU DU BRESIL** is a gorgeous looking horse who has developed physically since arriving from France. Unable to run last season, due to a slight setback, he is one to look forward to during the second half of the season. Runner-up on his only start at Auteuil, his form is strong – the winner, third, fourth and fifth have all won since. He is potentially a very nice horse. **FIGAROC** is a lovely horse who ought to be in action in the second half of the season. Runner-up over hurdles at Compiegne, he is a five year old by Masterstroke and his work last season was very good. He could run in a bumper before going novice hurdling depending on when he is ready. **FLY SMART** is another nice youngster who was second at Auteuil on his only run over hurdles (won on the Flat prior to that). His form is outstanding – the third, fourth, fifth, sixth, seventh, eighth and ninth have all won since - and we are hoping to have a full season with him. A five year old by Day Flight, he had a few issues last winter, hence he didn't run but we learned a lot about him. **GRAND BORNAND** won an AQPS Flat race at Senonnes in June last year and the plan was always to give him time. Only four, he was trained by Alain Couetil and is a fine big strong horse by Montmartre. He will go novice hurdling. **HOOK UP** is a lovely filly who won on the Flat in France and ran twice over hurdles for us last season. A daughter of No Risk At All, she finished a good third on her jumping bow in a Grade 3 juvenile hurdle at Fairyhouse in late February behind stablemate and subsequent Triumph Hurdle winner Burning Victory. Found to be sick after her run in the Triumph Hurdle at Cheltenham, she remains a novice and we certainly haven't lost faith in her. Not over big, she possesses plenty of speed and is one for mares' novice hurdles over two miles. **JON SNOW** is developing into the horse we always thought he was. A winner of his last three starts over hurdles, he won by 35 lengths at Killarney in August and has appreciated stepping up in trip this summer. Eligible for novice hurdles until the end of November, we will probably try and make the most of that before running in open company later on. Only five, he has the scope to jump fences eventually but will remain over hurdles this season. **N'GOLO** won over a mile and six on the Flat for Nicolas Clement before we bought him at the Arqana Sale in October 2018. An easy winner on his hurdles debut at the Galway Festival this summer, he pulled up next time at Kilbeggan, but I would put a line through that run. He has been fine since and remains a decent prospect.

We bought two very nice three year olds from France during the summer. **HA D'OR** was a six and a half lengths winner of an AQPS Flat race at Senonnes in July for Laurent Viel. By the same sire (Nidor) as Nicky Henderson's 150 rated chaser Valtor, he is one for the future and, while it is possible he could go juvenile hurdling this season, Willie (Mullins) may decide to give him time to mature and leave him off until next year. **HUBRISKO** is a half-brother to Grand Bornand and came from the same source, namely Alain Couetil. A son of Doctor Dino, he was an impressive eight lengths winner of an AQPS Flat race at Le Lion D'Angers in August and the form has already been boosted with the fourth winning next time by six and a half lengths. He has had a break since arriving but, like Ha D'Or, I don't know at this stage whether he will run in juvenile hurdles in the New Year or be saved for the following season. He looks a very exciting prospect though.

Novice Chasers

Despite the fact **ANTEY** has fallen on his latest two starts over fences, we haven't given up hope that he could develop into a nice chaser. Still in front when falling three out at Gowran in a race won by subsequent Grand Annual Chase winner Chosen Mate, he was rated 134 over hurdles and is still a novice over fences. **FIVE O'CLOCK** was placed twice over hurdles at Auteuil before we bought him. A dual winner at Limerick and Thurles, including the Grade 3 Michael Purcell Memorial Novice Hurdle at the latter track in February, he then ran well in the Martin Pipe Conditional Jockeys' Hurdle at the Cheltenham Festival. Beaten less than five lengths in seventh, he was hampered early on before running on strongly. Physically, he has done the best of all our horses during the summer and we think he is a proper horse and an exciting prospect for two and a half miles plus novice chases. **FRANCIN** is a horse we have had a while, but he started to come good over hurdles during the second half of last season. Third behind Cobbler's Way at Leopardstown over Christmas, he beat The Very Man (won four out of four since) at Navan next time over two miles. Stepping up to two miles six, he followed up at the same track in mid March. A big strong horse who handles soft ground and stays well, he is rated 141 over hurdles and is set to go chasing. **KARL DER GROSSE** has had plenty of issues since winning over hurdles at Tramore a couple of years ago. However, he finished third on his chasing debut at Galway in late July and we hope he will make his mark over fences. Still only six, he is a very good jumper and capable of winning races. **MONKFISH** is another one to look forward to over fences having won three out of four over hurdles last season, including the Grade 1 Albert Bartlett Novices' Hurdle at the Cheltenham Festival. Paul (Townend) loves him and we always thought he would make a better chaser because he is such a big horse who improved both physically and mentally last year. Even though stamina is his strong suit, he travels well in his races and showed a tremendous attitude on the run-in at Cheltenham to rally and get back up close home.

Hurdlers

BENIE DES DIEUX is in good form at home and, having won the Grade 2 Galmoy Hurdle at Gowran by twenty one lengths in January, she was second in the mares' hurdle at Cheltenham. It was unfortunate she never got the chance to go back to France to defend her crown in the Grande Course de Haies d'Auteuil at Auteuil in May. Willie (Mullins) is likely to have his eye on the new mares' chase at the Cheltenham Festival in March, otherwise she will be campaigned in the good hurdle races over two and a half miles plus. **SALDIER** produced a very good performance to win the Grade 1 Morgiana Hurdle at Punchestown in November, but incurred an injury afterwards and missed the remainder of the season. Still lightly raced, he is a horse with a huge engine and, while it remains to be seen whether he is ready in time for the Morgiana Hurdle in November once again, it is possible he will return at Leopardstown over Christmas. **SHARJAH** has won three Grade 1 hurdles for us, including twice at Leopardstown in December, and was runner-up in the Champion Hurdle at Cheltenham in March. Only seven, he gets on very well with Patrick (Mullins) and I would imagine he will be aimed at the Morgiana Hurdle at Punchestown (15th November), which he won in 2018.

Chasers

ANNAMIX won by eleven lengths on his chasing debut at Fairyhouse in January but hasn't run since, which means he is no longer a novice over fences. He therefore lacks chasing experience but has plenty of ability and will have no trouble stepping up in distance, if necessary. A winner over fences at Naas in December, **BAPAUME** jumps very well but the jury is out regarding his ideal trip. Not quick enough for the good two mile chases, I think three miles stretches his stamina, too. We haven't made any plans, but I wouldn't be surprised if he went back over hurdles at some stage and was aimed at conditions hurdles. **BRAHMA BULL** took well to chasing winning three times, including a Grade 3 novice at Cork in November. Absent since, he hurt himself that day but is back in work and in good form at home. Brian (Hayes) gets on well with him (2 from 2) and, while he is quirky and needs things to go his way, he is a capable horse who likes flat galloping tracks. From the family of Irish National winner Thunder And Roses, he stays well and wants two and a half miles plus. It is well documented we were aiming **BURROWS SAINT** at the Grand National last season and his whole campaign was geared around Aintree. Unfortunately, that didn't happen and whether we do the same again this year, I don't know but it is a long time to wait for one race. Rated 156 over fences, it is possible he will run in Pattern company instead. A winner over hurdles at Punchestown on New Year's Eve, he is still a young horse who has only had eight races over fences. **CHACUN POUR SOI** was very good at Leopardstown in February when winning the Grade 1 two mile chase at the Dublin Racing Festival. It was obviously disappointing and frustrating when withdrawn on the morning of the Queen Mother Champion Chase at Cheltenham but he is fine now and hopefully we will get a clear run with him this season. There is an obvious programme for him and Willie, being a creature of habit, will probably start him off in the Grade 1 chase at Leopardstown over Christmas, in which he was runner-up last season. **FAUGHEEN** is an extraordinary horse who gave us some incredible days out last season. A Grade 1 winner over fences at Limerick and Leopardstown last winter, the scenes in the winners' enclosure afterwards were incredible and those who were there will never forget it. Only beaten a length in the JLT Novices' Chase at Cheltenham, he is twelve years old and is back in the yard but we will see how he is in the Autumn before making any plans. **LIVELOVELAUGH** was running well in the Brown Advisory & Merriebelle Stable Plate at the Cheltenham Festival when badly hampered. He still ran a good race in eighth and we were aiming him at the Topham Chase at Aintree. He is a very good jumper and we thought the National fences would suit him. Two and a half miles on decent ground are his optimum conditions and we think he is capable of winning a good race. We were delighted with **MIN**'s victory in the Ryanair Chase at the Festival. Runner-up twice at Cheltenham in the past, the only time he had run below par there was when we got the tactics wrong in the Champion Chase. He is a horse with a huge amount of ability and when he is on song, he is very good indeed and it takes a fair horse to beat him. He has won the Grade 1 John Durkan Memorial Chase at Punchestown (6th December) for the last two seasons and it is possible he could reappear there again, although it is quite close to Leopardstown at Christmas. **SALSARETTA** is unbeaten in four runs over fences, although I think she would have struggled to have beaten Tintangle when left clear at the second last in a Grade 2 mares' novice chase at Limerick in March. She has won some black type, which is important, and we may bring her over to the UK for some of the valuable mares' chases at some stage. The key to her is the ground – the softer the better.

> **RICH'S HORSES TO FOLLOW: FLY SMART & FIVE O'CLOCK**
> **RACING MANAGER JOE CHAMBERS' HORSE TO FOLLOW: FIVE O'CLOCK**

Exclusive interview with

HENRIETTA KNIGHT

Three times Cheltenham Gold Cup winning trainer

Henrietta Knight will always be associated with three times Cheltenham Gold Cup winner Best Mate and Queen Mother Champion Chase and King George winner Edredon Bleu. Based at West Lockinge Farm near Wantage in Oxfordshire, Hen trained over 700 winners between 1989 and 2012, including seven at the Cheltenham Festival. Other Grade 1 winners included Karshi (Stayers Hurdle in 1997), Lord Noelie (Royal & Sun Alliance Chase (2000)), El Vaquero (Scilly Isles Novice Chase (2005)) and Somersby (Victor Chandler Chase (2012)). She won the Grade 2 Peterborough Chase at Huntingdon on no less than eight occasions (Edredon Bleu (4 times), Racing Demon (twice), Best Mate and Impek)) and, with her late husband and triple champion National Hunt jockey Terry Biddlecombe, formed a formidable partnership. Numerically, the yard's best season was in 1995/96 with 58 winners.

Since her retirement, Hen has been involved in the schooling and preparing of horses at West Lockinge and had 192 horses through her hands during the last twelve months. She has also recently formed an alliance with owner Mancunian businessman Mike Grech – who previously had horses in partnership with Stuart Parkin – and made a number of high profile purchases earlier this year. These youngsters are in training with Gordon Elliott, Nicky Henderson and Joseph O'Brien and are discussed below, plus a couple of exciting prospects owned by Harry Redknapp and Lord and Lady Vestey handled by Ben Pauling.

BALLINGERS CORNER (IRE) 5 br m Jeremy (USA) – Dances With Waves (IRE)
Trainer: N.J.HENDERSON. Lambourn, Berkshire.
She is a nice mare who I bought at the Cheltenham February Sale having won her only Irish point-to-point for Paurick O'Connor the previous month. Ridden to victory by his brother Derek, she has joined Nicky Henderson and has a lot going for her. I think she will go straight over hurdles this season and, although she may start off over two and a half miles, I expect her to stay all day.

BOWTOGREATNESS (IRE) 4 bb g Westerner – Miss Baden (IRE)
Trainer: B.PAULING. Bourton-on-the-Water, Gloucestershire.
A lovely unraced four year old who was due to run in an Irish point last spring. Bought privately since, he belongs to Harry Redknapp and is in training with Ben Pauling. I would imagine he will run in a bumper and I think he could be a bit special.

FILS D'OUDAIRIES (FR) 5 b g Saint Des Saints (FR) – Pythie D'Oudairies (FR)
Trainer: J.P.O'BRIEN. Piltown, Co.Kilkenny.
Previously trained in France by David Cottin, he raced twice over hurdles winning at Auteuil in November before we bought him. He is a fine big horse who was ready to run last spring before the season was cut short. I went to see him at Joseph's (O'Brien) in August and he has done very well physically during the summer. He is likely to go novice chasing and is suited by soft ground. Despite the fact he won over two miles one in France, I am expecting him to stay well.

56

FLOUEUR (FR) 5 b g Legolas (JPN) – Saraska D'Airy (FR)
Trainer: G.ELLIOTT. Longwood, Co.Meath.
Similar to Fils D'Oudairies, he is a big strong horse who won twice over hurdles in France, including at Auteuil in November. He ran a couple of times for Gordon Elliott winning at Navan in January before being placed in a Grade 3 novice hurdle over three miles at Punchestown the following month. He, too, has done well physically during the summer and is another who will go chasing. I would envisage him starting off over two and a half miles with a view to stepping up to three miles again later on. He wants soft ground.

GALLYHILL (IRE) 5 b g Getaway (GER) – Tanit
Trainer: N.J.HENDERSON. Lambourn, Berkshire.
A gorgeous looking horse who won his Irish point-to-point for Jamie Sloan in November. We bought him at the Cheltenham December Sale and he joined Nicky Henderson. He has needed time though so we have let him mature and he has summered very well. Suited by soft ground, he is not a bumper horse so I would expect him to go straight over hurdles. Even though he may start over shorter trips, he looks a stayer.

I AM MAXIMUS (FR) 4 b g Authorized (IRE) – Polysheba (FR)
Trainer: N.J.HENDERSON. Lambourn, Berkshire.
Another very nice unraced four year old, he has similar breeding to Goshen being out of a Poliglote mare. He is a very good jumper but Nicky (Henderson) will probably start him off in a bumper before going hurdling.

KESKONRISK (FR) 5 b g No Risk At All (FR) – La Courtille (FR)
Trainer: J.P.O'BRIEN. Piltown, Co.Kilkenny.
He is a lovely horse who was due to run in a bumper at the Punchestown Festival last spring. Having won on his debut at Fairyhouse on New Year's Day for Timmy Hyde, we bought him at the Goffs UK Sale at Doncaster three weeks later. A half-brother to Grade 2 winning hurdler Grand Sancy, he has schooled well over hurdles and is a horse with a lot of speed. I saw him during the summer and he looked great. He wants good ground and ought to running in October. Trips around two or two and a half miles will be ideal.

YOUR DARLING (IRE) 5 b g Shirocco (GER) – Carries Darling
Trainer: B.PAULING. Bourton-on-the-Water, Gloucestershire.
A very good horse who didn't surprise us when winning on his debut in a bumper at Newbury in January. He shouldn't have run the second time at Warwick because he was found to have an infection afterwards and wasn't himself. Ben (Pauling) has always thought he was a high-class horse and it wouldn't surprise me if he developed into a Ballymore Novices' Hurdle contenderat Cheltenham because I think trips around two and a half miles will be ideal.

TALKING TRAINERS

Kim BAILEY

Stables: Thorndale Farm, Withington Road, Andoversford, Cheltenham, Gloucestershire.
2019/2020: 32 Winners / 201 Runners 16% Prize-Money £453,641
www.kimbaileyracing.com

ADJOURNED 5 gr g Rip Van Winkle (IRE) – Bite of The Cherry
Despite finishing second on his hurdles debut at Stratford, he struggled with the testing ground last season. Lightly raced, I think he will do better this time around and, with his rating, we will be looking at novice handicap hurdles over two miles.

AJERO (IRE) 5 b g Red Jazz (USA) – Eoz (IRE)
A new arrival, he is a half-brother to Charbel (retired) and shaped with huge promise on his only start in a bumper at Thurles in February finishing third. The form is good and he will go novice hurdling.

BOBHOPEORNOHOPE (IRE) 5 b g Westerner – Bandelaro (IRE)
A nice young horse who won his only Irish point-to-point before we bought him at the Cheltenham April Sale last year. He shaped well on his first start for us finishing third in a bumper at Exeter on New Year's Day. However, he hated the ground next time at Warwick and got bogged down in it. He will go straight over hurdles and will be suited by two and a half miles.

CHAZZA (IRE) 6 b g Mahler – Presenting Proform (IRE)
Another former winning Irish pointer, he had a couple of runs last season winning a bumper at Bangor in November. Sent hurdling next time, he finished runner-up at Hereford. His future lies over fences but we may give him another run or two over hurdles beforehand. He wants two and a half miles plus.

COMMODORE BARRY (IRE) 7 br g Presenting – Specifiedrisk (IRE)
A four times winner over hurdles, he had a good season over fences last winter winning at Wetherby last time. Runner-up on his chasing debut at Exeter, he remains a novice until the end of October and I think he is the sort to win a decent staying handicap one day. We fitted him with cheekpieces last time and they definitely helped.

DANDY DAN (IRE) 7 b g Midnight Legend – Playing Around
He enjoyed a good season as a novice over fences a couple of years ago winning three times. However, it was a difficult year last season because he was high in the handicap and needs decent ground. Runner-up at Kelso in October, we will aim him at the good staying handicaps over three miles plus and hopefully everything will drop right for him one day.

DOES HE KNOW 5 b g Alkaased (USA) – Diavoleria
A winning UK pointer, he finished runner-up in both his starts over hurdles at Hereford and Ludlow. The form looks good, too, and he will continue to run in novice hurdles over two and a half miles. His future lies over fences, but I will be disappointed if he can't win over hurdles beforehand.

DONNIE BRASCO (FR) 7 b g Buck's Boum (FR) – Parislatino (FR)
He, too, won an English point-to-point before we purchased him at the Cheltenham February Sale last year. Placed in three of his four runs over hurdles last winter, he is a big horse and, given his size, I thought he did well to achieve what he did. Rated 115, he will go over fences and we will be looking at novice handicap chases over staying trips.

DUKE OF EARL (FR) 4 br g Noroit (GER) – Visiorienne (FR)
A big backward unraced four year old, we bought him at the Goffs UK Spring Sale at Doncaster last year. We haven't done a lot with him, but I hope he will develop into a nice horse and make his debut in a bumper in the spring.

EL PRESENTE 7 b g Presenting – Raitera (FR)
Produced an impressive performance to win at Market Rasen in July having undergone a wind operation beforehand. Who knows whether that made the difference but he certainly appreciated the better ground. Third next time off a nine pounds higher mark at Bangor, it was only his fifth run over fences and I hope he will continue to improve. Three miles handicap chases will be on his agenda.

ESPOIR DE ROMAY (FR) 6 b g Kap Rock (FR) – Miss Du Seuil (FR)
Lightly raced and progressive over hurdles last season, he won twice at Warwick and Wincanton and I was pleased with him. The plan is to send him novice chasing having schooled well at home. He has a good mix of speed and stamina and I think he is going to stay well over fences.

FIRST FLOW (IRE) 8 b g Primary (USA) – Clonroche Wells (IRE)
Had a wonderful season over fences winning four times. The ground is the key to him because soft and heavy suits him very well. We haven't made any plans because he is ground dependent and that will dictate where he runs. All four of his wins last year came over two miles, but I think he will stay two and a half miles, if necessary.

FLIRTATIOUS GIRL (IRE) 4 b f Flemensfirth (USA) – Another Gaye (IRE)
She is a nice unraced filly who we bought at the Goffs Land Rover Sale in Ireland last year. Well bred, she has shown promise at home and I like her. We will start her off in a mares' bumper.

GALANTE DE ROMAY (FR) 4 gr f Lord Du Sud (FR) – Miss Du Seuil (FR)
She is a nice unraced half-sister to Espoir De Romay. I have been pleased with her at home and, in all likelihood, she will start off in a mares' bumper next spring.

GERARD MENTOR (FR) 4 b g Policy Maker (IRE) – Trephine Du Sulon (FR)
A bonny horse, he has yet to run having been bought at the Goffs Land Rover Sale last year. I like him and I am hoping he will make his debut in a bumper around October/November. I think he will develop into a real fun horse.

GETAWEAPON (IRE) 5 b m Getaway (GER) – Milan Serenade (IRE)
She has had her training issues but possesses ability and is capable of winning races. Successful in her only UK point-to-point, the form is very good and I hope she will make her mark in novice hurdles this season.

HAPPYGOLUCKY (IRE) 6 br g Jeremy (USA) – Mydadsabishop (IRE)
Has schooled well over fences at home and is an exciting prospect for novice chases. Runner-up in an Irish point, he won over hurdles at Stratford and ran some very good races in defeat. Third a couple of times in Graded contests at Cheltenham and Sandown, I was delighted with his run at the Cheltenham Festival. Beaten three and a half lengths in fourth in the Martin Pipe Conditional Jockeys' Handicap Hurdle, it was an excellent performance considering his lack of experience. Staying on having been hampered at the last, he will stay three miles over fences.

HENDRA HOUSE (IRE) 4 b g Yeats (IRE) – Gold Strike (IRE)
A big backward unraced horse who was acquired as a three year old at the Goffs Land Rover Sale in Ireland. He is another who will make his debut in a bumper in the spring.

HOLLYMOUNT HOLLY (IRE) 6 ch m Doyen (IRE) – Parsee (IRE)
A twelve lengths winner of her only Irish point, we bought her soon afterwards at the Cheltenham November Sale. She then made all to win a bumper at Hereford. Runner-up over hurdles at Wincanton in March, she remains a novice and we will aim her at mares' events. She will be suited by a step up in trip because she stays well.

IMPERIAL AURA (IRE) 7 b g Kalanisi (IRE) – Missindependence (IRE)
He has done us proud and we were obviously delighted with his victory in the novices' handicap chase at the Cheltenham Festival in March. Having only had four races over fences, we are hoping he can improve again. He spent the summer with Kevin Ross in Ireland and the plan is to start him off in a Graduation chase at Carlisle and then we might consider races such as the BetVictor Gold Cup at Cheltenham (14th November). We will keep him over two and a half miles for the time being.

INCA ROSE 5 ch g Malinas (GER) – Cinderella Rose
From a family we know well, he is a half-brother to Rose To Fame. I thought he shaped well on his debut in a bumper at Huntingdon last spring. He will go novice hurdling and is capable of winning races.

INFLAGRANTE (IRE) 4 ch g Getaway (GER) – Maggie Connolly (IRE)
Another nice unraced four year old, he measures 17hh and was due to run in a bumper last spring. I like him and he ought to be in action in the Autumn.

JAVA POINT (IRE) 5 b g Stowaway – Classic Sun (GER)
Bought at the Cheltenham Festival Sale last year having won one of his two Irish points, I can't believe I didn't win a bumper with him last season. Switched to hurdles, he bumped into some good horses at Ludlow and Newbury and wasn't disgraced. He is now qualified for handicaps and, while he is a chaser in the making, he is capable of winning over hurdles beforehand.

LADY OF THE NIGHT 7 b m Midnight Legend – Even Flo
Lightly raced, she hasn't been the easiest to train and has had a few soundness issues. Placed twice in bumpers the previous season, she made her debut over hurdles at Huntingdon in February finishing a close second. She has ability and, provided she learns to settle, she will stay further and is certainly bred to.

LORD APPARELLI 5 ch g Schiaparelli (GER) – La Marette
A full brother to Prince Llewelyn, he has always looked useful at home. Fourth on his debut in a bumper at Ascot in November, he then finished second at Ludlow the following month. We were aiming him at the Goffs UK bumper at Newbury in March but that didn't happen. He is a nice horse who is good enough to win a bumper before going hurdling.

MR GREY SKY (IRE) 6 gr g Fame And Glory – Lakil Princess (IRE)
Unbeaten in two bumpers, he only raced once over hurdles at Ascot last season. He finished third but has been a big baby and I think he will improve a lot this year. Inclined to be keen last year, I put that down to immaturity. He is a big horse with plenty of potential and he is in good form at home.

NEWTIDE (IRE) 7 br g Getaway (GER) – C'est Fantastique (IRE)
Took well to fences winning twice, including the Grade 2 Towton Novices' Chase at Wetherby. Sixth in the National Hunt Chase at the Cheltenham Festival, I was very pleased with him because he lacked experience and just ran out of puff late on. He jumps and stays well and handles heavy ground. With that in mind, the Welsh National at Chepstow (27th December) is his target with one run beforehand. We are going to operate on his wind before he makes his reappearance.

PARTY FUZZ 5 b g Great Pretender (IRE) – Very Special One (IRE)
We trained the dam who was placed in the mares' final at Newbury and he has shown a good level of form. Placed in bumpers at Hereford and Wetherby from three starts, he will go hurdling and is a stayer. Three miles will be his trip.

PRINCE LLYWELYN 6 ch g Schiaparelli (GER) – La Marette
A smart bumper horse a couple of seasons ago, I was disappointed with him over hurdles last year. Runner-up at Wetherby in January, he has got ability and we are hoping a wind operation will make a difference. Two and a half miles is his trip and he could be on a good mark, if reverting to his bumper form.

RED RIVER (IRE) 7 ch g Beneficial – Socker Toppen (IRE)
Twice a winner over hurdles a few years ago, he has been unlucky since switched to fences. Restricted to a couple of outings, he is ready to run now and is in good form at home. Decent ground is ideal and he has the ability to win races over fences.

SAYADAM (FR) 3 b g Saint Des Saints (FR) – Catmoves (FR)
Only arrived in July, so we don't know a lot about him yet. Bought at the Arqana summer sale last year, he will start off in a bumper.

SHANACOOLE PRINCE (IRE) 7 ch g Primary (USA) – Shanacoole Rose (IRE)
A winning pointer in Ireland, he was a cheap buy and surprised us when winning over hurdles at Hereford in November. Runner-up at Leicester next time, he handles soft ground and we will send him chasing. He had eight runs in points so doesn't lack experience.

SHANTOU EXPRESS (IRE) 5 ch g Shantou (USA) – Spanker
He is a lovely horse who has only raced four times. I couldn't believe he got beaten on his debut at Ludlow but it turned out to be a decent race. An impressive winner on his return at Stratford, he beat the subsequent Grade 2 Dovecote Novices' Hurdle winner Highway One O Two by nine lengths. We then ran him in a Listed bumper at Ascot before Christmas and, despite finding the ground too soft, he still ran well in third. We purposely left him off after that and he finished second on his hurdles debut at Stratford in September. It hopefully won't be long before he goes one better, possibly over further.

SHINOBI (IRE) 4 ch g Iffraaj – Ninja Lady
Ran in three bumpers last season winning on his debut at Exeter before finishing fourth under a penalty at Huntingdon. The form is sound and he made a good start to his hurdles career when winning at Uttoxeter in early September. Two and a half miles on good ground is ideal.

STARVOSKI (IRE) 5 b m Aizavoski (IRE) – Telstar (IRE)
An old fashioned mare, she is a nice type who won her only Irish point-to-point by ten lengths. Bought at the Cheltenham February Sale, she is a big mare and I would imagine she will go straight over hurdles.

SUBWAY SURF (IRE) 6 b m Milan – Dante Rouge (IRE)
A useful mare in bumpers the previous season, she wasn't at her best over hurdles last winter. Placed at Warwick and Ludlow, she is a winning pointer and I think she will improve going over fences. We will aim her at mares' novice chases.

TALK OF FAME 5 b g Fame And Glory – Princess Oriane (IRE)
I thought he ran well on his debut in a bumper at Wincanton in November considering he didn't enjoy the ground. He will go novice hurdling.

THE BULL MCCABE (IRE) 6 b g Yeats (IRE) – Twilight View (IRE)
Bought at the Goffs UK Sale at Doncaster in the spring of last year having won an Irish point-to-point, he was disappointing on his first run for us over hurdles at Wincanton in November. Not right afterwards, he missed the remainder of the season, but has come back in looking a completely different horse. He will continue over hurdles for the time being.

THE EDGAR WALLACE (IRE) 5 b g Flemensfirth (USA) – Annalecky (IRE)
A half-brother to Cheltenham Festival winner Black Hercules, he is a lovely horse. Placed in his first two bumpers at Exeter and Doncaster, I couldn't believe he got beaten. An easy winner at Hereford next time, he will go novice hurdling and I don't think it matters what trip we run him over. He is a very nice horse.

TRWYN DU (IRE) 4 b g Valirann (FR) – Broken Thought (IRE)
I didn't know much about his sire but I loved him at the sales when we bought him last year. He goes nicely at home and we were going to run him in a bumper during the spring. He will therefore make his debut this Autumn and I like him.

TWO FOR GOLD (IRE) 7 b g Gold Well – Two Of Each (IRE)
Enjoyed a very good season over fences winning his first three starts, including a Grade 2 at Warwick in January. Runner-up in the Grade 2 Reynoldstown Novices' Chase at Ascot last time, we are hoping he will develop into a Grand National horse one day. The same owners had The Rainbow Hunter who ran in three Grand Nationals. Rated 146, we might look at the BetVictor Gold Cup at Cheltenham (14th November) for him.

VINNDICATION (IRE) 7 b g Vinnie Roe (IRE) – Pawnee Trail (IRE)
I have always thought the world of him and still feel he will win a very big race one day. Having said that, he has done well already winning a good chase at Ascot last December having had a wind operation beforehand. Fourth in the Ultima Handicap Chase at the Cheltenham Festival under top weight, I have been pleased with him since and we may start him off in the Charlie Hall Chase at Wetherby (31st October).

VOYBURG (IRE) 4 br g Sageburg (IRE) – Slevoy Ahoy (IRE)
A very nice unraced horse, we bought him at the Goffs UK Doncaster Spring Sale last year. Backward last season, he has grown during the summer and I like him.

YOUNEVERCALL (IRE) 9 b g Yeats (IRE) – Afarka (IRE)
Back in work having missed the whole of last season, he is a Grade 2 winner over hurdles and is rated 157. He is at his best racing right-handed but we are going to have to try him on a left-handed track at some stage. With that in mind, he could run in the Grade 2 West Yorkshire Hurdle at Wetherby (31st October).

TRAINER'S HORSE TO FOLLOW: VOYBURG

Harry FRY

Stables: Higher Crockermoor, Corscombe, Dorchester, Dorset.
2019/2020: 30 Winners / 169 Runners 18% Prize-Money £466,661
www.harryfryracing.com

ACTING LASS (IRE) 9 b g King's Theatre (IRE) – Darrens Lass (IRE)
A winner of the Welsh National Trial at Chepstow in December, he then finished runner-up in a valuable Listed chase at Ascot a fortnight later. Disappointing in the Peter Marsh Chase at Haydock last time, soft ground is the key to him. We may aim him at the Welsh National (27th December) with one run beforehand. Not the most robust of horses, he doesn't want over racing.

ASK ME EARLY (IRE) 6 gr g Ask – Cotton Ali (IRE)
A winning Irish pointer, we bought him at the Goffs UK Doncaster August Sale last year. Third on his hurdles debut at Chepstow in late January, I was very pleased with his run with the slow ground suiting him. A stayer, he wants cut in the ground and, while he may have another run over hurdles, it won't be long before he goes chasing. I think he will come into his own in staying novice chases.

BLACK MISCHIEF 8 b g Black Sam Bellamy (IRE) – Miss Mitch (IRE)
Missed the whole of last season, due to a leg injury, but he is back in work and will resume his chasing career. Runner-up at Uttoxeter on his only start over fences, he needs to jump better but will appreciate a return to two and a half miles. A three times winner over hurdles, he has the ability to win races over fences provided he gets his jumping together.

BOOTHILL (IRE) 5 bb g Presenting – Oyster Pipit (IRE)
Runner-up in a couple of Irish points, we purchased him at the Cheltenham November Sale. He did it well at Kempton in February winning a bumper at the first time of asking confirming what we thought of him beforehand. We are very much looking forward to him this season and he should be an exciting novice hurdler. However, he won't be in action until after Christmas, due to a minor niggle he incurred in the spring. We will start him off over two miles over hurdles.

BULLIONAIRE (IRE) 7 b g Gold Well – Dontcallerthat (IRE)
He won over hurdles at Uttoxeter in December and we were aiming him at the County Hurdle at Cheltenham but he was balloted out. We ran him at Kempton the following day instead, but the longer trip didn't suit him. He needs to learn to settle, if he is going to stay further. We are going to try him over fences.

BURROWS TREAT (FR) 4 b f Muhtathir – La Vie de Boitron (FR)
A nice unraced filly who was bought at the Arqana Sale in France as a yearling. Well related, she is a half-sister to Burrows Edge and Burrows Park. She has done well during the summer and we are looking forward to running her in a mares' bumper during the Autumn.

CAPTAIN DRAKE (IRE) 7 b g Getaway (GER) – Julika (GER)
Had a good season over fences winning at Exeter on New Year's Day and finishing runner-up in the Midlands National at Uttoxeter. We always thought that race would suit him and he ran a blinder. A proven mudlark, he is another we are likely to aim at the Welsh National at Chepstow (27th December) with one run beforehand. He stays very well.

ENA BAIE (FR) 6 b m Crillon (FR) – Trema Baie (FR)
She is rated nine pounds lower in Ireland compared to over here and she produced two good runs at Galway and Leopardstown last season. Pulled up at the latter track at the Dublin Racing Festival in February, it was one run too many. She will continue in mares' hurdles over two and two and a half miles.

FEHILY (IRE) 5 b g Asian Heights – Leahs Joy (IRE)
Unraced, he is a nice big horse who we have taken our time with. Back in work, I like him and we will aim him at a bumper in the Autumn.

FISHKHOV (FR) 5 ch g Sholokhov (IRE) – Kavalle (FR)
One to look forward to having finished second in his only Irish point for Robert Tyner in late December. Bought the following month at the Goffs UK January Sale at Doncaster, he is a nice big horse who will take another year to fill his frame. We haven't got stuck into him yet but he is an exciting recruit who could start off in a bumper or go straight over hurdles.

GENTLEMAN KAP (FR) 4 b g Kapgarde (FR) – Sabubelle (FR)
Purchased as a two year old at the Arqana Sale in France, he would have made his debut in the spring but the season was cut short. He has shown all the right signs though and will contest a bumper in the Autumn.

GET IN THE QUEUE 6 b g Mount Nelson – Amarullah (FR)
He is back in work having missed the whole of last season. Still a young horse, he was unbeaten in three bumpers the previous campaign and we are hoping he retains all his ability. He incurred a minor injury when winning at Newbury and we have purposely given him time because we didn't want to risk him. Novice hurdling will be his job this season.

GOLD IN DOHA (FR) 4 b g Spanish Moon (USA) – Utah Bald (FR)
A nice unraced four year old by Spanish Moon, he is another who could have run in the spring under normal circumstances. Still a youngster, he is a nice type to run in a bumper in the Autumn. I like him.

GRATIEN DE BRUZEAU (FR) 4 gr g Lord Du Sud (FR) – Rockbelle (FR)
A lovely unraced horse who I like a lot. He was in training with Christopher Barber last season and was due to run in a point-to-point. There is a possibility his name will be changed before he makes his debut in a bumper. He is a nice recruit.

GREEN DOLPHIN (IRE) 6 b g Oscar (IRE) – Shamrock Miss (IRE)
A promising bumper horse a couple of seasons ago, he didn't take to hurdling like we hoped last winter. Disappointing in two runs at Aintree and Taunton, we found he was suffering with kissing spines. We have worked on that and hopefully he will be able to reproduce his bumper form over hurdles.

HURRICANE MITCH (IRE) 5 b g Shirocco (GER) – Miss Mitch (IRE)
A half-brother to Black Mischief, he was as green as grass on his debut at Warwick on New Year's Eve. The penny dropped late on as he stayed on well at the finish. He confirmed that promise at Wincanton next time finishing second. The plan is for him to go novice hurdling and he will benefit from stepping up to two and a half miles.

IF THE CAP FITS (IRE) 8 b g Milan – Derravaragh Sayra (IRE)
I am delighted to retain him having been bought by Simon Munir and Isaac Souede during the summer. Purchased with chasing in mind, he won the Ascot Hurdle for the second consecutive season in November but was never at his best thereafter. A lot of my horses

were affected and he wasn't right when finishing fifth in the Cleeve Hurdle at Cheltenham in January. That run left its mark but we were preparing him for the Liverpool Hurdle at Aintree, which he had won the previous year. We have schooled him over brush fences in our outdoor school and I see no reason why he won't develop into a high-class chaser. Although he stays further, we will start him off over two and a half miles over fences and he could run at somewhere like Chepstow or Exeter in the Autumn.

IMPERIAL ESPRIT (IRE) 6 b g Scorpion (IRE) – Shesourpresent (IRE)
Pulled up on his hurdles debut at Plumpton in December, he was found to have an irregular heartbeat afterwards. He is fine now and has been in pre training. Very much a chaser in the making, he will run in a two and a half miles novice hurdle in the Autumn.

ISHKHARA LADY 6 b m Scorpion (IRE) – Loxhill Lady
She hasn't raced since winning on her debut at Plumpton in December 2018, but her owners have been very patient and she is back in work. We were looking forward to running her in the Listed mares' bumper at Cheltenham's November meeting last year, but she slipped a tendon off her hock a few days beforehand and therefore missed the whole of the season. A mare with a lot of ability, we are hoping she can stand training and fulfil her potential. We may run her in another bumper under a penalty before going hurdling.

JUST A STING (IRE) 8 b g Scorpion (IRE) – Shanann Lady (IRE)
Fourth in the Badger Ales Chase at Wincanton on his reappearance, his jumping let him down. However, he was much better next time when winning a valuable staying handicap at Kempton over Christmas, a race he had finished runner-up in the previous year. He tends to be best fresh in his first couple of runs each season and we may aim him at the Badger Ales Chase (7ᵗʰ November) once again, although he doesn't want it too soft.

KING ROLAND (IRE) 6 br g Stowaway – Kiltiernan Robin (IRE)
Back in work, he looks in great order and we are looking forward to sending him chasing this season. We have a strong team of novice chasers and everything has been geared towards his career over fences. Runner-up on his hurdles debut at Newbury in November, he was then an easy winner at Exeter on New Year's Day. We stepped him up in class in a Grade 2 novice at Cheltenham's Trials meeting and he looked like winning rounding the hometurn but weakened after the last. It transpired that he had suffered a pelvic injury, which meant he missed the remainder of the season. He isn't short of speed and I don't think he wants to be running beyond two and a half miles. He could start off at Exeter or Chepstow and then we may consider the Grade 2 Rising Stars Novices' Chase at Wincanton (7ᵗʰ November), a race we won with Bags Groove a couple of years ago.

LIGHTLY SQUEEZE 6 b g Poet's Voice – Zuleika Dobson
Very progressive last season, he was rated 110 when winning at Wincanton on Boxing Day and then followed up with victories at Taunton and Plumpton. Still in front when falling at the last in the *Betfair* Hurdle at Newbury, he is now rated 140. Thankfully, he was OK afterwards and we will aim him at the decent two and two and a half miles handicap hurdles. The Greatwood Hurdle at Cheltenham (15ᵗʰ November) is his first target, but he is only rated 77 on the Flat so we are keen to exploit that at some stage (third at Haydock in September). Still only six, he likes soft ground and I hope he can improve again.

LITTERALE CI (FR) 7 b m Soldier of Fortune (IRE) – Cigalia
Twice a winner over fences last season at Exeter and Warwick, she produced her best performance at the latter in March. We will mix and match between hurdles and fences but there is a good programme of mares' chases nowadays. Two and a half miles is ideal and, while she handles soft ground, she prefers a drier surface.

LONDON EYE (USA) 4 ch g Australia – Circle of Life (USA)
Showed promise on the Flat for Sir Michael Stoute before he joined us. He had his first run for us at Kempton in June finishing sixth in a twelve furlongs handicap. Only four, we have operated on his wind and the plan is to give him another couple of runs on the Flat before going hurdling.

METIER (IRE) 4 b g Mastercraftsman (IRE) – We'll Go Walking (IRE)
A winner on the Flat in Ireland, we bought him at the Tattersalls Horses in Training Sale last Autumn with a view to going juvenile hurdling. Entered in the Triumph Hurdle, we couldn't get a prep run into him and then decided rather than waste his novice status, we would give him time off and keep him as a novice for this season. He jumps very well and is one to look forward to in novice hurdles this year. Gelded since arriving, he enjoys cut in the ground and could also run on the Flat again at some stage. Indeed, he should make a very nice dual purpose horse.

MILLBANK FLYER (IRE) 5 b g Milan – The Last Bank (IRE)
A half-brother to Chantry House, he has only raced once but didn't deliver on the racecourse what he had been showing at home. Eighth in a bumper at Wincanton in November, he is a big horse who may have needed time. I have been pleased with him during the summer and he will go novice hurdling. If his homework is anything to go by, he is capable of winning races.

MILLE SUSSURRI (IRE) 5 b g Milan – Silent Whisper (IRE)
Third on his debut in a bumper at Ffos Las in October, I should have sent him hurdling after that. However, he ran in another bumper at Exeter on New Year's Day, but was too lit up and didn't finish his race. Switched to hurdles in the spring, we tried to get him to switch off and he ran well on both starts being placed at Exeter and Taunton over two miles. A chaser in the making, he wants further and we will be looking to exploit his mark of 107.

MISTY WHISKY 6 gr m Stowaway – Whisky Rose (IRE)
A smart mare in bumpers a couple of seasons ago winning a Listed event at Sandown, she wasn't disgraced over hurdles last year but lacked confidence with her jumping. Runner-up on all three starts, I think she will make amends this year and there are races to be won with her. Rated 112, she is on a good mark and we are going to aim her at the Richard Barber Memorial Mares' Handicap Hurdle at Wincanton (7th November) with one run beforehand.

MOMELLA (IRE) 8 ch m Sholokhov (IRE) – Missing Link (IRE)
Pulled up on her chasing debut at Ffos Las, she ran much better next time finishing second at Huntingdon under my sister-in-law (Aine O'Connor). She has dropped in the weights and, hopefully with her confidence boosted, she can win races over fences. We will be looking towards mares' chases.

MUY BIEN (IRE) 4 b g Cloudings (IRE) – Sari Rose (FR)
Half-brother to Geordie B, he is a nice unraced horse we bought at the Goffs UK Spring Sale at Doncaster as a three year old. We never got to run him last season but he should be running in a bumper in the Autumn.

OVER TO SAM 9 b g Black Sam Bellamy (IRE) – Lady Brig
Lightly raced for his age, he won over fences at Plumpton in January and was in the process of running a decent race at Exeter when jumping into the back of another horse. Third at Uttoxeter last time, I was pleased with him and he could be the sort of horse we may target at veterans' chases in the New Year. He stays well and loves soft ground and is another we could aim at the Welsh National at Chepstow (27th December).

PADSTOW HARBOUR 5 ch m Malinas (GER) – Cherry Pie (FR)
A half-sister to Stoney Mountain, she finished runner-up in an English point-to-point before joining us. Sixth in a bumper at Ludlow in January, she then had the misfortune to bump into a very useful looking mare at Taunton finishing second. She will be aimed at mares' novice hurdles over two and a half miles.

PARSONS PLEASURE (FR) 4 gr g Planteur (IRE) – Netrebko (IRE)
Another nice four year old who didn't get the opportunity to run last season. He will hopefully make up for lost time in a bumper during the Autumn.

PHOENIX WAY (IRE) 7 b g Stowaway – Arcuate
His whole season had been geared towards the Pertemps Final at the Cheltenham and, having won a qualifier at Huntingdon in January, it was very much the plan. Unfortunately, on the morning of declarations, he had a fibrillating heartbeat and therefore couldn't run. Thankfully it resetitself and, having spent the summer at Martinstown Stud in Ireland, we are looking forward to sending him novice chasing this season. A winning Irish pointer, he should be an exciting chaser who will start off over two and a half miles, although we know he stays further.

PURE BLISS 5 ch m Mount Nelson – Burton Ash
Another winning Irish pointer, she looked good when winning a bumper at Ffos Las on her first start for us in November. We feared the worst when she pulled up next time at Ascot when she wobbled under Sean (Bowen). It transpired that she had choked so we have operated on her wind since. Mares' novice hurdles over two and two and a half miles will be her target and we know she handles plenty of cut in the ground.

REVELS HILL (IRE) 5 b g Mahler – Chlolo Supreme (IRE)
Ran in two point-to-points for Chris Barber winning on the second occasion. Owned by the Noel Fehily Racing Syndicate, he spent the summer with Noel (Fehily) and will probably run in a bumper before going novice hurdling.

THE BIG STING (IRE) 5 b g Scorpion (IRE) – Glory Queen (IRE)
Well named measuring nearly 18hh, he ran in a couple of bumpers at Exeter last season. He has summered well and will benefit from stepping up in trip over hurdles this time around. Long-term, his future lies over fences because he is very much a chaser in the making.

UNOWHATIMEANHARRY 12 b g Sir Harry Lewis (USA) – Red Nose Lady
He has been a great horse for us winning thirteen races, including four Grade 1 hurdles. Runner-up at Wetherby and Leopardstown last season, he owes us nothing but is still full of enthusiasm. We haven't made any plans but he is a joy to have.

WHITE HART LADY (IRE) 6 b m Doyen (IRE) – Hats And Heels (IRE)
An impressive winner on her debut at Aintree in October, we then ran her in a Listed mares' bumper at Huntingdon but she got worked up in the horsebox on the way to the races. She got stressed before arriving at the track and never ran her race. She ran in another couple of Listed events at Market Rasen and Kempton and wasn't disgraced. She is a nice mare who will go novice hurdling and will be suited by a step up in trip.

WHITEHOTCHILLIFILI (IRE) 6 b m Milan – Mhuire Na Gale (IRE)
I didn't expect her to be running in the mares' novice hurdle at the Cheltenham Festival at the start of the season. However, she really progressed over hurdles winning at Wincanton and Exeter and travelled strongly at Cheltenham. Outstayed up the hill, she still ran well in sixth. Two miles on slow ground is ideal and we will aim her at the Listed mares' hurdle at Wetherby (31st October), which we won five years ago with Blue Buttons.

WINNINGSEVERYTHING (IRE) 6 b g Flemensfirth (USA) – Baliya (IRE)
Paul and Clare Rooney had four horses in training with us last season and we are lucky to retain three of them, including this horse who has done nothing wrong over hurdles. Unbeaten in two starts, he won in good style at Southwell and, while he didn't jump as well next time at Market Rasen, he still scored by eleven lengths. He didn't run again because a number of our horses weren't right, so we decided to be patient and left him off. Two and a half miles is his trip and he will go over fences. He should be an exciting novice chaser.

> TRAINER'S HORSE TO FOLLOW: WINNINGSEVERYTHING

Chris GORDON
Stables: Morestead Farm Stables, Morestead, Winchester, Hampshire.
2019/2020: 30 Winners / 188 Runners 16% Prize-Money £287,144
www.chrisgordonracing.co.uk

ALBERT HUCKLEBUCK (IRE) 4 b g Leading Light (IRE) – Queen of Cool (IRE)
Unraced, he has a nice pedigree and was bought for €15,500 as a yearling. He hasn't grown much during the summer but is a nice handy horse who was ready to run in a bumper last spring. He has had a couple of 'away days' at Lambourn and it will be all about educating him in bumpers before going hurdling.

ANNUAL INVICTUS (IRE) 5 b g Mahler – Shantou Rose (IRE)
He is a nice horse who won an Irish point-to-point for Cormac Doyle before joining us last Autumn. I was pleased with his first run in a bumper at Plumpton in December finishing second. Having led early on, he ran well until getting tired. He then finished fifth on his hurdles debut at Fontwell and I don't think it was a bad race. That run was over two miles three, but he is a staying horse who will benefit from stepping up in trip this season. He has strengthened up during the summer and I think he will improve.

BADDESLEY (IRE) 5 b g Presenting – Fox Theatre (IRE)
A lovely horse who has run three good races in bumpers, including when winning at Fontwell in October. His owner was keen for him to run in a Listed bumper at Ascot before Christmas but, unfortunately, the ground was too soft. He is a good moving horse who appreciates a sounder surface. Fourth at Wincanton last time under a penalty, he was lame afterwards and it transpired he had fractured his pelvis. Given plenty of time since, he is set to go novice hurdling and is a staying type. A very good jumper, he may start off in a two miles maiden hurdle at Fontwell (2nd October).

BADDESLEY KNIGHT (IRE) 7 b g Doyen (IRE) – Grangeclare Rhythm (IRE)
He is a really nice horse who is progressive and I hope he will be competitive off his mark over fences this season. Runner-up on his chasing debut at Market Rasen in October behind a subsequent Grade 2 winner and Arkle Trophy third (Rouge Vif), he then won a novices' handicap chase at Wincanton. Unfortunately, he bled last time when finishing second at Doncaster and hasn't raced since. We have given him a long break so hopefully it won't happen again, but it is always a concern. He has also been hobdayed, which we are hoping will make a difference. Well balanced and a very good jumper, he won a bumper and over hurdles earlier in his career and is a talented horse.

BLAME THE GAME (IRE) 5 b g Darsi (FR) – Lucy Walters (IRE)
We have bought the likes of Go Whatever, On The Slopes and Pres from Donnchadh Doyle in Ireland and this horse hails from the same source. A full-brother to Spiritofthegames, he finished fourth in his only point-to-point in January. Yet to run for us, he looks a good addition to the team and will either run in a bumper or go straight over hurdles.

BROTHER WINDSOR (IRE) 4 b g Valirann (FR) – Mrs Bukay (IRE)
Bought at the Tattersalls Ireland August Sale last year, he is a half-brother to Mount Windsor who has won a couple of times for us. Not the biggest, he is a bumper type and will start off in the Autumn.

CAN'T STOP NOW (IRE) 3 ch g Starspangledbanner (AUS) – Sorry Woman (FR)
A cheap buy at the Newmarket July Sales, he belongs to Alex Gorrie who is putting together a syndicate for him. Placed a couple of times on the Flat for Clive Cox, he was third at Leicester as a two year old and runner-up over a mile at Kempton in February. Given a break since arriving, he will go juvenile hurdling towards the end of September/early October.

COMMANCHE RED (IRE) 7 ch g Mahler – Auntie Bob
He is a promising young chaser who was very good at Kempton on Boxing Day when beating a subsequent Cheltenham Festival winner (Simply The Betts) by nine lengths in a novices' handicap chase. Third in the Grade 2 Pendil Novices' Chase at the same track in February, he was lame afterwards and we found he had pushed his hind shoe back and caused a lot of bleeding. He didn't appear to be happy during the race and he came back sore. The plan was to step him up to three miles in the Grade 1 novice chase at Aintree in April because Paddy (Brennan) felt he was ready for it. Rated 150, life isn't going to be easy this season but he is a big horse and still lightly raced. Therefore he will hopefully improve. We will step him up to three miles this season and I suppose we may consider races such as the Badger Ales Chase at Wincanton (7th November) and there is a valuable handicap chase at Ascot a week earlier (31st October).

GO WHATEVER (IRE) 6 b g Gold Well – And Whatever Else (IRE)
A lovely horse who gained plenty of experience in Irish points for Donnchadh Doyle. Bought with chasing in mind, I consider everything he achieved over hurdles last season as a bonus. Twice a winner at Plumpton and Sandown, he then finished third in a valuable Grade 3 handicap hurdle at the latter track in February. It was a particularly good run because he didn't have the best of preparations due to an abscess on the lead up to the race. We were then really looking forward to running him in the EBF Final at Sandown the following month, especially with the ground being very testing. Unfortunately, the meeting was abandoned and it was never going to suit him running in the rescheduled version at Kempton a week later. I have always viewed him as an out and out stayer who could be a Welsh National horse one day. He is a wonderful jumper and, with a rating of 125, he will start off over fences in a novices' handicap chase over three miles.

HIGHWAY ONE O ONE (IRE) 8 br g Stowaway – High Accord (IRE)
Despite running well in a valuable handicap chase at Kempton over Christmas, I was slightly disappointed with him last season. His jumping wasn't as a good as it had been as a novice chaser. A number of his races were in bad ground and that may explain his sticky jumping but we have also operated on his breathing, which will hopefully make a difference. Fourth at Newbury in late November, he stayed on well that day and he should have won at Kempton next time, but got racing too soon and was headed on the run-in. That was his first run over three miles. Disappointing on his next three starts, he lost his confidence a bit but I am expecting him to be competitive off his mark this season. He seems to be in good form at home.

HIGHWAY ONE O TWO (IRE) 5 bb g Shirocco (GER) – Supreme Dreamer (IRE)
A half-brother to Grade 3 winner Doctor Harper, I am very pleased with him and looking forward to sending him novice chasing. I have bought some very good horses from John Costello in Ireland over the years and he is another. I am able to go over there and watch them school and this horse is a wonderful jumper. Having run well in bumpers at Stratford and Ascot, he won three out of three over hurdles, including the Grade 2 Dovecote Novices' Hurdle at Kempton in February. Keen during his races, I wanted to get more experience into him over hurdles but the season was cut short. I think he will develop into a smart two mile chaser but I want him to back off at his fences. He appreciates cut in the ground and we hope to start him off around October/November time.

LORD BADDESLEY (IRE) 5 bb g Doyen (IRE) – Tropical Ocean (IRE)
Another promising young horse who ran very well first time out in a bumper at Worcester in October. The form is strong, too. Inclined to be quite keen, he was fifth next time at Kempton but the way the race was run didn't suit him. We were hoping for a proper gallop but they went steady and then quickened up. He is a horse who lacks an instant change of gear but we are teaching him to learn to settle and we have been pleased with him during the summer. I would like to start him off over two miles at somewhere like Fontwell or Plumpton and ride him handily.

MELLOW BEN (IRE) 7 b g Beneficial – Mellowthemoonlight (IRE)
Twice a winner over hurdles, I wasn't sure whether he would take to fences but he got his act together and won at Worcester and Fontwell. It isn't going to be easy off a rating of 137, but he came back in early because he is a better ground horse. Sixth on his return at Stratford in September, the handicapper has dropped him three pounds since. Trips around two and a half and three miles are ideal.

ON THE SLOPES 6 b g Librettist (USA) – Dalriath
A smashing horse who I ride every day, he has always felt like a stayer and his mother wasn't particularly quick. However, he hasn't stopped improving since we dropped him back in trip last season. Third over two and a half miles at Cheltenham on Trials day in January, Adam Wedge unleashed him and he immediately had everything in trouble but didn't get home and finished third. Dropped back to two miles two at Kempton next time, he made all and won easily. We were aiming him at the Grand Annual Chase at the Cheltenham Festival but he was balloted out. Rerouted to Kempton the following day, he won over two miles. I think two miles two is ideal, although two miles on a staying track is fine. I would like to aim him at the Haldon Gold Cup at Exeter (3rd November), although we have the option of waiting for the Cheltenham November meeting (13th). He is in good order following his summer break.

ONLY MONEY (IRE) 6 ch g Getaway (GER) – Kings Diva (IRE)
Raced in three bumpers the previous season winning at Fontwell last time. He was unable to run last season, due to a complication with his owner and legal issues. Thankfully, he has been sold to stay in the yard and finished fourth in another bumper at Stratford in September. Fitted with a hood, he raced keenly but we will send him hurdling now. He is a nice horse who is suited by better ground and is quick enough to start off over two miles.

PRES (IRE) 6 ch g Sans Frontieres (IRE) – Present Company (IRE)
Placed a couple of times in Irish points, he didn't win over hurdles but took well to chasing last season winning at Lingfield and Ffos Las. Runner-up on three other occasions, including at Newbury in February, I think he remains competitively handicapped and looks ideal for those provincial Nationals. The Southern National at Plumpton in early January is a possible target having finished second there last season.

PRESS YOUR LUCK (IRE) 5 b g Doyen (IRE) – Merry Gladness (IRE)
Bought at the Goffs UK Autumn Sale at Doncaster last year, he won one of his three Irish point-to-points for Donnchadh Doyle and is a lovely horse. He finished fifth in a decent bumper at Kempton in February. Leighton (Aspell) gave him a good ride and wasn't too hard on him once his chance had gone. He will go novice hurdling and will be suited by two and a half miles at somewhere like Plumpton. He is a nice horse and I will be disappointed if he doesn't win races.

REMILUC (FR) 11 b g Mister Sacha (FR) – Markene De Durtal (FR)
I bought him out of Paul Nicholls yard for £8,000 six years ago and he has been a stable star. Off the track for over eighteen months, he came back last season and ran a blinder to finish third in the *Betfair* Hurdle at Newbury in February. Only beaten three parts of a length, we only managed to get one run into him beforehand and I think that made the difference, plus the ground dried out on the day. It was one which got away and I will look back on that day at the end of my training career. Runner-up in the County Hurdle a couple of years ago, it won't be easy this season off 142. I suspect we will target him at the *Betfair* Hurdle once again.

SAMI BEAR 4 b g Sulamani (IRE) – Dalriath
A nice unraced half-brother to On The Slopes, we purchased him at the Goffs UK Spring Sale at Doncaster last year. He was ready to run earlier this year but never got the opportunity. We will start him off in a bumper in the Autumn and I think he is the sort to run well.

SMURPHY ENKI (FR) 5 b g Blue Bresil (FR) – Crème Veloutee (IRE)
Another former Irish pointer we bought off Donnchadh Doyle, he was placed twice in four starts. We ran him in a bumper at Wincanton in early March and I thought he would run well because of his experience in point-to-points, but was pleasantly surprised when he bolted up by eighteen lengths. The plan was to run him in the Grade 2 championship bumper at Aintree's Grand National meeting but that was cancelled. He wants some cut in the ground and is ready to go novice hurdling this season. However, if conditions were suitable, he could run in another bumper in the Autumn/early part of the winter. We will look to start him off in a small novice hurdle once sent jumping.

STORM DENNIS (IRE) 4 b g Libertarian – Lady Eile (IRE)
Another lovely unraced four year old who we like. He was due to run in March before racing was halted and is a horse who has pleased me. Broken in as a two year old, he has done well during the summer and will contest a bumper in October/November.

STRAIGHT SWAP (IRE) 5 bb g Yeats (IRE) – Alittlebitofheaven
From the family of Punjabi, he is another ex-Donnchadh Doyle trained horse who was placed in two of his three Irish points. He looks an interesting horse for bumpers and novice hurdles this season.

TOP MAN (IRE) 6 b g Milan – Get In There (IRE)
Won a point-to-point in Ireland before being acquired at the Goffs UK Spring Sale last year, he won over hurdles at Plumpton in December and ran well in a decent handicap at Kempton last time. Leighton (Aspell) looked after him and he wasn't beaten far. Rated 117 and from the family of Harbour Pilot, he will go over fences and be aimed at a two and a half miles novices' handicap chase.

TWOMINUTES TURKISH (IRE) 5 ch g Mahler – Kilbarry Cliché (IRE)
He is a nice horse and one to look forward to in novice hurdles this season. I was very pleased with his first run in a bumper at Newbury in November finishing fifth. We then took him to Huntingdon and he hung badly to his left and we don't know why. Given a break since, we haven't schooled him over hurdles on grass yet but I don't envisage any problems. Two miles on good to soft ground is probably ideal.

Unnamed 4 b f Doyen (IRE) – Grangeclare Rhythm (IRE)
Half-sister to Baddesley Knight, we bought her as an unbroken two year old and she is the most gorgeous filly. She will make her debut in a mares' bumper and is one to look forward to.

Unnamed 4 ch g Shirocco (GER) – Nodelay (IRE)
Bought privately off John Costello in Ireland, he is a nice four year old who had one or two niggly little problems last season. However, he is in good form now and will run in a bumper in the Autumn.

> **TRAINER'S HORSE TO FOLLOW: LORD BADDESLEY & TWOMINUTES TURKISH**

Philip HOBBS
Stables: Sandhill, Bilbrook, Minehead, Somerset.
2019/2020: 75 Winners / 419 Runners 18% Prize-Money £1,139,200
www.pjhobbs.com

ACROSS THE CHANNEL (FR) 5 b g Dunkerque (FR) – Aulne River (FR)
Ran in two Irish point-to-points falling on his debut before winning next time. He was bought at the Cheltenham December Sale but was light in condition when arriving, hence he has yet to run for us. Owned by Andrew Cohen and a half-brother to Wait For Me (5 wins) and That's A Given (3), who we have both trained, he could start off in a bumper or go straight over hurdles. He looks a nice horse in the making.

BIG SHARK (IRE) 6 b g Vinnie Roe (IRE) – Castlelost (IRE)
Runner in his only Irish point, he did well over hurdles last season winning twice at Worcester and Hereford before finishing runner-up at Haydock next time. Fifth in a competitive Grade 3 handicap at Sandown in February, he suffered with stomach ulcers and was light in condition afterwards. Given a break, he is likely to go straight over fences and should do well in staying novice chases on slow ground.

CAMPROND (FR) 4 b g Lope De Vega (IRE) – Bernieres (IRE)
A new arrival, he is a very nice horse who is owned by J.P.McManus. He won three times on the Flat in France, including by nine lengths over a mile and a half at Saint-Cloud in September last year. He is cantering at the moment and does everything easily at home.

DEFI DU SEUIL (FR) 7 b g Voix Du Nord (FR) – Quarvine Du Seuil (FR)
Everything went to plan last season, bar the Cheltenham Festival. He produced three very good performances to win the Shloer, Tingle Creek and Clarence House Chases. However, he never ran his race in the Queen Mother Champion Chase at Cheltenham and we don't know why. He didn't seem himself in the preliminaries and Barry (Geraghty) said he felt flat from the outset. We couldn't find anything wrong with him afterwards and he has had a long break having spent the summer at Martinstown Stud in Ireland. We haven't finalised plans, but I presume he will follow the same route and contest the top two mile chases once again. Therefore in all likelihood, he will start off in the Shloer Chase at Cheltenham (15th November). We know he stays further having won the Scilly Isles and JLT Novice Chases over two and a half miles and I think he will stay three miles, if necessary.

DEISE ABA (IRE) 7 b g Mahler – Kit Massini (IRE)
A progressive young chaser, he won twice over fences at Catterick and Sandown producing a very good performance at the latter. He then ran well at Cheltenham finishing fifth in the Kim Muir. Still lightly raced and green, he is open to further improvement and I have got the Welsh National at Chepstow (27th December) in mind. He will have one run beforehand.

DIPLOMATE SIVOLA (FR) 7 ch g Noroit (GER) – None De Sivola (FR)
Runner-up at Fontwell in December, he will continue in staying handicap chases during the first half of the season and then revert back to hunter chases in the New Year for his owner/ rider David Maxwell. Only seven, he could improve again and continue to go the right way. He stays well and handles soft ground.

DOLPHIN SQUARE (IRE) 6 b g Shantou (USA) – Carrig Eden Lass (IRE)
A lovely horse who also belongs to David Maxwell. He did everything right last year winning three times over hurdles at Newton Abbot, Wincanton and Ludlow. Runner-up at Newbury last time, he is a winning Irish pointer and will go novice chasing in the Autumn. Still improving, he should make a nice chaser and, while he has the speed for two and a half miles, he is most effective over three miles.

DOSTAL PHIL (FR) 7 b g Coastal Path – Quiphile (FR)
A dual winner over hurdles, he looked a nice horse when winning on his reappearance at Fontwell on Boxing Day. We then purposely saved him for the Imperial Cup at Sandown in March, but the meeting was abandoned and then he was balloted out at the Cheltenham Festival. Rerouted to Uttoxeter instead a few days later, he was disappointing and we don't know why. He is a big strong horse who will jump fences at some stage, but is capable of winning more races over hurdles in the meantime.

EARTH MOOR (IRE) 6 ch g Ask – Merrylas (IRE)
Enjoyed a good season having missed the previous campaign due to a tendon problem. Twice a winner at Taunton and Wincanton, he copes with soft ground and is suited by two and a half miles. Rated 134, he will probably have another run over hurdles before going novice chasing.

ECU DE LA NOVERIE (FR) 6 b g Linda's Lad – Quat'Sous D'Or (FR)
A big strong horse who has shown a decent level of ability since arriving from France. He won over fences at Wetherby in November before running two creditable races over hurdles at Cheltenham and Kempton. The plan is for him to continue in handicap chases before going hunter chasing in the New Year.

ESPION (FR) 6 ch g Coastal Path – Toutamie (FR)
An easy winner at Uttoxeter in March when stepped up to two and a half miles for the first time, it is a shame he isn't a novice for this season, but he remains eligible for novice events until the end of November. He is progressive and will stay three miles eventually. His long-term future lies over fences but he will continue over hurdles and I hope he is on a good mark.

EVERGLOW 5 br g Presenting – Cent Prime
An exciting prospect for novice hurdles, we have always thought he was a very nice horse. It therefore wasn't a surprise when he ran so well on his debut in a bumper at Chepstow finishing a close second. Third next time in a Listed event at Cheltenham's November meeting, we purposely saved him for the Goffs UK Doncaster Sales bumper at Newbury in March, but that never took place. Only five, he will improve with time and will go straight over hurdles. He will probably start off over two and a half miles.

FILOU DES ISSARDS (FR) 5 ch g Network (IRE) – Rapiere (FR)
Placed in an Irish point, he could be a big improver this season. Runner-up over hurdles at Taunton last time, he will appreciate a step up to two and a half miles.

FLINCK (IRE) 6 b g Fame And Glory – Princess Supreme (IRE)
Progressive over hurdles, he won twice at Warwick and Haydock. I am expecting him to improve again this year because he struggled to hold his condition last season, but looks stronger now following his summer break. Likely to go novice chasing, he will be campaigned over two and a half miles to start with, but I think he will stay three miles eventually.

FOREVER DES LONG (FR) 5 b g Blue Bresil (FR) – Fetuque Du Moulin (FR)
Previously owned by the Taunton Racecourse Owners Club, he now belongs to the Noel Fehilly Racing Club and could do well for them this season. Placed over hurdles at Wincanton and Ludlow, he was only narrowly beaten at the latter over a trip too sharp for him. I think he could be progressive once upped in distance and we will look for a suitable novices' handicap hurdle.

GOLDEN SOVEREIGN (IRE) 6 b g Gold Well – Fugal Maid (IRE)
A likeable and genuine horse, he isn't the quickest but stays well and will jump fences this season. Successful over hurdles at Uttoxeter and Warwick last winter, he copes with testing ground and wants three miles plus.

GOSHEVEN (IRE) 7 b g Presenting – Fair Choice (IRE)
Has been a very unlucky horse suffering a tendon injury a couple of seasons ago after finishing third in the Grade 2 Persian War Novices' Hurdle at Chepstow. He had a couple of runs last winter finishing third at Ludlow in January. We have operated on his wind since and I hope he will improve because he is a horse who has always had a lot of potential. Rated 122, he remains a novice and will continue over hurdles.

GUMBALL (FR) 6 gr g No Risk At All (FR) – Good Time Girl (FR)
He won a Listed handicap at Ascot in November before being narrowly denied in the Greatwood Hurdle at Cheltenham. Rated 152, he isn't the easiest the place because he isn't quite good enough for the championship races and is forced to carry big weights in handicaps. We haven't schooled him over fences yet, but it is something we are probably going to have to do at some stage to see how he gets on. He has won three out of four on the Flat, including when beating Verdana Blue at Kempton last year, and is rated 90. We therefore may aim him at a decent staying handicap before going back over jumps.

HOPE YOU DO (FR) 3 b g Boris De Deauville (IRE) – Une Tournee (FR)
Owned by J.P.McManus, he arrived in late summer having won his only AQPS Flat race at Angers in May. His win came on soft ground and, while we haven't done a lot with him yet, he looks a nice prospect for juvenile hurdlers this season.

JATILUWIH (FR) 6 ch g Linda's Lad – Jaune De Beaufai (FR)
Had a good season over hurdles winning three times, including at Cheltenham's November meeting. I thought he ran well, too, in the Pertemps Final at the Festival. A winner over fences in France prior to joining us, he may have a run in a handicap chase but his main target is likely to be the Foxhunters' Chase at Cheltenham in March. We are hoping he may be his owner/rider David Maxwell's best chance in the race to date. Therefore to qualify, we may decide to run him in an open point-to-point before the hunter chases start in the New Year.

JERRYSBACK (IRE) 8 b g Jeremy (USA) – Get A Few Bob Back (IRE)
Third in a valuable Listed handicap chase at Ascot before Christmas, his main target last season was the Irish National but that never took place. He is capable of winning a good staying handicap chase but I am not sure he wants extreme distances. We haven't made any plans but three miles on a right-handed track is ideal.

KALOOKI (GER) 6 b g Martaline – Karuma (GER)
Progressive over hurdles, he won easily at Ludlow and Wetherby before finishing runner-up in a Grade 2 novice at Haydock in February. It was heavy ground and it is debatable whether he stayed three miles having travelled strongly for a long way. Perhaps trips around two miles six are ideal and it is likely he will go over fences. He should make a nice novice chaser.

KEEP WONDERING (IRE) 6 b g Scorpion (IRE) – Supreme Touch (IRE)
A big strong horse who won an Irish point and ran well in three starts over hurdles for us. Switched to fences in January, he produced a good performance to win by ten lengths at Ffos Las before unseating his rider at Kempton last time. Two and a half miles handicap chases are on his agenda and, having only raced twice over fences, he ought to improve.

KEPY BLANC (FR) 5 ch g Kapgarde (FR) – Villemanzie (FR)
A new arrival from France, he finished second on his only start over hurdles at Fontainebleau in October. Beaten a couple of lengths, he was subsequently bought by David Maxwell and will be campaigned in novice hurdles.

LARKBARROW LAD 7 b g Kayf Tara – Follow My Leader (IRE)
Won the Fixed Brush series final at Worcester in October and then we decided to operate on his wind, which has made a difference. Fifth in the Lanzarote Hurdle at Kempton next time, he wants fences and will benefit from a return to three miles. However, he doesn't want the ground too soft.

LE LIGERIEN (FR) 7 b g Turgeon (USA) – Etoile De Loir (FR)
Placed three times at Taunton during the first half of last season, he surprised me at Newbury in January winning by nineteen lengths. It was staggering. He followed up under a penalty three days later at Haydock, but had probably had enough by the time he ran in the County Hurdle at the Festival. We will run him in another handicap hurdle before switching to fences. Two miles on a left handed track are his optimum conditions.

LITTLE RIVER BAY (IRE) 5 b m Shirocco (GER) – Penneyrose Bay
A half-sister to Imperial Presence, she has only raced twice and I hope she will improve. Fifth in a bumper at Plumpton on her debut, she was then third over hurdles at Wincanton in the spring and it was a step in the right direction. She will be suited by a step up to two and a half miles and will be aimed at mares' novice hurdles.

MASTERS LEGACY (IRE) 5 br g Getaway (GER) – Gently Go (IRE)
Looked good last season winning two of his three starts over hurdles. It's just a shame we didn't get the opportunity to run him again because he needs more experience. We nearly ran him in a bumper but decided to go straight over hurdles and he improved with each run. Still green, he is rated 136 and we will be looking towards some decent two and a half miles handicap hurdles.

MELEKHOV (IRE) 6 b g Sholokhov (IRE) – Yorkshire Girl (IRE)
Progressive in bumpers and novice hurdles, he disappointed on his reappearance at Sandown and we don't know why. Given time, he was ready to run in the spring but the season was cut short. Prior to Sandown, he was going the right way and could improve again. Two and a half miles handicap hurdles on better ground will be his target.

MUSICAL SLAVE (IRE) 7 b g Getaway (GER) – Inghwung

I was pleased with him last season progressing with each run over fences. A winner at Exeter on New Year's Day, he was then third at Haydock before running well on bad ground at Uttoxeter in March. It was his first run over three miles and he stayed on well. Three miles on better ground will be ideal and he is the sort to continue to improve.

NO COMMENT 9 br g Kayf Tara – Dizzy Frizzy

Suffered two nasty falls at Leopardstown over Christmas and in the Ultima Handicap Chase at the Cheltenham Festival. Still a maiden over fences, he is rated 137 and isn't the easiest to place. Ideally, we could do with finding a small field novice chase and get a win into him over fences. Prior to his falls, his jumping had been good and he has plenty of ability.

OAKLEY (IRE) 7 b g Oscar (IRE) – Tirolean Dance (IRE)

Placed three times last season, including when narrowly beaten at Cheltenham in December. He ran creditably in the *Betfair* Hurdle at Newbury and County Hurdle at the Festival. We may give him one more run over hurdles before sending him chasing. Two miles is his trip because he has plenty of speed.

OFF THE PLANET (IRE) 5 ch g Presenting – Kings Diva (IRE)

Ran promisingly on his debut in a bumper at Worcester in October. Richard (Johnson) couldn't pull him up afterwards and the race has worked out well. Absent since, we were waiting to run him again on better ground in the spring but never got the opportunity. Previously owned by the Rooneys, he now belongs to David Rees and The Brushmakers, who owned Balthazar King. He could have another run in a bumper or go straight over hurdles over two and a half miles.

ONE FOR YOU (IRE) 5 b g Yeats (IRE) – Tempest Belle (IRE)

An unraced half-brother to Grade 1 winning chaser Monalee, he has done everything nicely at home. Like Off The Planet, he was formerly owned by the Rooneys but will carry the colours of Tim Syder and Martin St Quinton this year. He is a nice horse with ability and is likely to start in a bumper in the Autumn.

ORBYS LEGEND (IRE) 4 b g Milan – Morning Legend (IRE)

A very nice horse who finished runner-up in his only point-to-point in Ireland. Bought at the Cheltenham February Sale on behalf of Highclere Thoroughbreds, he worked well at home last spring. Back in work, he is only four and could start off in a bumper in the Autumn. He is a big strong horse and I like him.

PILEON (IRE) 6 b g Yeats (IRE) – Heath Heaven

A dual winner over hurdles at Catterick and Ffos Las, he then ran a cracking race in the Martin Pipe Conditional Jockeys' Handicap Hurdle at Cheltenham. Beaten a short head in second, he remains unexposed and open to further improvement. Rated 143, he will continue over hurdles and could reappear in the Silver Trophy at Chepstow (10th October).

POTTERS VENTURE (IRE) 6 b g Arcadio (GER) – Starventure (IRE)

He is potentially a very nice horse who produced a good performance to win over hurdles at Chepstow in November. Unfortunately, he suffered a tendon injury and hasn't raced since. However, his leg has been scanned and he will hopefully be back in action in December. He lacks experience over hurdles but his mark looks fair and there should be more to come.

ROCK THE KASBAH (IRE) 10 ch g Shirocco (GER) – Impudent (IRE)
He has been a very good horse for us winning nine races but isn't easy to place off his rating of 150. Runner-up in a Grade 3 handicap chase at Cheltenham in December and the Portman Cup Chase at Taunton the following month, he stays well but doesn't want the ground too soft. Back in work, he will be in action in October over three miles plus.

RONDE DE NUIT (FR) 3 b f Doctor Dino (FR) – Nuit De Guerre (FR)
She is another nice prospect for juvenile hurdles owned by J.P.McManus. She finished fourth on her only start on the Flat at Angers in France in early June. Beaten less than two lengths against colts, she arrived in late summer.

SMARTY WILD 6 b g Fair Mix (IRE) – Blaeberry
A four times winner over hurdles, including at Exeter in November, he is a big strong horse who ought to continue to improve. Fourth a couple of times at Sandown last winter, including in a Listed handicap hurdle, we haven't decided whether he will stay over hurdles or go chasing. Two and a half miles is his trip. He should make a nice chaser.

SPORTING JOHN (IRE) 5 bb g Getaway (GER) – Wild Spell (IRE)
Looked so promising when winning his first three starts over hurdles. Unfortunately, Cheltenham proved a disaster only finishing seventh in the Ballymore Novices' Hurdle. It was very odd because he wasn't sound immediately after the race, but was OK within an hour. His performance was too bad to be true because he was never travelling. Anyway, he has had a long break at Martinstown Stud during the summer and the plan is to send him novice chasing. A horse with lots of ability, he was impressive at Ascot in February and, while he may start off over two miles, we know he stays further. He remains an exciting prospect.

SPRINGTOWN LAKE (IRE) 8 b g Gamut (IRE) – Sprightly Gal (IRE)
A twenty lengths winner of a decent handicap chase at Warwick in February, his form is in and out and I don't know why. He appears to be at his best following a break and I hope he will continue to make an impact in the good two and a half miles handicap chases.

ST BARTS (IRE) 6 b g High Chaparral (IRE) – Lindeman (IRE)
I think he could be a very good horse in the making. Twice a winner over hurdles last season at Wincanton and Ascot, he appreciated the step up to three miles at the latter track. I thought it was a good performance and the plan is to send him chasing. Already a point-to-point winner, he is rated 125 and we will look for a suitable novices' handicap chase to begin with.

STEELY ADDITION (IRE) 8 b g Craigsteel – Blond's Addition (IRE)
Only raced twice last year and, having run OK on his return at Sandown in a Listed Intermediate chase, we were aiming him at the Welsh National. However, he was lame a couple of days beforehand and was forced to miss that engagement. Disappointing in the Grand National Trial at Haydock in February, he has form on testing ground but I am not sure he wants it too deep. He stays well and will be aimed at three miles plus handicap chases.

SURTITLE (IRE) 4 b g Presenting – Annabaloo (IRE)
Purchased at the Land Rover Sale in Ireland last year, he is a very nice unraced horse who has worked well at home. From the family of Oscar Whisky, he will start off in a bumper in the Autumn.

THYME HILL 6 b g Kayf Tara – Rosita Bay
He is in good form at home having enjoyed an excellent season over hurdles winning three times, including the Grade 1 Challow Hurdle at Newbury. Fourth in the Albert Bartlett Novices' Hurdle at Cheltenham in March, I thought he was a bit unlucky not to finish even closer. We have schooled him over fences and he was very good, but the plan is to remain over hurdles and aim him at the top staying events. With the exception of Paisley Park, it looks an open division and he doesn't have to improve too much to become a contender. The plan is for him to return in the Grade 2 West Yorkshire Hurdle at Wetherby (31st October).

TIDAL FLOW 7 b g Black Sam Bellamy (IRE) – Mrs Philip
Took well to fences winning at Uttoxeter and Stratford and is going the right way. It won't be easy this season off his rating of 148 and he may prefer smaller fields. However, he has only had four starts over fences and is open to further improvement. Trips around two and a half miles suit him.

TRUCKERS PASS (IRE) 6 br g Kalanisi (IRE) – Lady Knightess (IRE)
He is a very nice horse who was unlucky not to win a bumper last season. Runner-up at Warwick and Exeter, he showed signs of greenness on both occasions. Richard (Johnson) thought he was going to win last time but he went left and may be at his best on left-handed tracks. He will go novice hurdling and I hope he will do well.

TRUCKIN AWAY (IRE) 7 br g Getaway (GER) – Simons Girl (IRE)
Still a novice over fences, he finished third at Taunton and Ludlow. We have operated on his wind, which will hopefully make a difference. With his rating of 127, we will look for a novices' handicap chase.

WILDFIRE WARRIOR (IRE) 5 b g Flemensfirth (USA) – Lady of Fortune (IRE)
A nice horse who had two runs in bumpers last season finishing runner-up on his debut at Warwick in January. Fourth at the same track next time, he will go hurdling and will be suited by two and a half miles.

WINTER GETAWAY (IRE) 7 b m Getaway (GER) – Galzig (IRE)
She won two Irish points before joining us and had a good season over hurdles last winter. A dual winner at Stratford and Warwick, she was also placed at Taunton and I hope she will progress further this season. She will jump fences eventually but we will keep her to mares' handicap hurdles over trips around two miles six for now.

YOUNG WILLIAM (IRE) 4 b g Yeats (IRE) – Full of Fruit (FR)
A nice unraced four year old who is a three parts brother to Pileon. He was due to run in an Irish point for Tom Keating last spring and was reportedly going well. Owned by Tim Syder, he is likely to make his debut in a bumper.

ZANZA (IRE) 6 b g Arcadio (GER) – What A Bleu (IRE)
A winner at Newbury in November, he ran some good races in defeat notably finishing sixth in the Greatwood and *Betfair* Hurdles at Cheltenham and Newbury respectively. He has plenty of speed for two miles but doesn't want the ground too soft. We have the option of going novice chasing but he will probably have another run or two over hurdles beforehand.

ZIZANEUR (FR) 5 b g Planteur (IRE) – Zitana (FR)
Unlucky when set to win at Taunton in January, he unseated his rider at the third last and then he made a mistake at Haydock when still in contention. A novice over fences, we will probably mix and match between the two and he is capable of winning races off his mark.

ZOFFEE 4 b g Zoffany (IRE) – Mount Crystal (IRE)
Runner-up on his first two races over hurdles, he then won in good style at Doncaster appreciating the better ground in the process. Pulled up in the Boodles Juvenile Hurdle at the Cheltenham Festival, he is high enough in the handicap. We have therefore schooled him over fences and he has been good, so we may decide to make the most of his four year old allowance. He looks to have improved over the summer and ran well on the Flat at Thirsk in September finishing third.

> **TRAINER'S HORSE TO FOLLOW: PILEON**

Anthony HONEYBALL
Stables: Potwell Farm, Mosterton, Beaminster, Dorset.
2019/2020: 36 Winners / 126 Runners 29% Prize-Money £412,750
www.ajhoneyballracing.co.uk

ACEY MILAN (IRE) 6 b g Milan – Strong Wishes (IRE)
Runner-up in the Grade 3 staying handicap hurdle at Haydock in November, he ran a blinder and looked like winning for most of the race until he was headed close home on the long run-in. Unfortunately, that run really tore the guts out of him and he was never the same thereafter last season. He has had a good break after his last run at Newbury though and will go novice chasing. Not over big, he has schooled very well and is a horse with a lot of ability. Depending on what races are available at the time, he is likely to start off over two and a half miles, although we know he stays further.

BELLE DE MANECH (FR) 4 gr f Vision D'Etat (FR) – Noor Forever (FR)
A very nice filly with a good mind and a bit of quality. She beat Coquelicot on her debut at Warwick and then wasn't beaten far in a Listed four year old bumper at Cheltenham on New Year's Day. Runner-up on heavy ground at Ascot, she got wound up before her final start at Kempton and was probably over the top, in any case. She travels well in her races and is versatile groundwise. We have schooled her and she jumps great and we will be aiming her at mares' novice hurdles. Her owner had Ms Parfois with us and he is keen for this filly to win some black type, too.

BLEUE AWAY (IRE) 6 b m Getaway (GER) – Majorite Bleue (FR)
A dual English point-to-point winning mare, we bought her at the Cheltenham May Sale last year and she finished fifth on her only start for us in a bumper at Ffos Las in November. She was then due to go mares' novice hurdling but suffered a stress fracture with a joint and hasn't raced since. Back to full fitness, she is ready to go hurdling and jumps very well. Another mare with some quality, I don't think she will want to go any further than two and a half miles for the time being because she isn't slow.

CALL ME CRACKER 4 b f Black Sam Bellamy (IRE) – Cream Cracker
An unraced full-sister to Sam Brown, she is a nice filly but a different type of model to her older sibling. A strong filly, she is a smaller version and more of a hurdler. We will start her off in a mares' bumper in the Autumn and I think she possesses the engine to win or at least be placed in one before she goes hurdling.

COQUELICOT (FR) 4 b f Soldier of Fortune (IRE) – Moscow Nights (FR)
Half-sister to the Ebor winner and Melbourne Cup runner-up Heartbreak City, she is a cracking filly who I think is very good. She has a good cruising speed and loads of stamina and has done nothing wrong either at home or on a racecourse. Runner-up on her first couple of starts in bumpers at Warwick and Newbury, the further she has gone, the better she has looked winning her next three races over two miles. She still had the speed to win around Taunton and Huntingdon though before winning a Listed mares' bumper at Kempton last time. We have done a lot of schooling with her and, while she jumps well, I think she may take a couple of runs before her jumping becomes really slick. She has a big engine though and her ultimate aim is the Grade 2 Dawn Run Mares' Novices' Hurdle at the Cheltenham Festival in March. Long-term, I think she will be even better over two and a half miles. She copes with heavy ground but is versatile and doesn't need it bottomless.

DEJA VUE (IRE) 6 b m Fame And Glory – Westgrove Berry (IRE)
Twice a winner over hurdles at Ffos Las, she has a high cruising speed on soft and heavy ground. A free going mare who likes to race prominently, she is a bit one dimensional and isn't as fast as she thinks she is. A winning Irish pointer, she will go novice chasing and I think she will jump fences better than hurdles. She stays three miles but two and a half miles on very testing ground is ideal. I will be disappointed if she doesn't win mares' novice chases.

DON LAMI (FR) 7 ch g Honolulu (IRE) – Toutamie (FR)
Lightly raced, he won on his chasing debut at Taunton in November but then suffered a strain to his suspensory ligament and hasn't raced since. He is 100% now though and, while he lacks experience over fences, he will be aimed at some decent three miles handicap chases. A strong stayer, he is at his best on flat tracks.

DREAMING BLUE 3 b g Showcasing – Got To Dream
A new arrival, we bought him at the Tattersalls Horses in Training Sale at Newmarket in August with a view to him going juvenile hurdling. Rated 72 on the Flat, he won over a mile and a half at Wolverhampton in August for Richard Fahey and has shown he handles soft ground earlier in his career.

FANFARON DINO (FR) 5 gr g Doctor Dino (FR) – Kadjara (FR)
A half-brother to the Champion Hurdle winner Epatante, he finished second on her debut in a bumper at Ffos Las behind a potentially very useful horse (Easy As That). Quite a nervy sort, he had a couple of runs over hurdles at Exeter but has taken time to get to grips with jumping. Qualified for handicaps following one more run, he stayed well in his bumper and will be suited by two and a half miles on a galloping track. He has shown enough to suggest he can win races.

GABRIEL'S GETAWAY (IRE) 3 b g Getaway (GER) – Chosen Destiny (IRE)
He is a lovely unraced three year old from the family of Burton Port. I have ridden him myself and really like him. He has got a great attitude and is one to look out for in a bumper next spring. Long-term, he is very much a chaser in the making.

GUSTAVIAN (IRE) 5 b g Mahler – Grange Oscar (IRE)
Runner-up in a couple of bumpers at Chepstow and Ffos Las, he won well on his hurdles debut at Exeter in January. We then had his palate fired but he was a bit disappointing at Uttoxeter next time. We stepped him up in trip but he was too keen and I think he was over the top by that stage of the season, in any case. A horse with a big engine, he is capable of winning off his mark of 120 and will benefit from being dropped in over shorter trips. Two miles two at somewhere like Exeter would be fine for him and, once he learns to settle, I envisage him staying three miles. He handles soft and heavy ground.

HIDEAWAY VIC (IRE) 7 b g Stowaway – Cailin Vic Mo Cri (IRE)
Very consistent, he won a bumper at Plumpton a few seasons ago and, while he has run well over hurdles, I am disappointed we haven't managed to win with him over jumps so far. Runner-up twice at Ffos Las and Plumpton, he was below par at Hereford last time. He had his third wind operation of his career this summer so it is a big season for him this time around. The plan is to go over fences and aim him at novice handicap chases off his mark of 120. Two and a half to three miles is ideal and, if he puts his mind to the job, he could do well.

JEPECK (IRE) 11 b g Westerner – Jenny's Jewel (IRE)
Did very well last season winning novice hurdles at Bangor and Chepstow and then the veterans' chase final at Sandown in early January. That was his Gold cup and he did a great job. Fourth at Ascot next time in a Listed handicap chase, the veterans' final, for which he is already qualified, will once again be his big target but he needs to drop a few pounds in the ratings.

KID COMMANDO 6 b g Robin Des Champs (FR) – Banjaxed Girl
An exciting horse who looked very good on occasions last season. A former winning Irish pointer, he won his bumper in impressive fashion at Fontwell and I thought he won well on his hurdles debut at Plumpton. Third next time in the Grade 2 Dovecote Novices' Hurdle at Kempton, his jumping was good and the plan was to step him up to two and a half miles and aim him at the Grade 1 novice hurdle at Aintree in April. We were expecting a big run there, too. He will benefit from running over further and ought to be very competitive off his mark of 136. If he is ready in time, a race such as the Silver Trophy at Chepstow (10th October) could suit him. Longer-term, it wouldn't surprise me if he ran in something like the Grade 2 National Spirit Hurdle at Fontwell in February because I think he is that level. He copes with soft ground.

KILCONNY BRIDGE (IRE) 6 b m Stowaway – Wattle Bridge (IRE)
She has done extremely well since we bought her at the Cheltenham May Sales last year. A half-sister to Benny's Bridge, she won her only point-to-point in Ireland for Colin Bowe and kept improving for us last season. A bumper winner at Plumpton, she has won three out of four over hurdles, including handicaps at Exeter and Ludlow. She stays well and handles soft ground and I hope she will continue to progress. Rated 126, we might aim her at a mares' handicap hurdle at Wincanton (7th November). Whilst she isn't over big, she should jump fences later on.

LILITH (IRE) 5 b m Stowaway – Flirthing Around (IRE)
A new arrival, we purchased her at the Goffs UK Summer Sale at Doncaster in July having won one of her three English point-to-points for Philip Rowley. We haven't done much with her yet, but she looks nice and I am hoping she proves a bit of value. She has size and scope for fences eventually and was progressive in her points. A ready made mare, jumping looks to be her forte, but we may try her in a mares' bumper before she goes novice hurdling.

MARILYN MONROE (IRE) 7 b m Scorpion (IRE) – Go On Eileen (IRE)
A well bred mare, she is a half-sister to Regal Encore and The Organist and won a point-to-point in Ireland before we bought her. A bumper winner at Fontwell for us the previous season, she found the ground too soft over hurdles last winter. She wants good or good to soft and is well handicapped off 82. I view her as a 110 or 115 mare and she will benefit from stepping up to two and a half miles.

MIDNIGHT CALLISTO 5 br m Midnight Legend – Carrigeen Queen (IRE)
We have always loved her and she looked very good when winning easily on her debut in a bumper at Fontwell. Her victory wasn't a surprise and we thought she would win the Listed mares' bumper at Cheltenham's November meeting. Aidan (Coleman) said she didn't handle the ground but I think the race came too soon. We gave her a break and then she finished third in another Listed bumper at Market Rasen in January. Despite the fact she ran well, I was disappointed she didn't win but at least she picked up some black type. We have schooled her over hurdles and she jumps fantastically. She will make a cracking mares' novice hurdler and, while she will probably start over two miles, I don't think it would matter what trip she ran over. Good or good to soft ground is probably ideal because she doesn't want it too testing or tacky.

MIDNIGHT TUNE 9 b m Midnight Legend – Harmonic Motion (IRE)
This is likely to be her final season, so we are hoping she can win a decent race before she is retired to stud. Three times a winner over fences last season, we thought she would go close in the Peter Marsh Chase at Haydock in January. She stays well and loves soft/heavy ground and everything appeared to be in place for a big run. However, she dropped away tamely before pulling up. It was a similar story at Uttoxeter last time and, having made a noise on her final two starts, we decided to operate on her wind. Rated 135, I don't think she has shown her true ability over fences yet.

MONT SEGUR (FR) 5 ch g French Fifteen (FR) – Vie De Reine (FR)
Half-brother to Grade 1 winning chaser Terrefort and Vino Griego, he is a very nice horse with a big engine. Third on his debut in a bumper at Wincanton in November, he was very green and threw the race away by hanging left inside the final furlong. However, he went to Ludlow next time and won well from a highly regarded horse trained by Kim Bailey (Lord Apparelli). Put away after that, we haven't done a lot of schooling with him yet and there is a possibility we will aim him at the Listed bumper at Cheltenham's November meeting. He has shown enough to suggest he would have a realistic chance in that. A horse with a bit of speed, he stays well too and copes with good to soft and soft ground.

OSCAR MARTINI (IRE) 5 b g Oscar (IRE) – Stickwithmenancy (IRE)
From the family of Oscar Whisky, he is a nice quality unraced horse who was ready to run in a bumper last spring. He had done some work in Ireland before we bought him and I view him as a 120 – 130 horse in the making. I would expect him to be competitive in a bumper in the Autumn before going novice hurdling. He jumps well.

PRECIOUS (IRE) 4 b f Midnight Legend – Carrigeen Queen (IRE)
A full-sister to Midnight Callisto, she is a nice big unraced filly who has been straightforward. A different type to her sister, she is more robust and a tank of a filly. A real galloper, she looks capable of winning a mares' bumper.

PURE VISION (IRE) 9 b g Milan – Distillery Lane (IRE)
Absent for nearly two years, he has had his share of niggles but I still think he could win a high-class staying handicap chase. Runner-up at Cheltenham in April 2018, he handles any ground and stays well and could be one for the Welsh National at Chepstow (27th December).

REGAL ENCORE (IRE) 12 b g King's Theatre (IRE) – Go On Eileen (IRE)
Spent the summer with his owner in Ireland, he looks great for his age. His palate was tightened up during the summer and has been fired and I would imagine he will follow a similar programme. He won the Listed handicap chase at Ascot before Christmas for a second time and there is every chance he will go back in December and attempt to win it for a third time. Then, if he gets in, all roads will lead to Aintree for a third tilt at the Grand National.

SAM BROWN 8 b g Black Sam Bellamy (IRE) – Cream Cracker

Rated 152 over fences, he lacks experience having only had three runs. Returning from a long absence, he won on his chasing debut at Lingfield and then followed up in a Grade 2 at Haydock. He then blew out in the Grade 2 Reynoldstown Novices' Chase at Ascot and we don't really know why. It is possible he 'bounced' after his Haydock win. Given a break since, he enjoys soft and heavy ground and stays well. I don't think he has enough experience for the Ladbrokes Trophy at Newbury but we could aim him at the Welsh National over Christmas. Eligible for Graduation chases, it is not beyond the realms of possibility we will enter him in the Grade 1 *Betfair* Chase at Haydock (21st November). He might be outclassed but it is usually testing ground, a small field and we know he handles the track. I have been pleased with him during the summer and he seems in good form.

SOJOURN (IRE) 7 b g Getaway (GER) – Toscar (IRE)

He is a lovely horse who has only raced twice over fences winning on his chasing debut at Market Rasen in November. Runner-up at Chepstow next time, he jumps very well and copes with soft and heavy ground. A straightforward horse, it wouldn't surprise me if he developed into a Welsh National contender one day. Rated 129, he remains well handicapped and we will try and win a 0-130 handicap chase and then aim him at a big staying handicap.

SULLY D'OC AA (FR) 6 b g Konig Turf (GER) – Samarra D'Oc (FR)

Despite the fact he remains a maiden over fences, I think there is a decent handicap to be won with him. A bit fresh on his chasing debut at Ascot, he blew up but still ran well in sixth. Runner-up at Newbury next time, the trip was on the short side, plus he was beaten by a useful horse (Fanion D'Estruval). Sixth at Cheltenham on Trials day in January, he hated the ground but it was still a solid run. He jumps well and is still lightly raced but doesn't want soft or heavy ground. Good or good to soft is ideal with two and a half or two miles five being his trip. He doesn't want any further.

SWINCOMBE FLEAT 4 b f Yeats (IRE) – Swincombe Flame

A very nice unraced filly with a good pedigree. A full-sister to Master Debonair, her dam won the Lanzarote Hurdle. I have ridden her at home and she feels like a lovely mare with some quality. She has plenty of size and scope measuring 16.3hh and has something about her. We will start her off in a mares' bumper in the Autumn.

UCANAVER 4 bl f Maxios – Purely By Chance

Runner-up on her debut in a mares' bumper at Huntingdon in February behind Coquelicot, we bought her at the Cheltenham Sale later the same month. Last off the bridle that day, the form is strong and she looks a nice quality filly. A half-sister to Golden Spread who has won three times for Willie Mullins in Ireland, she is capable of winning a mares' bumper and may prove Listed class. We have already schooled her over hurdles and she jumps nicely.

WAGNER (IRE) 5 b g Mahler – Astalanda (FR)

Ran in three English point-to-point winning once before we purchased him at the Cheltenham May Sale last year. Third on his hurdling debut at Taunton in January, we operated on his wind and he won very well next time at Fontwell. He jumped with a lot of zest and accuracy and I was delighted with his performance. A big strong horse, he is still a novice until the end of November but it won't be long before we send him chasing. Effective on testing ground, he will stay two and a half miles in time.

WINDANCE (IRE) 5 b g Shirocco (GER) – Maca Rince (IRE)

Out of a Grade 3 winning hurdler, he could be an interesting one to follow over hurdles this season. Once raced, he finished fourth in a bumper at Wincanton in March. Off the bridle down the backstraight, he kept galloping and will have learned a lot. We might give him another run in a bumper at one of the smaller tracks before going hurdling. He jumps really well.

WINDSWEPT GIRL (IRE) 5 ch m Getaway (GER) – Chicago Vic (IRE)
Hadn't shown a great deal at home prior to her debut in a bumper at Taunton in February. It was therefore a pleasant surprise when she won by thirteen lengths coping with the heavy ground in the process. We were hoping she would run well but weren't expecting that. The further she went, the better she looked. She has schooled well over hurdles but we might try her in a Listed bumper and see how good she could be. Once hurdling, she will want two and a half miles and will stay three.

WORLD OF DREAMS (IRE) 4 b g Kayf Tara – Rose of The World (IRE)
A nice unraced four year old with a decent pedigree, he isn't over big (15.3hh) but has a good confirmation. He has worked nicely on the grass at home and ought to run well in a bumper in the Autumn.

YOU CAUGHT MY EYE (IRE) 6 b m Court Cave (IRE) – Didn't You Know (FR)
An easy winner on her debut in a bumper at Uttoxeter during the summer of last year, she hasn't run since but came back into work quite late and was due to run in the spring. The plan was to run her in February/March and then aim her at the Grade 2 mares' bumper at Aintree in April. The form of her win isn't anything special but she won very well and deserves a crack at a good bumper. It is possible she will go for the Listed mares' bumper at Cheltenham (14th November). Otherwise, she will go mares' novice hurdling. She has schooled well.

Unnamed 3 b g Yeats (IRE) – Swincombe Flame
A full-brother to Swincombe Fleat and Master Debonaire, I bought him this summer and he looks a lovely three year old with a high quality pedigree.

> **TRAINER'S HORSE TO FOLLOW: KID COMMANDO**

Alan KING
Stables: Barbury Castle Stables, Wroughton, Wiltshire.
2019/2020: 41 Winners / 339 Runners 12% Prize-Money £644,470
www.alankingracing.co.uk

ALARGEDRAM (IRE) 3 ch g Lope De Vega (IRE) – Myrica
The plan is to send him juvenile hurdling having been schooled at home. Fourth a couple of times on the Flat last year, he has only run once this season but we will give him some more experience before going jumping. He doesn't want the ground too quick.

BALLYWOOD (FR) 6 b g Ballingarry (IRE) – Miss Hollywood (FR)
He is in good form at home and, although he didn't win last season, I thought he ran some solid races finishing third at Cheltenham in December and he wasn't disgraced in the Grand Annual Chase at the Festival. Suited by good ground, he never got his conditions last winter. Runner-up on his reappearance at Fontwell in September, he will follow a similar programme, although I am keen to try him over two and a half miles at some stage.

BERINGER 5 b g Sea The Stars (IRE) – Edaraat (USA)
Depending on how he performs on the Flat during the Autumn, there is a possibility he will go hurdling this season. We schooled him last year and he jumps very well. Runner-up in the Cambridgeshire last Autumn, his form is strong and I was pleased with his reappearance at Pontefract in July finishing runner-up in a Listed race. He will need a sharp track, if he goes jumping.

BLACKO (FR) 4 gr g Balko (FR) – Ascella (FR)
I like him, he joined us from France last season and won twice at Taunton and Warwick. We ran him in the Boodles Juvenile Hurdle at the Cheltenham Festival but he wasn't quite right. He has done well during the summer and could start off in the four year old hurdle at Chepstow (9th October).

CANELO (IRE) 7 ch g Mahler – Nobody's Darling (IRE)
It took him a while to get used to jumping fences but he came good at Huntingdon on his final start. I thought Tom (Cannon) gave him an excellent ride and he remains a novice until the end of November. He wants two and a half miles plus.

COLOURS OF MY LIFE (IRE) 5 b m Arcadio (GER) – Lough Roe Lady (IRE)
A likeable mare with a good staying pedigree, I was very pleased with her debut run in a bumper at Newbury in late February. She looked like winning before getting tired late on. She has strengthened up during the summer and will have another run in a bumper before being aimed at mares' novice hurdles. Her schooling has gone well.

DAL HORRISGLE 4 b g Nathaniel (IRE) – Dalvina
He only arrived in August so we are still feeling our way with him. A three times winner on the Flat for William Haggas, he is rated 95 and has shown a good level of form. We have operated on his breathing and he will be having a run or two on the Flat in the Autumn but we have the option of sending him jumping later on.

DEYRANN DE CARJAC (FR) 7 b g Balko (FR) – Queyrann (FR)
A bit behind some of the others, he had an operation on his knee after his run at the Cheltenham Festival. Therefore he won't be in action until November onwards. He took well to chasing winning at Cartmel and Huntingdon and was third in Grade 2 novice events at Newbury and Cheltenham. Trips around two and a half miles to two miles six suit him and he may even stay three miles eventually.

DIDONATO (IRE) 5 b m Milan – Dream Lass (IRE)
I like her, she is a lovely mare who showed progressive form in bumpers last season. Fourth a couple of times at Bangor and Ludlow, she wasn't beaten far at Newbury last time. She takes a bit of getting fit and will be aimed at mares' novice hurdles over two and a half miles.

DINGO DOLLAR (IRE) 8 ch g Golden Lariat (USA) – Social Society (IRE)
Ran some solid races finishing fifth in the Ladbrokes Trophy at Newbury. Rated 142, he is high enough in the weights. We might try him over the National fences at Aintree in the Grand SeftonChase (5th December).

EDWARDSTONE 6 b g Kayf Tara – Nothingtoloose (IRE)
Looks marvellous following his summer break, he was a high-class novice hurdler last season winning at Wincanton and Aintree before being narrowly beaten in a Grade 2 event at Haydock. Sixth in the Supreme Novices' Hurdle at Cheltenham, he is going to stay over hurdles and we may give him one run and then aim him at the Greatwood Hurdle at Cheltenham (15th November). He is going to make a gorgeous chaser eventually, but he hasn't had a lot of racing and we haven't seen the best of him yet. Inclined to tank through his races, he will stick to two miles for the time being. However, once he learns to relax, he is bred to stay further.

ES PERFECTO (IRE) 5 ch g Shirocco (GER) – Shadow Dearg (IRE)
A lovely horse whom we bought at the Cheltenham December Sale having won an Irish point-to-point a few days earlier. We gave him one run in a bumper at Kempton in February and, while he ran well in third, the race wasn't run to suit him. Tom (Bellamy) educated him and he stayed on well at the finish. I have been pleased with him during the summer because he has thickened out and is ready to go novice hurdling. We will start him off over a stiff two miles.

FRATERNEL (FR) 5 b g Kap Rock (FR) – Valence (FR)
Placed over hurdles in France, he looks promising and was still a big weak horse last season. We had a bit of a hold up with him, but I thought he was good at Fakenham winning over two and a half miles. Given a workable mark, he is still a novice until the end of November. He will stay over hurdles this season but will make a lovely chaser next year. He wants two and a half miles plus.

GRISBI DE BERCE (FR) 4 b g Tin Horse (IRE) – Volupia De Berce (FR)
Ran with a lot of promise on his debut in a bumper at Kempton in February. However, he pulled hard and hung to his right. We have done some work on his teeth since and we have given him a good break, which has done him good. He seems more relaxed and is a horse with a big engine. He will go novice hurdling.

GROSVENOR COURT 4 b g Shirocco (GER) – Hurricane Milly (IRE)
Sixth on his only run in a bumper at Market Rasen in February, he was green and will have learned plenty for the experience. Given time off since, he has been in pre training and will have another run in a bumper before going hurdling.

GROUP STAGE (GER) 4 b g Maxios – Good Hope (GER)
I am pleased with him because he has done very well during the summer. He enjoys soft ground and took well to jumping last season winning at Ludlow and finishing second in the Listed Scottish Triumph Hurdle at Musselburgh. We ran him in the Boodles Juvenile Hurdle at Cheltenham but found things happening a bit quick for him. The plan is to step him up to two and a half miles, but we will give him a run on the Flat beforehand.

HACKSAW RIDGE (IRE) 5 b g Stowaway – Erins Lass (IRE)
A winning Irish pointer, he had a couple of runs over hurdles last season but was a bit disappointing. It was bad ground at Warwick last time though and we have given him a long break since. He looks well and there is better to come. Two and a half miles novice hurdles will be on his agenda this season.

HARAMBE 7 br g Malinas (GER) – Crystal Princess (IRE)
Produced a very good performance to win the Greatwood Hurdle at Cheltenham in November. He was then in the process of running well in the *Betfair* Hurdle at Newbury when being brought down at the last. He was lucky to survive, too, but thankfully he is OK now and still hasn't had a lot of racing. Very useful, there is a possibility he will go novice chasing.

HARROWBY 4 b g Gentlewave (IRE) – Cutielilou (FR)
Made his debut in a Listed four year old bumper at Cheltenham on New Year's Day but was very green. He has had a few muscular issues since, but is in good form now and is quite forward. We will run him in another bumper in the Autumn.

HEART OF A LION (IRE) 5 b g Yeats (IRE) – Lady Secret (FR)
I think he is very good. An impressive winner on his debut at Southwell in July last year, he was held up with a joint issue last season but was ready to run in the spring. We haven't decided whether he will have another run in a bumper or go novice hurdling. He's very exciting.

HER INDOORS (IRE) 3 b f Raven's Pass (USA) – Superfonic (FR)
She has schooled well and will go juvenile hurdling this Autumn. A winner on the Flat at Lingfield, I would like to aim her at the Listed juvenile fillies' hurdle at Aintree (5th December), which we have won three times, including Midnights' Gift last season.

HOSTILE 6 ch g Malinas (GER) – Skew
A half-brother to Valdez, he finished runner-up in a bumper at Warwick in the spring of last year. Unable to run last winter having damaged his pelvis, he would have run last spring before the season was cut short. A bit of a playboy at home, he loves his jumping and will go novice hurdling over two and a half miles.

ISOLATE (FR) 4 b g Maxios – Unaided
Ran well on his hurdling debut at Doncaster in February and it was a blessing he didn't run again because it means he is still a novice for this season. Given a break since, he is more relaxed now.

JAY BEE WHY (IRE) 5 b g Yeats (IRE) – Lady Bernie (IRE)
We bought him at the Cheltenham November Sales having won his only Irish point. I think he is a good horse but he boiled over before his debut in a bumper at Newbury in January, which surprised me because he had done everything right at home. I like him but he needs to grow up. He will go novice hurdling.

JERMINNIE GREEN (IRE) 6 b m Jeremy (USA) – Minnie Maguire (IRE)
Another winning Irish point-to-pointer, we purchased her at the Cheltenham December Sale. I made the mistake of running her in a bumper at Taunton in March when the ground was too soft. She is in good form now though and will be campaigned in mares' novice hurdles.

JUST IN TIME 6 b g Excelebration (IRE) – Flying Finish (FR)
We schooled him over hurdles a couple of years ago and the intention is to send him novice hurdling this time. He has some good form on the Flat winning six times, including the Mallard Handicap at Doncaster in 2018. Off the track for over eighteen months, he has run well at Newbury and York this summer. He stays well and likes cut in the ground.

LISP (IRE) 6 ch g Poet's Voice – Hora
Is in great form at home and I am very pleased with him. He took well to chasing winning at Plumpton and ran a good race in the Grand Annual Chase at the Cheltenham Festival finishing seventh. I am looking forward to stepping him up to two and a half miles and I think there is a good race to be won with him over fences.

LORD LAMINGTON 4 b g Australia – Lady Éclair (IRE)
Has enjoyed a good break this summer having had a busy time in the past running on the Flat for Mark Johnston and then going jumping with us last winter. A winner over hurdles at Market Rasen, he was runner-up a couple of times in a Grade 2 at Doncaster and then Kempton. Back in strong work, he may have a run on the Flat before going handicap hurdling over two miles.

MAJOR DUNDEE (IRE) 5 b g Scorpion (IRE) – Be My Granny
A bumper winner at Southwell, he was running well on his first start over hurdles at Warwick when falling at the last. Only sixth at Ludlow next time, the race came too soon. Off since, he has had a break and will continue in two and a half miles plus novice hurdles.

MESSIRE DES OBEAUX (FR) 8 b g Saddler Maker (IRE) – Madame Lys (FR)
A Grade 1 winning novice hurdler and placed at Cheltenham and Aintree that season, he was off the track for nearly three years before finishing fourth at Huntingdon in February. He travelled well for a long way until getting tired. The plan was to run him again in the spring but we were unable to. He has been doing some roadwork and will go novice chasing. He still shows plenty at home.

MIDNIGHT GINGER 4 ch f Midnight Legend – Calamintha
A full-sister to William H Bonney and Midnight Maestro, she is a lovely filly who won a bumper first time out at Newbury in December. Fourth next time in a Listed mares' bumper at Market Rasen, the form is strong. She has done well during the summer and we may run her in another Listed mares' bumper at either Cheltenham (14th November) or Huntingdon (6th December).

MIDNIGHTREFERENDUM 7 b m Midnight Legend – Forget The Ref (IRE)
Twice a winner over hurdles, she finished third at Cheltenham in December and then fifth at Kempton in another decent handicap. We have schooled her over fences with a view to her going mares' novice chasing over two and a half miles plus.

MIDNIGHTS' GIFT 4 gr f Midnight Legend – Giving
Took well to jumping last season winning her first two starts at Fakenham and Aintree, including a Listed event at the latter venue in December. Fifth at Newmarket and sixth at Kempton on the Flat during the summer, her mark looks OK and she will be campaigned in handicap hurdles over two miles.

MIDNIGHTS LEGACY 3 b c Midnight Legend – Giving
A full-brother to Midnights' Gift and from a family we know very well, he is a lovely horse. A three times winner on the Flat, he has won twice at Haydock this season over ten and twelve furlongs and stays well. He then found the ground too slow in the Melrose Stakes at York in August. He has been schooled over hurdles and could be an exciting prospect for juvenile hurdles this season.

NEBUCHADNEZZAR (FR) 5 b g Planteur (IRE) – Trexana
Runner-up over hurdles at Wincanton and Sandown, he appreciated the better ground when winning at Fakenham last time. Rated 124, he is another who remains a novice until the beginning of December. He will continue over two miles but will stay further in time.

NOBBY 6 b g Authorized (IRE) – Magic Music (IRE)
Back in work having missed last season, we have taken our time with him because he is a very good horse. Twice a bumper winner, he was unlucky not to win a third time in a Listed event at Newbury, but he broke down and was caught close home. It was a serious injury but fingers crossed he is OK now and we are looking forward to sending him hurdling.

NOTACHANCE (IRE) 6 b g Mahler – Ballybrowney Hall (IRE)
Narrowly beaten on his chasing debut at Southwell, he won next time at Exeter. Runner-up at Newbury on his latest start, we fitted him with cheekpieces but I don't think they made a lot of difference. We may try him in a visor because it could make him travel a bit better in his races and help his jockey. I think he wants better ground, which he never got last season, with three miles plus being his trip.

ON TO VICTORY 6 b g Rock of Gibraltar (IRE) – Clouds of Magellan (USA)
He has run two very good races on the Flat over a mile and a half at York and Ascot this summer.Despite the fact he failed to complete in two of his four starts over hurdles last season, he has always been a very good jumper. Unlucky on his hurdling debut at Haydock, he would have finished second behind a useful mare (Marie's Rock) but unseated his rider at the last. Placed on his next two runs at Newbury and Kempton, he fell last time at the latter track. Still a novice, he doesn't want the ground too quick and is capable of winning races.

OUTONPATROL (IRE) 6 gr m Stowaway – Burnt Oil Babe (IRE)
She has done well during the summer and showed promise over hurdles at Plumpton and Wincanton finishing second and fourth respectively. We have operated on her wind since her last run and she will be aimed at novices' handicap hurdles off her mark. A winning Irish pointer, she is one to look forward to over fences eventually.

SAN RUMOLDO 5 ch g Malinas (GER) – Ancora (IRE)
A bumper winner at Southwell a couple of seasons ago, he had three runs over hurdles last winter and will go for a novices' handicap hurdle off his mark of 107. He has done well for his summer break and will be suited by two and a half miles plus this season.

SANTON (IRE) 5 b g Scorpion (IRE) – Nutmeg Tune (IRE)
He is a fine big horse who was green on his debut in a bumper at Southwell in November. Sent hurdling, he stayed on at the finish at Market Rasen and will be suited by further than two and a half miles in time. A chaser in the making, he will spend this season over hurdles.

SCARLET DRAGON 7 b g Sir Percy – Welsh Angel
Has been an amazing horse winning the Duke of Edinburgh Stakes at Royal Ascot this summer. He also ran well in both the Old Newton Cup at Haydock and *Skybet* Ebor at York, on ground which was too soft for him. A Listed winner over hurdles at Market Rasen last Autumn, he will go back over jumps and aimed at decent handicap hurdles.

SCEAU ROYAL (FR) 8 b g Doctor Dino (FR) – Sandside (FR)
He has undergone wind surgery since his last run in the Queen Mother Champion Chase at Cheltenham and is in good form at home. Runner-up in the Grade 2 Game Spirit Chase at Newbury prior to that, we are keen to step him up to two and a half miles this season. We haven't discussed plans but something like the Grade 2 Old Roan Chase at Aintree (25th October) could be a suitable target. Good ground is ideal and, while he handles slow ground, he doesn't want it very soft as it was in the Tingle Creek Chase last season.

SENIOR CITIZEN 7 b g Tobougg (IRE) – Mothers Help
Went chasing last season and, having finished second at Doncaster, he won next time at Fakenham. We then ran him back too soon at Stratford, but we were trying to get him qualified for the novices' handicap at Ayr's Scottish National meeting so needed to get another run into him. I have been pleased with him during the summer and he is still a novice until the end of November. We will start him off over two and a half miles but he will stay further.

SHESHOON SONNY (FR) 5 b g Youmzain (IRE) – Minnie's Mystery (FR)
Placed over hurdles at Stratford and Market Rasen, he has been a slow learner but I have always liked him. He is rated 117 and we will look for a suitable novices' handicap hurdle.

TALKISCHEAP (IRE) 8 b g Getaway (GER) – Carrigmoorna Oak (IRE)
Only raced twice last season and he was hobdayed after his run at Sandown in November. Returning at Kempton in February, I thought he ran OK but we probably made too much use of him. He has had a long break and done some roadwork. Rated 155, he will be aimed at the good staying handicap chases and his owner is keen to have a crack at the Grand National.

THE GLANCING QUEEN (IRE) 6 b m Jeremy (USA) – Glancing (IRE)
A high-class bumper mare a couple of seasons ago, she won a Listed mares' bumper at Cheltenham and a Grade 2 at Aintree. Things didn't go to plan last season though because she was held up with a splint problem and didn't reappear until March. I thought she ran well in the Cheltenham Festival bumper until getting tired late on. She has had a couple of runs on the Flat at Kempton during the summer but the track hasn't suited her. A winning Irish pointer, she jumps well and will go novice hurdling in the Autumn. She is a very good mare and one to look forward to.

THE KICKING QUEEN (IRE) 4 b f Beat Hollow – Shivermetimber (IRE)
A half-sister to The Pirate's Queen who we used to train, she is a lovely filly who had worked very well prior to her debut in a mares' bumper at Newbury in February. She had done everything easily at home but got a bit lost during the race when she came off the bridle. I think she is a smart filly who will have another run in a bumper before going hurdling.

THE UNIT (IRE) 9 b g Gold Well – Sovana (FR)
Absence since December 2018 due to injury, he was ready to run last spring before the season was cut short. Twice a winner over fences, he wants good ground and will be aimed at two and a half miles handicap chases.

TREMWEDGE 4 b g Foxwedge (AUS) – Tremelo Pointe (IRE)
Placed a couple of times over hurdles in Ireland, he joined us halfway through last season. Disappointing at Newbury first time, I thought he ran well next time in the Grade 2 Adonis Hurdle at Kempton. He has had a good summer break and I am looking forward to stepping him up to two and a half miles this season.

TRONADA 4 b f Toronado (IRE) – Manbaa (USA)
Fourth on her three starts over hurdles, she has been in good form on the Flat this summer winning over a mile and a half at Lingfield, Chepstow and Bath. Still a novice, she will go back over hurdles and doesn't look to be on a bad mark.

VALLERES (FR) 5 b g Coastal Path – Duchesse Pierji (FR)
He won a point-to-point in Ireland in December and we bought him shortly afterwards at the Cheltenham Sales. We gave him one run in a bumper at Kempton in February and he ran well in third. A straightforward horse, he has schooled well at home and will go novice hurdling over two and a half miles.

WYNN HOUSE 5 ch m Presenting – Glorious Twelfth (IRE)
She is a lovely mare who won a bumper first time out at Uttoxeter and was subsequently second twice, including in a Listed mares' bumper at Huntingdon in December. Schooled over hurdles, she jumps well and will run in mares' novice hurdles. She will start off over two miles but will stay further in due course. She doesn't want it too soft though.

TRAINER'S HORSE TO FOLLOW: MIDNIGHTS LEGACY

Tom LACEY

Stables: Cottage Field Stables Ltd., Sapness Farm, Woolhope, Herefordshire.
2019/2020: 20 Winners / 152 Runners 13% Prize-Money £272,727
www.cottagefield.co.uk

ADRIMEL (FR) 5 bb g Tirwanako (FR) – Irise De Gene (FR)
He has come back in following his summer break looking fantastic and will go novice hurdling. A winning Irish pointer, he was impressive on his first start for us in a bumper at Uttoxeter before Christmas scoring by twenty six lengths. I thought it was a great performance to follow up under a penalty at Doncaster because Kim Bailey thinks the world of the runner-up (The Edgar Wallace) with the pair pulling over twenty lengths clear of the third. We then let him take his chance in the Cheltenham Festival bumper but he went very wide and was always in the firing line, which was never going to bring out the best in him. There is a huge amount to look forward to with him but we will start low key and hopefully progress as the season goes on. I envisage him starting off over two miles at somewhere like Chepstow or Exeter and, while he copes with deep ground, he will be fine on good to soft.

ARGONAUTA (IRE) 4 b g Getaway (GER) – Oscar Ladensa (IRE)
A lovely unraced four year old who is a very good work horse. There is plenty of Oscar in his nature and he may take a run or two mentally before the penny drops. However, I like him and we have the option of running him in a bumper or going straight over hurdles.

DORKING BOY 6 ch g Schiaparelli (GER) – Megasue
From the family of Ballyandy, he had a good season over hurdles winning at Taunton and Newbury. Stepped up to three miles at Huntingdon next time, they went no gallop which didn't suit him and he finished fourth. Dropped back in trip at Ascot last time, I thought he ran OK for a long way but the bad ground wasn't to his liking. The plan is to send him chasing and, while we haven't schooled him yet, I think he will improve for going over fences. Two and a half miles plus is ideal.

DORKING ROGUE 4 b g Dunaden (FR) – Megasue
An unraced half-brother to Dorking Boy, he goes nicely at home and will run in a bumper during the Autumn. Straightforward at home, I am hopeful he will put up a good account on his debut and we will take it from there.

FAIR KATE 6 b m Fair Mix (IRE) – Silver Kate (IRE)
Half-sister to Kateson, she produced a good performance to win over hurdles at Newbury over Christmas. Runner-up at Taunton last time, she appears to be at her best over a strongly run two miles. She will continue over hurdles for the time being, although we could try her over fences at some stage. We are keen to aim her at some of the British bred bonus races for mares, which she is eligible for.

FLOATING ROCK (GER) 5 b g It's Gino (GER) – Fly Osoria (GER)
A bumper winner at Catterick the previous season, he was placed over hurdles at Taunton and Doncaster last winter. Disappointing at Market Rasen in January, he wasn't right afterwards and must have been feeling something during the race. He was quite sore and required physio. Third at Newton Abbot in August, we dropped him back to two miles one at Fontwell in September and he made all.

GINFLIX (FR) 4 b f Al Namix (FR) – Une Tournee (FR)
She is a beautiful filly with loads of quality. Having won a bumper in France, she joined us last season and I thought she would win on her first start at Newcastle in February. However, she was still very green and finished fourth. She covers the ground so well and is a lovely filly for the future. Two miles mares' novice hurdles are likely to be her target.

GLORY AND FORTUNE (IRE) 5 b g Fame And Glory – Night Heron (IRE)
A big raw horse, he won over hurdles at the first time of asking at Huntingdon. Third in a Listed novice at Haydock in November, I thought he ran very well at Doncaster last time finishing a neck second behind Buzz. He is growing up all the time and going the right way. We are going to send him novice chasing starting off over two miles, although he will stay further in due course. We want to get more experience into him, but I think he is a lovely horse for the future.

GOLD CLERMONT (FR) 4 b f Balko (FR) – Une Dame D'Or (FR)
She won her only point-to-point in bad ground at Brocklesby Park in mid February. A filly with a very good attitude, she is as hard as nails. The intention is to send her over hurdles and aim her at mares' only novices over two miles plus. Two and a half miles may prove to be her optimum trip this season.

GRIZZMAN (FR) 4 gr g Al Namix (FR) – Lavi (FR)
Another lovely young horse who won on his only point-to-point for us over two and a half miles at Larkhill in March. He won by three parts of a length from Adjourned, who is highly regarded by Francesca Nimmo and Charlie Poste, with twenty five lengths back to the third. Third in a bumper at Fontwell in September, he jumps very well and is likely to go hurdling now.

HAZZAAR (IRE) 6 b g Flemensfirth (USA) – Una Sorpresa (GER)
I am delighted he has rejoined us during the summer having won a bumper at Ascot a couple of seasons ago. Rated 117, he has only raced three times over hurdles and I will be disappointed if he can't win races this winter. I think he will appreciate running on better ground and is a horse I have always liked.

HIGHSTAKESPLAYER (IRE) 4 b g Ocovango – Elivette (FR)
A gorgeous horse, he is unraced but has a fantastic attitude and could be anything. We have given him time and he has done very well during the summer. Schooled over hurdles, he jumps well and we will look to start him in a novice hurdle around October/November time.

HUNTING PERCIVAL 5 b g Sir Percy – Motcombe (IRE)
Half-brother to Coningsby, he won a bumper on his debut at Wincanton in October last year before finishing third over hurdles at Ludlow in January. Back in action during the summer, he won at Uttoxeter before finishing fourth at the same track. Capable of winning a novices' handicap hurdle off his rating of 113, he wants top of the ground and will be suited by a step up to two and a half miles.

IMMORTAL FLAME (IRE) 4 b g Fame And Glory – Calverleigh Court (IRE)
A nice unraced horse who I like, he went weak on us last season so we have brought him along slowly. Quite gassy, he is by Fame And Glory and there is a bit of Montjeu in him. All being well, he will run in a bumper in the Autumn.

JOHNBB (IRE) 6 b g Stowaway – Flemins Evening (IRE)
Successful over fences at Sandown in December, he doesn't want over racing because he appears to be best fresh and hasn't always backed up next time. I also think he will benefit from some nicer ground. Despite his win at Sandown being gained over two miles, he needs further. Two and a half miles handicap chases will be on his agenda and I would love to try him over the National fences at Aintree one day.

KAPHUMOR (FR) 4 b g Kapgarde (FR) – Money Humor (IRE)
Purchased at the Goffs Land Rover Sale in Ireland as a three year old, he won by four lengths at Larkhill in March on the same card as Grizzman. He has bags of ability but everything was an effort for him last year. However, he has returned from his summer break a different horse and could be a proper racehorse. We will start him off in a two and a half miles novice hurdle.

KATESON 7 gr g Black Sam Bellamy (IRE) – Silver Kate (IRE)
Despite running well on his chasing debut at Exeter in December finishing second, things didn't work out for him on his subsequent two starts over fences. I thought small fields novice chases, where they don't go too quick early on, would have suited him. We operated on his wind and he ran well back over hurdles in a valuable handicap at Uttoxeter in March. I think he is capable of winning a nice race over hurdles but we will try fences once again at some stage.

KIMBERLITE CANDY (IRE) 8 b g Flemensfirth (USA) – Mandys Native (IRE)
We are looking forward to seeing him back in action having done so well last season. Runner-up in the Becher Chase over the National fences at Aintree in December, he then won the Grade 3 Warwick Classic by ten lengths the following month. The Grand National was his ultimate target so it was very disappointing when the season was cut short. He spent the summer in Ireland and I would imagine he will follow a similar route starting with the Becher Chase (5th December) with all roads leading to a return to Aintree next April for the Grand National. Good fresh, the ground is always a worry because he wants it soft and we are hoping he will encounter such conditions next spring.

KING FERDINAND (IRE) 4 b g Milan – Nobody's Darling (IRE)
Purchased at the Tattersalls Derby Sale in Ireland last year, he is a lovely unraced horse who we have given time and aren't going to rush. A half-brother to Alan King's three times winner Canelo, I really like him and the plan is for him to run in a bumper in October/ November.

KYNANCE COVE 5 ch g Midnight Legend – Tante Sissi (FR)
His dam won the mares' final over hurdles at Newbury for Alan King and is from the family of Epatante. He finished fifth on his only start in a point-to-point for Ciaran O'Brien and gives the impression he will be suited by decent ground. Two and a half miles plus novice hurdles will be his initial target.

LAGONDA 5 b m Great Pretender (IRE) – Lago D'Oro
A half-sister to six times winner Spirit of Shankly, she is a nice mare who I really like, but I think she is ground dependent. She ran in a couple of point-to-points last season finishing third on her debut at Barbury in December before galloping her opponents into the ground next time. She won an open maiden over three miles at Milborne St Andrew in early February by twenty five lengths. She jumps very well and loves soft ground. Her owner has been patient and I hope we can win one of the mares' bonus races with her this season. We may run her in a mares' bumper on soft ground at a stiff track like Chepstow or Exeter before going hurdling.

LAMANVER STORM 5 b g Geordieland (FR) – Lamanver Homerun
He is another who loves soft/heavy ground and I am keen to win a race over hurdles before he goes chasing. Fences will bring out the best in him, but he ran well at Exeter last time finishing second in a two miles two novice hurdle in February. He is a three miles chaser in the making.

LE GRAND FROMAGE 5 b g Kayf Tara – Megalex
Full-brother to Ballyandy and Megastar, I think he is potentially well treated off 117. Runner-up on his hurdles debut at Hexham last Autumn, we operated on his wind and he finished fourth at Doncaster. The ground was against him at Newbury last time and we will try and win over hurdles and then send him chasing. Two and a half miles is his trip.

L'INCORRIGIBLE (FR) 5 b g No Risk At All (FR) – Incorrigible (FR)
Absent since winning a bumper on his debut in November 2018, he was due to run over hurdles last season but unfortunately fractured his pelvis. He is a horse with a lot of ability and, if we can keep him in one piece, he is capable of doing well in novice hurdles.

MARTY TIME (FR) 4 gr g Martaline – Shahwarda (FR)
A gorgeous unraced four year old we bought at the Tattersalls Derby Sale in Ireland last year. We didn't run him last season because he had a couple of minor bumps in the road, but he looks great and I absolutely love him. In all likelihood, he will start in a two miles novice hurdle and learn his trade. He could run over any trip because I think he is very good.

NEVILLE'S CROSS (IRE) 5 b g Stowaway – Dancing Bird (IRE)
His future ultimately lies over fences but we may keep him over hurdles for the time being having won at Uttoxeter in September. I was disappointed with him last season but he benefited from stepping up in trip last time and I think he is capable of defying his rise in the weights.

QUICK DRAW (IRE) 4 b g Getaway (GER) – Sept Verites (FR)
I think he is a nice horse who has schooled well over hurdles and will be suited by two and a half miles. Runner-up on his debut in a junior bumper at Aintree in November, he finished well. He then ran in a Listed bumper at Cheltenham on New Year's Day and I was pleased with him. He is a lovely horse.

RED NIKA (FR) 5 br g Denham Red (FR) – Nika Glitters (FR)
A winning pointer, he finished runner-up in two of his three starts over hurdles last season and could prove well handicapped. I think he appreciates nicer ground and we will continue to campaign him over two and two and a half miles.

SEBASTOPOL (IRE) 6 b g Fame And Glory – Knockcroghery (IRE)
Did nothing wrong last season winning twice over hurdles, including the Scottish County Hurdle at Musselburgh in February. His only defeat came at Huntingdon when he was found to have swallowed his tongue. Despite the fact he has had a handful of races over hurdles, I still don't think he has learned to race properly yet. Therefore I am hoping he is open to more improvement and we will aim him at the decent two mile handicap hurdles, although he will have no trouble staying further. He doesn't want it too soft though.

TEA CLIPPER (IRE) 5 b g Stowaway – A Plus Ma Puce (FR)
A very nice horse who I have always liked. He did well over hurdles last season winning his first three starts at Warwick, Kempton and Huntingdon before finishing runner-up at the latter venue last time. He has already won a point-to-point and the plan is to send him novice chasing. We will probably start him off over two miles, but he stays well and I am excited about him for this season. Good or good to soft ground is ideal because he is another who doesn't want it too slow.

THAIS TOIR (FR) 5 b g Diamond Boy (FR) – Scotland Act (FR)
He is a gorgeous horse who I like a lot. Following a couple of runs in bumpers at Warwick and Ascot, he made his hurdles debut at Huntingdon in February finishing fifth. Keeping on in the closing stages, he is crying out for a step up in trip and I think he will win over hurdles before going chasing. He needs a fence to bring out the best in him.

THOMAS PATRICK (IRE) 8 b g Winged Love (IRE) – Huncheon Siss (IRE)
A smart chaser a few years ago, he reached a mark of 148 but rather lost his way. The handicapper has dropped him to a reasonable rating now and I hope he can make an impact in three miles plus chases. Ideally, he wants a small field and I may give him an entry in the Becher Chase at Aintree (5th December) because I think those fences could suit him.

UNOHU 5 b g Kayf Tara – Little Miss Flora
Raced three times in bumpers last season and did nothing wrong. A winner on his debut at Newcastle in November, he ran very well under a penalty at Chepstow next time finishing third before filling second position at Uttoxeter on his latest start. Two and a half miles plus on soft ground over hurdles will suit him.

VADA FORTE (FR) 7 b g Walk In The Park (IRE) – Gloire (FR)
Unlucky not to win over fences last season, he was narrowly beaten at Newbury over Christmas and finished second at Ludlow last time. Rated 130, the handicapper didn't cut him any slack for running so consistently. A strongly run two miles on a galloping track such as Chepstow or Newbury is tailormade for him.

VELASCO (IRE) 4 b g Sholokhov (IRE) – Bilboa (FR)
Very well bred being out of a top-class mare who was placed in the Champion Hurdle, he is a half-brother to The West's Awake, who was fourth in the Galway Plate in July. He is a lovely horse who was a wide margin winner of a two and a half miles point-to-point at Milborne St Andrew in early February. Not the quickest, he galloped his opponents into the ground and will be contesting two and a half miles plus novice hurdles on soft ground this winter.

YES NO MAYBE SO (IRE) 6 br g Stowaway – Godlylady (IRE)
Joined us during the spring having previously won a bumper and been placed over hurdles. He has been in very good form winning four times at Uttoxeter (twice), Southwell and Fontwell with his rating climbing from 107 to 123. He has appreciated the step up to three miles. We will give him a few more runs over hurdles but he wants a fence and I think he will improve once sent chasing.

Unnamed 4 b g Fame And Glory – Liss Na Tintri (IRE)
Another gorgeous unraced four year old who was bought at the Tattersalls Derby Sale last year. From the family of Liss A Paoraigh, he is still a frame of a horse and won't be over raced this season. He will start in a bumper and I like him a lot.

> **TRAINER'S HORSE TO FOLLOW: MARTY TIME**

> ## Please see page 195
> ## for details of
> # *Ahead on the Flat 2021*

Olly MURPHY

Stables: Warren Chase Stables, Wilmcote, Stratford Upon Avon.
2019/2020: 67 Winners / 351 Runners 19% Prize-Money £613,394
www.ollymurphyracing.com

AFRICAN DANCE (IRE) 5 br g Shirocco (GER) – Dani California
Third on his debut in a bumper at Fakenham in February, he has a good pedigree and I think he will benefit from racing on nicer ground. I am keen to try and win a bumper with him before going hurdling. We may start him off over two miles over hurdles, but he will stay two and a half miles in time.

ALLAVINA (IRE) 5 b m Getaway (GER) – One Cool Kate (IRE)
A smart mare who was very green on her debut at Huntingdon in February, plus I think the winner is very good (Coquelicot). She won next time at Market Rasen and is one for mares' novice hurdles this season. She is another who will start off over two miles and I think she is one of our nicest mares.

ALPHA CARINAE (IRE) 5 ch m Robin Des Champs (FR) – Annas Present (IRE)
A winning Irish pointer, she won an all-weather bumper at Newcastle in January but had a small issue with her wind. We have therefore operated on her and it appears to have transformed her. She is another who will appreciate some nicer ground and we will therefore get her started early on and I think she will pay her way in mares' novice hurdles.

BLAZER'S MILL (IRE) 6 b g Westerner – Creation (IRE)
A bumper winner at Fontwell the previous season, he is a lot better than he showed in two starts over hurdles last term. Both races at Ayr and Wincanton were over two and a half miles but I am not sure he stayed. We are therefore going to drop him back to two miles and send him chasing. He could prove well treated in a novices' handicap because he has always worked well at home, plus he was runner-up in an Irish point behind Birchdale.

BREWIN'UPASTORM (IRE) 7 b g Milan – Daraheen Diamond (IRE)
He is in good form at home having summered well. Having won his first two starts over fences at Carlisle and Taunton, he gave himself a knock at the latter track and, as a result, missed the middle part of the season. We therefore took him to Cheltenham for the Arkle Chase lacking a bit of experience. However, he was just starting to get into the race when unseating Richard (Johnson) at the fourth last, which was frustrating. Unable to run again due to the coronavirus, we had planned to take him to Aintree. He remains a horse to look forward to though and we may start him off in the Colin Parker Memorial Chase at Carlisle (1st November) or the Grade 2 Skymas Chase at Down Royal the previous day. Although two miles on soft ground is OK for him, I think he will benefit from stepping up to two and a half miles this season.

CALIPSO COLLONGES (FR) 8 b g Crossharbour – Ivresse Collonges (FR)
Only rated 94 when he joined the yard a couple of seasons ago, he has developed into a decent staying handicapper. The softer the ground the better for him and I thought he ran well in the Tommy Whittle Chase at Haydock last time finishing second. He has learned to relax now and wants three miles plus. He will follow a similar programme and I hope he can drop on one of the good staying handicaps this winter.

CAPTAIN BIGGLES (IRE) 5 gr g Milan – Timon's Present
He made his debut in a bumper at Hereford in November at a time when my horses weren't at their best, plus the ground was very soft. I have always thought a bit of him and I will be disappointed if he isn't better than he showed that day. We have operated on his wind since and he will start off in a maiden hurdle over two and a half miles on some better ground in September/October.

CHAMPAGNESUPEROVER (IRE) 5 b g Jeremy (USA) – Meldrum Hall (IRE)
One of our nicest novice hurdlers for this season, I think he is a very good horse. An impressive winner on his debut at Ayr in January, it was testing ground but he handled it very well. Stepped in grade, he ran in a Listed bumper at Newbury the following month and looked like winning at one stage. It turned into a bit of a sprint inside the final couple of furlongs and his effort flattened out late on. Brewin'upastorm ran in the same race a couple of years ago and, while this horse wouldn't be quite as sharp as him, I think he is very smart. We will start low key, but I view him as a Graded novice hurdler in the making and a race such as the Grade 1 Tolworth Hurdle at Sandown in January could suit him because it is invariably soft ground for that meeting. Alternatively, if we think he wants two and a half miles, the Grade 1 Challow Hurdle at Newbury (29th December) could be a target.

CHOSEN PORT (IRE) 4 b f Well Chosen – Despute (IRE)
Purchased at the Cheltenham Festival Sale in March, she belongs to Noel and Valerie Moran having won her only Irish point for Colin Bowe a few days earlier. Well bred, she is a half-sister to triple Grade 2 winning chaser Burton Port and is an exciting prospect for mares' bumpers. I would like to think she will gain black type in bumpers at some stage this season.

COLLOONEY (IRE) 6 b g Yeats (IRE) – Amber Trix (IRE)
Lightly raced, he only had a couple of runs last season finishing runner-up at Wincanton in March. We were thinking in terms of running him at Aintree but never got the opportunity. Yet to race beyond two miles five over hurdles, I think he will stay further and has the ability to win more races. There is a possibility we will send him chasing having finished second in his only Irish point-to-point.

COPPERLESS 5 b g Kayf Tara – Presenting Copper
From a good family being a half-brother to Copper Kay, I thought he would win on his debut in a bumper at Lingfield in November, but the all-weather didn't suit him and he finished third. Off since, we will run him in another bumper on decent ground before going hurdling. He is a horse I like a lot.

DUBAI GUEST (IRE) 5 b g Dubai Destination (USA) – Formidable Guest
A nice staying type, he ran well first out at Warwick before winning at Musselburgh next time. The form received a boost with the third winning subsequently. He will go novice hurdling and will be suited by two and a half miles plus.

DUNDRUM WOOD (IRE) 6 b g Flemensfirth (USA) – Ruby Isabel (IRE)
Despite winning over hurdles at Market Rasen last season, he has disappointed me because he works like a Graded horse at home. Unfortunately, he has yet to reproduce his homework on the track. He has undergone wind surgery during the summer and we are hoping he will come to himself this season. We are also going to change the way we have been riding him. The plan is to drop him in this time around and see if that makes a difference. He is going over fences and, if he puts it all together, then he could be a very well handicapped horse.

ENDLESSLY (IRE) 5 b g Nathaniel (IRE) – What's Up Pussycat (IRE)
Has done well since joining us winning twice on the Flat and two out of three over hurdles. A very keen horse, he possesses a big engine and, if he learned to settle, he could win a good race one day. Well treated on the Flat, we will explore that route at some stage and I would love to see him in something like the Greatwood Hurdle at Cheltenham (15th November) off a low weight. A fast run two miles is ideal.

ENEMY COAST AHEAD 6 br g Malinas (GER) – Penang Princess
Has done well since joining us winning three out of three over hurdles during the summer. Suited by nicer ground, he won a couple of times at Southwell and one at Uttoxeter and he has had a wind operation since his last run. He could be one for the two and a half miles novice hurdle at Cheltenham's first meeting (23rd October). He is a nice horse.

EWOOD PARK (IRE) 5 b g Shirocco (GER) – Windfola (FR)
We have a very nice collection of unraced bumper horses, many of whom would have run last spring but the season was ended prematurely due to the coronavirus. Owned by the McNeill Family, he is a horse I like a lot. He has shown us plenty at home and will start off in a bumper in the Autumn.

FABRIQUE EN FRANCE (FR) 5 b g Yeats (IRE) – Knar Mardy
Purchased at the Goffs UK July Sale at Doncaster this summer on behalf of Noel and Valerie Moran, he was placed in two of his three Irish points. Runner-up last time, the winner (Killer Kane) was subsequently sold for £300,000 and Jamie Codd rode him and recommended we buy him. He appears to be another who appreciates nicer ground and I think there is plenty of improvement to come from him. There is every chance he will run in a bumper before going hurdling.

FEARLESS (IRE) 5 b g Arakan (USA) – La Spezia (IRE)
Has only raced three times for us winning over hurdles at Market Rasen in March. Rated 122, I think he is well handicapped, but I am not sure which route we are going to take with him because he is still eligible for novice hurdles until the end of November. Yet to race beyond two miles, he will want two and a half miles in time. He is a massive horse and I can't believe he won a three year old bumper.

FINAWN BAWN (IRE) 7 b g Robin Des Champs (FR) – Kayanti (IRE)
Third in the Grade 2 Leamington Novices' Hurdle at Warwick a couple of seasons ago, he made his chasing debut at Chepstow in October. Third behind the subsequent Midlands National winner and Welsh National runner-up Truckers Lodge (Grade 2 Reynoldstown Chase winner Copperhead was fifth), he unfortunately incurred a tendon injury and has been sidelined since. All being well, he will be back in action around Christmas time and I would like to get a couple of runs into him before something like the National Hunt Chase at the Cheltenham Festival. He is a horse with a lot of ability and his form is strong.

FITZROY (IRE) 6 b g Fame And Glory – Forces of Destiny (IRE)
Ran well without winning over hurdles last season. Placed three times, including at Ludlow on his latest start, we will try and win a race over hurdles before going chasing. He will make a nice chaser eventually. Fame And Glory's stock appear to need a bit of time before they show their best form.

FLETCH (FR) 5 b g Kayf Tara – Oeuvre Vive (FR)
A lovely unraced gelding by Kayf Tara, we bought him as a three year old at the Tattersalls Derby Sale in Ireland. It took him a long time to come to himself last year but he has shown us plenty at home and is one to watch out for in a bumper in the Autumn.

FUSIONICE (FR) 5 b g Coastal Path – Oasice (FR)
Well bred, he is a full-brother to Bacardys, but has yet to run for us having been held up with a few niggles last season. Fourth in his only Irish point-to-point for Denis Murphy, he wants decent ground and may have a run in a bumper before going hurdling.

GARRETTSTOWN (IRE) 7 b g Doyen (IRE) – Azur (IRE)
Runner-up over hurdles on his reappearance at Aintree, we then sent him chasing and, having finished fourth at Wetherby, he was brought down at Ludlow and frightened himself. Pulled up at Doncaster last time, we need to build his confidence up and therefore he will have a run over hurdles before going back over fences. Two and a half miles is ideal and he is a horse with plenty of ability.

GETAWAY LUV (IRE) 5 b g Getaway (GER) – Ut Love (FR)
Third on his debut in a bumper at Lingfield in November, I thought he was unlucky because it was a typical all-weather bumper, where they went no pace early on. He finished strongly though and we expected him to go close next time at Ludlow, but he raced too keenly early on. Capable of winning a bumper before he embarks on his hurdling career, he should win plenty of races.

GO DANTE (IRE) 4 b g Kayf Tara – Whoops A Daisy
A half-brother to Angel of Harlem, he is a very nice unraced horse we bought at the Tattersalls Derby Sales in Ireland last year. His dam was a useful mare for Nicky Henderson winning a Listed race over hurdles. He will start off in a bumper and is a lovely horse.

GRACES ORDER (IRE) 5 b m Mahler – Janebailey
Full-sister to the Troytown and Red Mills Chase winner Chris's Dream, she is a sweet mare who always tries to please. Having run creditably on her first couple of starts, she won a mares' bumper at Sedgefield in March and is a staying type who handles heavy ground. Mares' novice hurdles will be her target this season.

GRANDADS COTTAGE (IRE) 5 ch g Shantou (USA) – Sarah's Cottage (IRE)
A dark horse and one to look forward to. A winning Irish pointer for Donnchadh Doyle, he is a full-brother to Cheltenham Festival runner-up Super Duty. It was heavy ground when he finished third on his first run for us in a bumper at Uttoxeter in November. I couldn't believe he got beaten at Stratford next time being denied by a head. He jumps very well and will go novice hurdling over two miles, although he will step up to two and a half miles later on.

GUNSIGHT RIDGE 5 b g Midnight Legend – Grandma Griffiths
He, too, won his only Irish point-to-point for Donnchadh Doyle before joining us last season. He has always shown a lot at home since arriving and we therefore expected him to run well on his first start for us in a bumper at Southwell. However, he only finished fourth finding the ground too testing. The form of the race has worked out well though and he remains a nice horse for novice hurdles this season.

HERE COMES JOHNY (IRE) 5 b g Yeats (IRE) – Strike An Ark (IRE)
Bought at the Cheltenham February Sale, he hails from the same source in Ireland as Notre Pari. Yet to run for us, he ran in three point-to-points winning on his latest start. Very much a future chaser, he will run in a bumper and then go novice hurdling.

HERE COMES MCCOY (IRE) 5 br g Dylan Thomas (IRE) – Is It Here (IRE)
Despite the fact he has always shown ability at home, he surprised me when winning on his debut in a bumper at Warwick in January. He is owned by my yard's sponsors and I would have been pleased if he had finished in the first half a dozen because he was still green at home. However, I was very impressed with him, especially as it took Aidan (Coleman) a long time to pull him up afterwards. I think he is a cracking prospect and one to look forward to. He is a big strong horse who will start off over hurdles over two miles, but may want two and a half miles later in the season. He is a lovely horse for the future.

HERE COMES TRUBLE (IRE) 5 b g Flemensfirth (USA) – Old Moon (IRE)
A full-brother to Noble Endeavor, who I was associated with during my time as assistant to Gordon (Elliott), he is a grand horse who has yet to race. Unable to run last season due to an injury, he is back in work and is a lovely horse who will start off in a bumper.

HOGAN (IRE) 4 b g Fame And Glory – Don't Be Upset (IRE)
Another nice unraced four year old who was bought at the Tattersalls Derby Sale last year. Unlikely to jump hurdles this season, he will run in a bumper around Christmas time.

HUNTERS CALL (IRE) 10 b g Medaaly – Accordingtogelica (IRE)
He has been a very good horse for us even though he has only raced three times winning twice. He won a valuable Grade 3 handicap hurdle at Ascot in December 2017, but was then absent until July this year. I was delighted with his win at Southwell before finishing fourth in the Galway Hurdle later the same month. The race didn't work out as planned as he ended up making the running. but he still ran a very good race. The Greatwood Hurdle at Cheltenham (15th November) is his target.

I K BRUNEL 6 b g Midnight Legend – Somethinaboutmolly (IRE)
I think he could develop into a very good staying novice chaser this season. Twice a winner over hurdles and rated 140, anything he achieved last year was a bonus. We stepped him up to three miles for the first time at Musselburgh in February and fitted him with a hood in the preliminaries beforehand. Everything went to plan and he ran out a convincing winner of the Scottish Stayers' Novices' Hurdle. He is capable of even better over fences and I have been very pleased with him during the summer. We will start him off over two and a half miles before stepping up in distance as the season goes on.

ITCHY FEET (FR) 6 b g Cima De Triomphe (IRE) – Maeva Candas (FR)
Took well to chasing winning at Leicester before providing us with our first Grade 1 winner in the Scilly Isles Novices' Chase at Sandown in February. It was such a shame what happened in the JLT Novices' Chase at Cheltenham. Blinded going into the fence, he made a mistake and unseated Gavin (Sheehan). He is likely to reappear in the Grade 2 Old Roan Chase at Aintree (25th October) and then we will make a plan thereafter. Two and a half miles suits him well but I wouldn't rule out trying him over an easy three miles because he was strong at the finish at Sandown.

JETAWAY JOEY (IRE) 5 b g Getaway (GER) – Present Your Own (IRE)
Green on his debut in a bumper at Market Rasen, he then won over an extended two miles one at Fontwell three months later. The runner-up was fancied that day, too. A half-brother to Getaway John, he stays well and enjoys soft ground. He is a horse I like a lot who should do well in staying novice hurdles.

KAPROYALE 5 gr g Kapgarde (FR) – As You Leave (FR)
Unraced, we purchased him at the Goffs Land Rover Sale in Ireland a couple of years ago. Given time, he will run in a bumper in the Autumn and then go novice hurdling.

LINELEE KING (FR) 5 gr g Martaline – Queen Lee (FR)
A winning Irish pointer, he has always worked well at home and I was surprised when he finished second in a bumper at Chepstow in October. A comfortable winner at Sedgefield next time, he is a lot better than he showed in the Cheltenham Festival bumper. Not right afterwards, he looks well at home and I think he is above average. He jumps very well and will run in a two miles novice hurdle but will be suited by two and a half miles later on.

MON PORT (IRE) 8 b g Scorpion (IRE) – Sounds Charming (IRE)
A three times winner over hurdles, he got a fright when falling over fences at Warwick in November and hasn't raced since. He is a horse with a lot of ability and we will probably switch him back to hurdles. Decent ground suits him with two miles being his trip.

MOORE MARGAUX (IRE) 5 b g Flemensfirth (USA) – Omas Glen (IRE)
He is a very nice unraced horse who does everything easily at home. We will run him in a bumper before Christmas and then go novice hurdling. He has shown us plenty and is a lovely horse.

NICKOLSON (FR) 6 b g No Risk At All (FR) – Incorrigible (FR)
I love him and even though he has won two of his three starts, we haven't seen the best of him yet. An easy winner on his hurdles debut at Wincanton in October, he then had a few niggles and didn't run again until March finishing second at Warwick. Rated 135, I think he is on a good mark and I would like to give him one more run before targeting the Listed Gerry Feilden Hurdle at Newbury (28th November). Although he will stay further in time, he is quick enough for two miles and I view him as a Graded horse in the making.

NO RISK DES FLOS (FR) 5 b g No Risk At All (FR) – Marie Royale (FR)
A half-brother to Vision Des Flos and Umndeni, he is a very nice unraced horse who was an expensive buy at the Tattersalls Derby Sale a couple of years ago. He has a big engine and will run in a bumper in October/November.

NOTRE PARI (IRE) 6 br g Jeremy (USA) – Glynn Approach (IRE)
Progressive last season, he appreciated the step up to two and a half miles winning at Aintree and Fontwell, plus he was in the process of running very well in the Lanzarote Hurdle at Kempton when falling at the last. The plan is to send him chasing this season but we will give him another run over hurdles first. The Silver Trophy at Chepstow (10th October) could suit him. Runner-up in an Irish point, he should make a nice chaser later on.

OVERTHETOP (IRE) 6 br g Flemensfirth (USA) – Dawn Bid (IRE)
Won twice over hurdles at Carlisle and Newcastle but each time we stepped up in grade he was disappointing. The ground was desperate at Haydock last time, which may explain his performance. He will go chasing and I hope he will improve over fences. Two and a half miles suits him but I think he will stay three miles in time.

PLENTY IN THE TANK (IRE) 5 b g Champs Elysees – Lunathea (IRE)
He beat Linelee King on his debut in a bumper at Chepstow last Autumn and we therefore bought him at the Cheltenham November Sale. We were going to run him in the Festival bumper at Cheltenham and I thought he would run well. Unfortunately, he had a setback about a fortnight beforehand hence he has yet to run for us. We might run him in another bumper, but it won't be long before he goes hurdling. He jumps well and has shown enough to suggest he is above average.

PORT OF MARS (IRE) 6 b g Westerner – Sarahall (IRE)
A winning English pointer, he missed the previous season but had three runs over hurdles last winter. Runner-up at Leicester over Christmas, he then produced a good performance to win at Chepstow next time. He underperformed in a Grade 2 at Haydock on his latest start though and will go novice chasing this Autumn. A staying chaser in the making, he seems to handle any ground.

PRESENCE OF MIND (IRE) 5 b g Presenting – Alleygrove Lass (IRE)
Like Port of Mars, he also won an English point and did nothing wrong in three races for us last season. Unlucky not to win all three, he was narrowly beaten in a bumper at Fakenham. He then went one better at Huntingdon before winning on his hurdles debut at Catterick on New Year's Day. We were waiting to run him on some nicer ground in the spring, but that never happened and unfortunately he has lost his novice status. Although he lacks experience over hurdles, we are forced to run him in handicaps before he goes chasing eventually. Two and a half to three miles will be his trip ultimately.

ROCK THE HOUSE (IRE) 5 b g Scorpion (IRE) – Holiday Time (IRE)
Half-brother to Pistol Whipped, he ran well on his only start in a bumper at Warwick finishing sixth. It looked a good race, too, and I think he is capable of winning a bumper this Autumn. He jumps well and will go hurdling later on.

SANGHA RIVER (IRE) 7 br g Arcadio (GER) – Hidden Reserve (IRE)
He has obviously been fragile but is a horse with a massive engine. A bumper winner at Doncaster in December 2017, he was unlucky not to follow up at Lingfield before being sidelined with injury for nearly two and a half years. Back in action during the summer, he won twice at Southwell and Market Rasen in July before finishing second at Uttoxeter the following month. We are going to aim him at a Listed novice hurdle at Kempton (18th October), but he doesn't want the ground too slow.

SKANDIBURG (FR) 6 b g Sageburg (IRE) – Skandia (FR)
A strong stayer, he did well when stepping up to three miles winning handicap hurdles at Aintree and Cheltenham. High enough in the ratings when running in the Pertemps Final at the Cheltenham Festival, he will go novice chasing this season and it wouldn't surprise me if he ended up in the National Hunt Chase at the Festival in March. Stamina is his forte.

STRONG GLANCE 7 bl g Passing Glance – Strong Westerner (IRE)
Joined us last season and, having finished a close second at Fakenham, he won nicely next time at Market Rasen in January. He hated the heavy ground at Sedgefield last time and I think he is on a lovely mark for handicap hurdles. He will go novice chasing later on and is capable of winning plenty of races.

TAMAR BRIDGE (IRE) 5 b g Jeremy (USA) – Mise En Place
Another nice unraced youngster who could be very good. Bought at the Tattersalls Derby Sale as a three year old, he does everything easily at home and looks capable of winning a bumper before going hurdling.

THE BUTCHER SAID (IRE) 7 b g Robin Des Champs (FR) – Georgina Valleya (IRE)
A progressive type who won four times over hurdles during his first season with us. He produced a career best when runner-up in a valuable prize at Kempton in March. A twelve lengths winner at Southwell on his chasing debut in August, he ran well in defeat next time at Uttoxeter under a penalty. He jumps well and I am expecting him to improve again as a chaser.

THE WOLF (FR) 6 ch g Kapgarde (FR) – Ges (FR)

Another who joined us last season, he did well winning twice at Fakenham and Newcastle before finishing seventh in the Grade 1 Albert Bartlett Novices' Hurdle at Cheltenham. He fared the second best of the British runners (Thyme Hill fourth) and we are looking forward to sending him chasing, too. We have operated on his wind and I am hoping he will prove Graded class over fences. He wants two and a half miles plus.

THOMAS DARBY (IRE) 7 b g Beneficial – Silaoce (FR)

A top-class novice hurdler a couple of seasons ago, we tried him over fences a couple of times last winter. Although he didn't look the most natural, he ran at a time when our horses weren't at their best. Switched back to hurdles, he produced a very good performance to win a Grade 3 handicap at Ascot over two and a half miles in January before finishing third in the Grade 2 National Spirit Hurdle at Fontwell. We are going to start him off in a two and a half miles conditions hurdle at Aintree (7th November) and then step him up in trip. We are hoping he will develop into a stayers' hurdle contender because it looks an open division. His half-brother Muirhead stayed three miles.

THUNDER ROCK (IRE) 4 b g Shirocco (GER) – La Belle Sauvage

Derek O'Connor recommended we buy him at the Goffs UK Doncaster July Sale having finished runner-up on his debut in an Irish point. From the family of Lady Rebecca, he has a good pedigree and comes from a small yard. He looks well bought and is open to plenty of improvement.

TIGERBYTHETAIL (IRE) 4 b g Yeats (IRE) – Talktothetail (IRE)

Purchased at the Goffs UK Spring Sale as a three year old, he is a lovely unraced horse and a half-brother to Grade 1 Cheltenham Festival winner Roksana. We have been very pleased with him and he does everything easily at home. He will run in a bumper in October/November.

VINNIE'S GETAWAY (IRE) 6 b g Getaway (GER) – Trixskin (IRE)

A winning pointer, he won a bumper at Stratford last year before finishing runner-up in both his starts over hurdles. A half-brother to Cheltenham Festival bumper winner Cousin Vinny, I think he is on a nice mark over hurdles and will jump fences eventually.

TRAINER'S HORSE TO FOLLOW: CHAMPAGNESUPEROVER

Don't forget to read my Diary @
www.mhpublications.couk

Paul NICHOLLS

Stables: Manor Farm Stables, Ditcheat, Somerset.
2019/2020: 96 Winners / 445 Runners 22% Prize-Money £2,341,313
www.paulnichollsracing.com

ACCOMPLICE (FR) 6 gr g Network (GER) – Miss Vitoria (FR)

A nice horse who won over hurdles in France before joining us. Unfortunately, he sustained an injury on his first run for us at Exeter eighteen months ago. Off since, he is back in work and may have another run over hurdles, but it won't be long before he goes chasing.

ASK FOR GLORY (IRE) 6 b g Fame And Glory – Ask Helen (IRE)

He is a lovely horse who has only raced twice over hurdles winning at Wincanton in February. Due to the new rule, which was brought in during the summer, he remains a novice until the beginning of December, which is good news. A winning Irish pointer, his future lies over fences but we will give him at least one more run over hurdles before deciding whether to send him chasing. He is a two and a half miles plus chaser in the making and is a very nice horse who copes well with soft ground.

ATHOLL STREET (IRE) 5 b g Jeremy (USA) – Allthewhile (IRE)

An expensive buy from the Goffs Land Rover Sale a couple of years ago, he is from the family of Kicking King. Sixth in a bumper at Exeter on New Year's Day, we have operated on his wind since and he will go novice hurdling this season.

BARBADOS BUCK'S 5 b g Getaway (GER) – Buck's Blue (FR)

Runner-up in his only Irish point-to-point, he had a couple of runs in bumpers at Cheltenham and Wincanton but was still big and backward last winter. I think he will benefit from racing on better ground over hurdles this time around.

BLACK CORTON (FR) 9 br g Laverock (IRE) – Pour Le Meilleur (FR)

Despite the fact he didn't get his head in front last season, he still ran some very good races in defeat. Runner-up in the Galway Plate off top weight, he was also placed in Grade 3 handicap chases at Ascot and Kempton. It isn't going to be easy for him off a mark of 161, but we have operated on his wind for the first time during the summer and we think that may make a difference. He will follow a similar campaign this season.

BLACKJACK KENTUCKY (IRE) 7 b g Oscar (IRE) – My Name's Not Bin (IRE)

Goes novice chasing and likes soft ground and stays well. He is a winning pointer and was consistent over hurdles last season. A winner at Chepstow in January, he finished runner-up on his three other starts last winter. I hope he will make an even better chaser.

BRAVEMANSGAME (FR) 5 b g Brave Mansonnien (FR) – Genifique (FR)

Bought at the Cheltenham Festival Sale last year having won his only Irish point-to-point a few days earlier, he is a lovely horse who has needed time. We ran him in a couple of bumpers at Ascot finishing third in November before we tried him in a Listed event before Christmas. Off since, he is ready to go novice hurdling and is a horse I like.

BREWERS PROJECT (IRE) 6 b g Aizavoski (IRE) – Shaylee Wilde (IRE)
Back in action following a spell on the sidelines due to injury, he finished fourth on his hurdles debut at Newbury in November. Reappearing at Taunton in early February, he was leading when falling at the third last. He will therefore continue in novice hurdles but is a chaser in the making.

CALVA D'AUGE (FR) 5 b g Air Chief Marshal (IRE) – Hill Ou Elle (FR)
Ex-French, he had a good season over hurdles winning three times at Plumpton twice and Wincanton. Runner-up in a Listed novice hurdle at Haydock in between, he isn't the biggest and will therefore contest the decent two miles handicap hurdles off his mark of 136.

CAP DU MATHAN (FR) 5 b g Kapgarde (FR) – Nounjya Du Mathan (FR)
A beautiful horse who improved with each start over hurdles last season. Placed a couple of times at Chepstow, he then won nicely at Plumpton in January. Only five, he could have another run over hurdles before going chasing. Rated 128, he is on a good mark and I think he will continue to improve, especially when he goes over fences.

CAPELAND (FR) 8 b g Poliglote – Neiland (FR)
Did well winning a valuable two miles handicap chase at Ascot in November having been unlucky at the same track on his previous start. Not disgraced in the Grade 2 Desert Orchid Chase at Kempton over Christmas, he tends to show his best form during the first half of the season and we will aim him at a similar programme during the Autumn/early winter.

CELESTIAL FORCE (IRE) 5 b g Sea The Stars (IRE) – Aquarelle Bleue
Yet to run for us, he won three times on the Flat for Tom Dascombe and is rated 84. We have schooled him over hurdles and, while he hasn't been a natural, he is getting there but we will give him a run on the Flat before going jumping.

CHRISTOPHER WOOD (IRE) 5 b g Fast Company (IRE) – Surf The Web (IRE)
A smart juvenile hurdler a couple of seasons ago winning twice and finishing third in Grade 1 company at Aintree, he benefited from a wind operation last season. An easy winner at Musselburgh in February, he then took his chance in the County Hurdle at the Cheltenham Festival but failed to get involved. Successful back on the Flat at Pontefract in June, he will follow a similar programme over jumps.

CILL ANNA (IRE) 5 b m Imperial Monarch (IRE) – Technohead (IRE)
She is a lovely mare who progressed throughout last season. A three times winner over hurdles, including a Listed mares' event at Doncaster in February. Rated 135, we will aim her at mares' conditions hurdles before going chasing. She is a very nice mare who ought to make a smashing chaser. Two and a half miles plus is her trip.

CLAN DES OBEAUX (FR) 8 b g Kapgarde (FR) – Nausicaa Des Obeaux (FR)
He is in great form at home and I am delighted with him. His main target once again is the King George at Kempton (26th December), which he has won for the last two years. There is a possibility he could start off in the Charlie Hall Chase at Wetherby (31st October) but the *Betfair* Chase at Haydock (21st November) is more likely. He won't be going to Cheltenham again so we will aim him at Aintree and Punchestown during the spring.

CONFIRMATION BIAS (IRE) 5 b g Presenting – Bonnie Parker (IRE)
A half-brother to El Bandit, he has a staying pedigree and is a nice horse for novice hurdles. A winner on his debut in a bumper at Wincanton in November, he then finished runner-up over the same course and distance under a penalty on Boxing Day. He may start off over two miles but will be suited by further in time.

CUT THE MUSTARD (FR) 8 br m Al Namix (FR) – Tadorna (FR)
I am delighted to be training for owner Jared Sullivan once again having had a lot of success with his horses over the years. His string only arrived during the summer, so we are still getting to know them and haven't made any definite plans yet. Rated 137 over fences, she won two mares' chases last season, including a Listed event at Naas in February. I would imagine she will be aimed at mares' conditions chases.

CYRNAME (FR) 8 b g Nickname (FR) – Narquille (FR)
Looks fantastic and is in great format home following his summer break. He produced a very good performance to beat Altior in the Grade 2 Christy 1965 Chase at Ascot in November but endured a hard race and wasn't at his best in his two subsequent starts in the King George at Kempton or the Ascot Chase in February. He was, however, ready to run again in the spring but the season was cut short due to the coronavirus. The plan is to start him off in the Grade 1 JNWine Champion Chase at Down Royal (31st October) over three miles. That will tell us whether he stays the trip and also give him a good break before a crack at the King George on Boxing Day. If he doesn't stay, then we will drop him back to two and a half miles.

DANNY KIRWAN (IRE) 7 b g Scorpion (IRE) – Sainte Baronne (FR)
Only raced once last season finishing sixth at Exeter in February. A horse with a lot of ability, he is still a novice over hurdles and I would like to win one before he goes chasing. A winning Irish pointer, he should make a lovely chaser.

DANNY WHIZZBANG (IRE) 7 b g Getaway (GER) – Lakil Princess (IRE)
He won a Grade 2 novice on his chasing debut at Newbury in November before finishing third in the Grade 1 Kauto Star Novices' Chase at Kempton on Boxing Day. He filled the same position in the Grade 2 Reynoldstown Novices' Chase at Ascot last time and is a horse who stays well. Rated 145, we are likely to enter him in races such as the Ladbrokes Trophy at Newbury (28th November) and Welsh National at Chepstow (27th December).

DANSE IDOL (IRE) 7 b m Dansant – Screen Idol (IRE)
Twice a winner over hurdles, she was placed a couple of times at Kempton and Wincanton last season. She won a point-to-point in Ireland and will go novice chasing and we will aim her at mares' only races over two and a half miles plus.

DIEGO DU CHARMIL (FR) 8 b g Ballingarry (IRE) – Daramour (FR)
Enjoyed a good season winning a valuable Listed chase at Ascot in November on his reappearance. Runner-up behind Capeland in a similar event later the same month, he was only beaten half a length in the rescheduled Grade 2 Kingwell Hurdle at Kempton in February. Rated 156 over fences and a few pounds lower over hurdles, we will probably mix and match between the two once again this season.

DOLCITA (FR) 5 b m Saint Des Saints (FR) – Orcantara (FR)
Another very nice mare owned by Jared Sullivan, she has only raced a handful of times over hurdles finishing runner-up in the Grade 2 Dawn Run Mares' Novice Hurdle at the Cheltenham Festival in March. She is rated 136 and we are likely to aim her at mares' handicap hurdles but we are still getting to know her.

DOLOS (FR) 7 b g Kapgarde (FR) – Redowa (FR)
A dual winner last season at Kempton and Ascot, he finished runner-up in the Haldon Gold Cup at Exeter (3rd November) and that will be his target once again. Rated 161, he isn't the easiest to place but is tough and I am sure he will continue to run well in the good two mile chases.

DORRELLS PIERJI (FR) 7 br g Coastal Path – Playa Pierji (FR)
Absent since November, he arrived during the summer and is a lovely horse to send novice chasing this season. He is already a point-to-point winner, plus he won twice in bumpers and over hurdles.

DUC DES GENIEVRES (FR) 7 gr g Buck's Boum (FR) – Lobelie (FR)
A horse with some top-class form having won the Arkle Trophy a couple of seasons ago. Runner-up in the Grade 2 Desert Orchid Chase at Kempton over Christmas, we have operated on his wind since he arrived in the summer and hopefully we can get him back to his best.

ECCO 5 b g Maxios – Enjoy The Life
A useful horse on the Flat in Germany, he benefited from a wind operation last year and won twice over hurdles at Wincanton and Ascot. Runner-up at Kempton on Boxing Day, he wasn't disgraced in the *Betfair* Hurdle at Newbury in February. Suited by better ground, he will be running in handicap hurdles during the Autumn and could be one for the Greatwood Hurdle at Cheltenham (15th November).

EGLANTINE DU SEUIL (FR) 6 b m Saddler Maker (IRE) – Rixia Du Seuil (FR)
A previous Cheltenham Festival winner, she is a smart mare who finished fourth in a valuable handicap hurdle at the Dublin Racing Festival at Leopardstown in February. It is early days with her because she only arrived in August but there is a possibility she will go mares' novice chasing. She is a lovely mare.

ENRILO (FR) 6 bl g Buck's Boum (FR) – Rock Treasure (FR)
He is a nice horse who will go novice chasing over two and a half miles plus. A dual winner over hurdles last season, including a Grade 2 at Sandown in December, he was third in the Grade 1 Challow Novices' Hurdle at Newbury last time. Rated 140 over hurdles, he has always looked a chaser in the making.

ERITAGE (FR) 6 b g Martaline – Sauves La Reine (FR)
A winner over hurdles at Taunton in November, he was runner-up at the same track next time. He is another who has undergone surgery on his wind since his last run and the intention is to send him novice chasing. Quite a free going type, he will stay further provided he learns to settle.

ESTELLE MA BELLE (FR) 6 ch m Air Chief Marshal (IRE) – Ozalid (FR)
Twice a winner on the Flat in France, she has only raced once over hurdles finishing runner-up at the Galway Festival last year. Another new recruit during the summer, she will be campaigned in mares' novice hurdles and looks a nice type.

FAMOSO (IRE) 4 b g Fame And Glory – Mucho Macabi (IRE)
He is a very nice unraced horse we bought at the Goffs Land Rover Sale in Ireland last year. From a good family, he is a half-brother to Tornado Flyer and we like him. He will start off in a bumper in the Autumn.

FAST BUCK (FR) 6 br g Kendargent (FR) – Juvenil Delinquent (USA)
He won a couple of times over hurdles last season, including a Listed novice at the Galway Festival. Having only joined us during the summer we haven't done a lot with him, but he looks the sort to jump fences and is likely to go novice chasing.

FIDELIO VALLIS (FR) 5 b g Saint Des Saints (FR) – Quora Vallis (FR)
A lovely young horse who was runner-up over hurdles at Auteuil in France before we bought him. He really got his act together over hurdles during the second half of the season winning at Wincanton and Kempton. Similar to Ask For Glory, he remains a novice until the end of November and could be one for the Cheltenham November meeting. I would imagine he will go over fences later on because he is very much a chaser for the future.

FLIC OU VOYOU (FR) 6 b g Kapgarde (FR) – Hillflower (FR)
Twice a bumper winner, I can't believe he is still a maiden over hurdles. Runner-up on four occasions, he is a big strong horse who ought to improve. I would like to win over hurdles with him before embarking on his chasing career. He is a horse with plenty of ability.

FORCE TEN (FR) 5 b g Al Namix (FR) – Quick Siren Mae (FR)
From the family of New Little Bric, who won the Grade 1 Scilly Isles Novices' Chase for us in 2007, he is a nice big horse who ran in a couple of bumpers at Newbury and Kempton. Third at the latter track, he will go novice hurdling.

FRIEND OR FOE (FR) 5 b g Walk In The Park (IRE) – Mandchou (FR)
Missed the whole of last season having won a couple of times as a juvenile hurdler the previous year. Rated 128, he had his wind operated on following his victory at Chepstow in the spring of last year. Back in work, he doesn't want the ground too soft and will probably have one more run over hurdles before going chasing. His mark looks fair.

FRODON (FR) 8 b g Nickname (FR) – Miss Country (FR)
Has been a fantastic horse for us over the years and he benefited from being treated for ulcers last season. He won the Grade 2 Silviniaco Conti Chase at Kempton in January before finishing fourth in the Ryanair Chase at Cheltenham. We are going to campaign him more over three miles this season because I think he wants a trip nowadays.

GALA DE CORTON (FR) 4 b g Secret Singer (FR) – Pour Le Meilleur (FR)
Bought at the Goffs Land Rover Sale in Ireland last year, he is a half-brother to Black Corton. He is a nice youngster who will run in a bumper in the Autumn.

GALOPIN D'AINAY (FR) 4 b g Fame And Glory – Tornade D'Ainay (FR)
From the family of Crystal D'Ainay, he was bought at the Tattersalls Derby Sale in Ireland as a three year old. He is a lovely horse and is another who will start off in a bumper in October/November.

GELINO BELLO (FR) 4 b g Saint Des Saints (FR) – Parade (FR)
Bought as a two year old at the Arqana Summer Sale, he is a nice unraced young horse who will make his debut in a bumper in the Autumn.

GETAWAY TRUMP (IRE) 7 b g Getaway (GER) – Acinorev (IRE)
We sent him chasing last season and, although he ran well twice at Cheltenham, the ground was too soft for him. Pulled up in the Christmas Hurdle last time, he will go back over fences but will be running early on, provided the ground is suitable. We have operated on his wind and I still have high hopes for him as a chaser because we know he is a smart horse.

GIVE ME A COPPER (IRE) 10 ch g Presenting – Copper Supreme (IRE)
Produced a good performance to win the Listed Badger Ales Chase at Wincanton and he will go back there for a repeat bid in November (7th). I would then like to aim him at either the Grand Sefton or Becher Chase at Aintree (5th December) and, in all likelihood, he will get an entry in the Grand National. I think he wants a flat track but doesn't want the ground too soft.

GLAJOU (FR) 4 br g Network (GER) – Toscane (FR)
Placed twice over hurdles in France, he was bought at the Arqana Sale in November last year. Disappointing on his only start for us at Taunton in March, he was a big backward horse last season and I think he will improve enormously this time around. He will continue in novice hurdles.

GLENLIVET (IRE) 5 b g Flemensfirth (USA) – Gleaming Spire
He has always worked like a very nice horse at home and I was therefore disappointed when he didn't win on his debut in a bumper at Chepstow last Autumn. He travelled strongly but didn't finish his race off. We have operated on his wind and I hope he repeats his homework on the track because he shows us plenty. We may give him one more run in a bumper before going hurdling.

GOLDEN GIFT (IRE) 6 b g Gold Well – Five Star Present (IRE)
Runner-up in a couple of bumpers the previous season, he was third on his hurdles debut at Chepstow in November. A staying type, he has the ability to win over hurdles before going chasing.

GRAND SANCY (FR) 6 b g Diamond Boy (FR) – La Courtille (FR)
Runner-up in the Elite Hurdle at Wincanton in November, we switched him to fences soon afterwards. Third in the Grade 1 Henry VIII Novices' Chase at Sandown on his chasing debut, he filled the same position in the Grade 2 Wayward Lad Novices' Chase at Kempton over Christmas. He won over fences at Fontwell in February and is therefore another who benefits from the new ruling, which means he is still a novice until the end of November. With that in mind, he could go to Chepstow (10th October) for a two and a half miles novice chase. He will then have to go into open company from December onwards.

GREANETEEN (FR) 6 b g Great Pretender (IRE) – Manson Teene (FR)
A smart novice chaser last season, he won three times at Ascot, Musselburgh and Fakenham before finishing fourth in the Grand Annual Chase at the Cheltenham Festival. He was due to run in the Grade 1 novice chase at Aintree but the season was cut short. The plan is for him to start off in the Haldon Gold Cup at Exeter (3rd November) and we have got high hopes for him this season. I think there is a huge amount of improvement to come and, all being well, he will be contesting the top two mile chases.

GREAT GABLE (IRE) 4 b g Fame And Glory – Mistress Mole (IRE)
Purchased as a three year old at the Tattersalls Derby Sale in Ireland, he is another promising youngster who will make his debut in a bumper. We like him.

HACKER DES PLACES (FR) 3 b g Great Pretender (IRE) – Plaisance (FR)
We have bought some potentially exciting juvenile hurdlers from France during the summer, including this former Francois Nicolle trained three year old. He has raced twice finishing third on his debut before winning at Dax in June. Given a month off since arriving, he looks a nice horse.

HELL RED (FR) 3 gr g Martaline – Queen Margot (FR)
Another nice French recruit who finished runner-up on his debut over hurdles at Auteuil in March for Guillaume Macaire. Beaten two and a half lengths, we bought the winner (Monmiral), too, and they are both lovely prospects. We may start him off in the juvenile hurdle at Chepstow (10th October), which we have done well in over the years.

HIGHLAND HUNTER (IRE) 7 gr g Subtle Power (IRE) – Loughine Sparkle (IRE)
Has only raced twice for us winning a Pertemps qualifier at Musselburgh in February. He is a strong stayer and we are going to send him novice chasing. A winning Irish pointer, he copes well with soft ground.

HITMAN (FR) 4 b g Falco (USA) – Tercah Girl (FR)
A lovely horse who ran three times over hurdles for Guillaume Macaire in France winning on his latest start at Pau in January. He joined us soon afterwards, but has yet to run over here. Very much a chaser in the making, he will send this season over hurdles and we will look for a suitable four year old hurdle to begin with.

IS A REAL CHAMP (IRE) 6 ch g Getaway (GER) – Siobhans Charm (IRE)
Back in work having missed last season, he was runner-up in a point-to-point in Ireland before we bought him. He ran well in third in a bumper at Chepstow during the spring of last year and will go novice hurdling.

KANDOO KID (FR) 4 gr g Kapgarde (FR) – Scarlett du Mesnil (IRE)
From the family of Politologue, he was purchased as a two year old at the Arqana Summer sale in France. He is another very nice youngster for bumpers in the Autumn.

KILMINGTON ROSE (IRE) 5 ch m Presenting – Robyn's Rose (IRE)
She is a lovely mare who finished second on her debut in a bumper at Taunton in January. I think she will improve when encountering better ground and we will try and win a mares' bumper with her before going hurdling.

KNAPPERS HILL (IRE) 4 b g Valirann (FR) – Brogella (IRE)
A half-brother to dual Listed mares' chase winner Rene's Girl, he is a very nice unraced gelding who was acquired at the Goffs Land Rover Sale in Ireland as a three year old. He will run in a bumper in the Autumn and I like him a lot.

LAURINA (FR) 7 b m Spanish Moon (USA) – Lamboghina (GER)
She is a high-class mare and we are very pleased to have been sent her during the summer. A former Cheltenham Festival winner, we haven't made any definite plans but we have operated on her wind since she arrived. We are still getting to know her and, while we have the option of going back over fences because there is a good chase programme for mares', it is possible something like the Grade 2 Ascot Hurdle (21st November) might suit her.

LUCKY ONE (FR) 5 br g Authorized (IRE) – Lady Anouchka (IRE)
Another one of Jared Sullivan's who joined us this summer, he finished runner-up twice over hurdles in France and fourth on his only run in Ireland last season. Still a novice, he will continue over hurdles.

LYDFORD LAD (IRE) 5 b g Yeats (IRE) – Shannon Rose (IRE)
Half-brother to Minella Foru, he was fifth on his debut in a bumper at Wincanton in January. He will go straight over hurdles and ought to develop into a nice staying novice.

LYONS (IRE) 4 ch g Australia – Light Quest (USA)
Bought at the Arqana Sale in France last November, he has yet to run for us but will go novice hurdling. Gelded during the winter, he won three times on the Flat for Carlos Laffon-Parias, including over ten furlongs at Longchamp in July last year.

MAGIC SAINT (FR) 6 b g Saint Des Saints (FR) – Magic Poline (FR)
He will follow a similar programme and contest the good two mile handicap chases. We were pleased with his win at Newbury in November and, having missed the Cheltenham Festival, we were aiming him at Aintree but that never happened.

MALAYA (FR) 6 b m Martaline – Clarte D'Or (FR)
Runner-up over hurdles at Ascot in February, she was due to defend her crown in the Imperial Cup at Sandown the following month but the meeting was abandoned. Rated 138, we may try her over fences once again having finished third on her chasing debut at Market Rasen last Autumn. She loves soft ground.

MANORBANK (IRE) 5 b g Arcadio (GER) – Kind Word (IRE)
A four lengths winner of a bumper on his debut at Kelso last winter, we subsequently bought him at the Cheltenham February Sale. His long-term future is as a staying chaser but he will go novice hurdling this season.

MASTER TOMMYTUCKER 9 b g Kayf Tara – No Need For Alarm
He is a horse with a huge amount of ability but endured a frustrating season. Successful over fences on his reappearance at Kempton in November, he then fell when leading in the Grade 1 Kauto Star Novices' Chase at the same track on Boxing Day. It was a similar story in the Grade 2 Pendil Novices' Chase at Kempton last time because he was still in front when falling at the same fence (fourth last). We have operated on his wind since because his breathing may have been an issue as he was about to come under pressure. We could start him off in the Grade 2 Skymas Chase at Down Royal (31st October), which we have won seven times, and it wouldn't surprise me if we entered him in the King George on Boxing Day.

MCFABULOUS (IRE) 6 b g Milan – Rossavon (IRE)
An exciting prospect who remains a novice over hurdles until the end of November. He appreciated the step up to two and a half miles winning at Market Rasen in February. He then followed up in the rescheduled EBF Final at Sandown the following month producing an awesome performance off a mark of 132. His first target is the Grade 2 Persian War Novices' Hurdle at Chepstow (9th October). It wouldn't surprise me if he developed into a stayers' hurdle horse. The original plan was to aim him at the Grade 2 West Yorkshire Hurdle at Wetherby (31st October) until they changed the rules regarding novices. He is a very nice horse.

MICK PASTOR (FR) 4 b g Meshaheer (USA) – Mick Oceane (FR)
He won over hurdles at Ludlow in January on his second start for us before undergoing wind surgery. Tenth in the Boodles Juvenile Handicap Hurdle at the Cheltenham Festival, I think he wants a flat track and better ground. Rated 139, he will be aimed at the decent handicap hurdles.

MONDORA (FR) 3 gr f Montmartre (FR) – Clarte D'Or (FR)
She is a very nice unraced half-sister to Malaya. We may start her off in a mares' bumper before going juvenile hurdling.

MON FRERE (IRE) 4 b g Pour Moi (IRE) – Sistine
A stayer on the Flat for Sir Mark Prescott, he won twice on the all-weather at Chelmsford and Lingfield last year and has joined us with a view to going novice hurdling.

MONMIRAL (FR) 3 bl g Saint Des Saints (FR) – Achere (FR)
As discussed, he beat Hell Red on his debut over hurdles at Auteuil in the spring when trained by Francois Nicolle in France and will go juvenile hurdling. He is a lovely big strong horse and very much a chaser in the making.

MONT DES AVALOIRS (FR) 7 b g Blue Bresil (FR) – Abu Dhabi (FR)
Still a novice over fences, he ran well in a Grade 2 event at Newbury in November on his reappearance and was runner-up at the same track last time. I would like to find a small novice chase somewhere to begin with, but I think he will be suited by a strongly run handicap when they go flat out from the outset.

MR GLASS (IRE) 4 b g Sholokhov (IRE) – Maryota (FR)
Bought at the Goffs UK Doncaster Spring Sale last year, he is a very nice horse who will be aimed at a bumper to start with in the Autumn.

MY WAY (FR) 6 ch g Martaline – Royale Majesty (FR)
He, too, remains a novice over fences but we are going to step him up to three miles this season. The plan is to give him a run in a novice hurdle before aiming him at the Badger Ales Chase at Wincanton (7th November).

NEXT DESTINATION (IRE) 8 b g Dubai Destination (USA) – Liss Alainn (IRE)
A Grade 1 winning novice hurdler, he is a lovely horse who arrived during the summer. Absent for a couple of years, he has had a few issues but is in good form now and we are looking forward to sending him chasing. We will start him off low key and take it from there.

ONETHREEFIVENOTOUT (FR) 4 b g Blue Bresil (FR) – Maralypha (FR)
Well related, he is an unraced half-brother to Listed bumper winner Eden Du Houx. An expensive purchase at the Tattersalls Derby Sale in Ireland as a three year old, he is another for bumpers in October/November.

PIC D'ORHY (FR) 5 b g Turgeon (USA) – Rose Candy (FR)
He looks great and we can't wait to send him over fences this season. He produced a very good performance to win the *Betfair* Hurdle at Newbury in February off a mark of 146. Runner-up in Grade 1 company in France before joining us, we are hoping he will develop into an Arkle horse this season, although we will try and find a small race to begin with. Two miles is his trip and I think he is a proper horse.

POLITOLOGUE (FR) 9 gr g Poliglote – Scarlet Row (FR)
We were delighted with his victory in the Queen Mother Champion Chase at Cheltenham in March. We learned the key to him is to give him a good break between his races and keep him fresh. We will therefore space his races out this season with the Champion Chase once again his ultimate target. The Grade 2 Shloer Chase at Cheltenham (15th November), a race in which he finished second last year, is a possible starting point, although we may decide to go straight to Sandown for the Grade 1 Tingle Creek (5th December), which he won three years ago.

POSH TRISH (IRE) 7 b m Stowaway – Moscow Demon (IRE)
A useful mare, she is a dual Listed winner over hurdles but hasn't raced since finishing third on her chasing debut at Chepstow last Autumn. However, she is back in work now and will continue in novice chases.

POZO EMERY (FR) 5 b g Le Havre (IRE) – Chic Et Zen (FR)
He is a very nice horse who finished second in his only Irish point-to-point in January. Novice hurdles will be on his agenda this season.

QUEL DESTIN (FR) 5 ch g Muhtathir – High Destiny (FR)
Had another good season over hurdles winning twice, including the Listed Contenders Hurdle at Sandown in February. Runner-up in the Grade 2 National Spirit Hurdle at Fontwell last time, he is tough and loves soft ground. We are going to send him novice chasing but I am going to run him on the Flat beforehand. I can't believe he got beaten at Bath last October off a mark of 66 and we are going to aim him at the same race (14th October).

REAL STEEL (FR) 7 b g Loup Breton (IRE) – Kalimina (FR)
A lovely horse who has some top-class form over fences. A dual Grade 2 winner in Ireland last season, he ran a cracker in the Cheltenham Gold Cup finishing sixth. We are therefore delighted to be training him and he has plenty of options. The Charlie Hall Chase at Wetherby (31st October) is a possible starting point. Alternatively, he could wait for the Grade 2 Christy 1965 Chase at Ascot (21st November), which Cyrname won last season. The King George at Kempton (26th December) could definitely come into the equation later on. Still only seven, he is an exciting addition to the team.

RED RISK (FR) 5 b g No Risk At All (FR) – Rolie De Vindecy (FR)
A winner over hurdles and fences in France, he was bought in the Autumn and has only raced twice for us. Third at Hereford over two miles in January, he then stepped up to two and a half miles at Ludlow and won easily. Raised nine pounds since, he will be aimed at the decent handicap chases off his mark of 144.

ROCHESTON (FR) 5 b g Kapgarde (FR) – Ravna (FR)
Another new arrival, he finished third on his only start over hurdles for Guillaume Macaire in France as a three year old. Absent since, he looks a nice novice hurdler for this season.

ROQUE IT (IRE) 6 b g Presenting – Roque De Cyborg (IRE)
Yet to run for us, he ran in a couple of bumpers for Olly Murphy winning at Huntingdon in March last year. Off the track since, he joined us in the summer and is another who will spend this season in novice hurdles.

SABRINA (IRE) 5 b m Yeats (IRE) – En Vedette (FR)
Runner-up on her debut in a bumper at Taunton last Autumn, she then won impressively at Ascot in February. Over the top by the time she ran in a Listed mares' bumper at Kempton the following month, she is a nice mare for novice hurdles.

SAGLAWY (FR) 6 b g Youmzain (IRE) – Spasha
A Grade 2 winning hurdler in Ireland, he has some good form on the Flat, too, and we are going to enter him in the Cesarewitch at Newmarket (10th October). Then, he will go back over hurdles and, with a rating of 146, we will target the good handicaps.

SAINT DE REVE (FR) 6 b g Saint Des Saints (FR) – Ty Mat (FR)
A winner over hurdles at Wincanton in November, we have operated on his wind since his last run at Kempton and hopefully that will make a difference. Rated 125 over hurdles, he will go over fences and be aimed at a novices' handicap chase. I think there is plenty of improvement in him.

SAINT SONNET (FR) 5 b g Saint Des Saints (FR) – Leprechaun Lady (FR)
He is a very nice horse who had some smart form over hurdles and fences in France. He only arrived halfway through last season winning at Catterick in late February before running well in the Grade 1 JLT Novices' Chase at the Cheltenham Festival. I think there is a lot of improvement to come from him and we will give him an entry in the BetVictor Gold Cup at Cheltenham (14th November).

SECRET INVESTOR 8 b g Kayf Tara – Silver Charmer
Rated 153 over fences, he isn't the easiest horse to place but ran well in the Grade 2 Denman Chase at Newbury in February finishing second behind Native River. Runner-up behind the aforementioned Real Steel at Down Royal in another Grade 2 on his reappearance, he prefers good ground. The Charlie Hall Chase at Wetherby (31st October) is a possible target.

SECRET POTION (GER) 4 bb g Dabirsim (FR) – Sola Gratia (IRE)
He is a nice horse who won on the Flat in Germany and was placed at Listed level. Gelded since joining us, he is a big strong horse and will go novice hurdling.

SHEARER (IRE) 4 b g Flemensfirth (USA) – The Crown Jewel (IRE)
A very nice unraced four year old who belongs to the McNeill Family. Given time to mature, he will run in a bumper in the Autumn. I like him.

SILVER FOREVER (IRE) 6 gr m Jeremy (USA) – Silver Prayer (IRE)
She is a very good mare who won three of her four races over hurdles last season. A Listed winner at Sandown in early January, she then had a tiny setback but we were preparing to run her in the spring but the season was cut short. A winning pointer, she will go over fences and ought to make a very nice chaser.

SIROCO JO (FR) 3 ch g Hurricane Cat (USA) – Diana Vertica (FR)
Trained in France by Mickael Seror, he was beaten narrowly on his only start over hurdles at Clairefontaine in early August. He looks a lovely prospect for juvenile hurdles.

SIR PSYCHO (IRE) 4 b g Zoffany (IRE) – Open Book
A three times winner over hurdles before running well in the Triumph Hurdle at Cheltenham. Similar to Quel Destin, he is a very nice horse who I think will continue to improve. We will start him off in a four year old hurdle, possibly at Cheltenham (24th October) in the Autumn. It wouldn't surprise me if he was contesting something like the Grade 2 National Spirit Hurdle at Fontwell in February.

SKATMAN (IRE) 5 br g Mustameet (USA) – Maid For Action (IRE)
Bought at the Goffs UK Doncaster Spring Sale last year having won his only Irish point-to-point, he was a big backward horse last season. We decided to give him time to mature after his run in a bumper at Ascot and he will go novice hurdling this season.

SOLO (FR) 4 b g Kapgarde (FR) – Flameche (FR)
He is in very good form at home and we are looking forward to seeing him again this season. A winner over hurdles at Auteuil in November, he joined us halfway through last season and was impressive when winning the Grade 2 Adonis Hurdle at Kempton in February. I think he was over the top by the time he ran in the Triumph Hurdle at Cheltenham, having been on the go for a long time. He is a lovely horse and very much one for fences in the future. However, he will stay over hurdles this season and we may have a look at the Grade 1 Prix Renaud du Vivier at Auteuil (8th November), which we won with Ptit Zig in 2013. He will then be campaigned in the good hurdle races before going chasing next season.

SONNY CROCKETT (IRE) 5 b g Robin Des Champs (FR) – Onewayortheother (IRE)
A half-brother to Grade 2 winner Birchdale, he is a very nice unraced horse who is owned by Malcom Denmark. He will go straight over hurdles.

SOUTHFIELD HARVEST 6 b g Kayf Tara – Chamoss Royale (FR)
Half-brother to Southfield Theatre and Southfield Vic, he is a very nice horse who is on a good mark. A bumper winner the previous season, he has only raced twice over hurdles. Runner-up at Wincanton in January, he won next time at Ludlow in February and is still eligible for novice hurdles until the end of November. He will go over fences later on and I think he will make a very good chaser.

SOUTHFIELD STONE 7 gr g Fair Mix (IRE) – Laureldean Belle (IRE)
A winner over fences at Musselburgh in February, he was narrowly beaten in the Grade 2 Pendil Novices' Chase at Kempton later the same month. Still a novice until the start of December, we have tweaked his wind since his last run and I think two and a half miles is his trip.

STORMY IRELAND (FR) 6 b m Motivator – Like A Storm (IRE)
Rated 153, she is a very good mare who won three times last season, including Grade 3 mares' hurdles at Leopardstown and Naas. She has settled in well since arriving during the summer, but we haven't made any plans for her. Although not the biggest, we may send her novice chasing. Otherwise, she will continue in the Graded mares' hurdles.

STRATAGEM (FR) 4 gr g Sunday Break (JPN) – Our Ziga (FR)
A half-brother to *Skybet* Chase winner Ziga Boy, he is a lovely horse who won over hurdles at Auteuil in October. Bought at the Arqana Sale the following month, he has needed time and took a while to acclimatise. However, he was an easy winner at Kelso in late February. He won't be the easiest to place over hurdles off a mark of 141, but we have the option of sending him novice chasing and receive an age allowance.

TAKE YOUR TIME (IRE) 5 b g Dubai Destination (USA) – Don't Be Bleu (IRE)
A wide margin winner of an English point-to-point last winter, he was bought at the Goffs UK Doncaster January Sale. Given time, he will spend this season in novice hurdles.

TAMAROC DU MATHAN (FR) 5 b g Poliglote – Thisbee Du Mathan (FR)
He is a nice horse who ran some good races in defeat last season. Runner-up at Ascot on his reappearance, he ran very well in the *Betfair* Hurdle at Newbury finishing a close fifth. A winner over hurdles in France, he will go over fences and should make a nice chaser.

THREEUNDERTHRUFIVE (IRE) 5 b g Shantou (USA) – Didinas (FR)
A very nice horse who has been big and backward. Runner-up in a bumper at Fontwell on his debut, he won next time and Chepstow. All set to go novice hurdling, he will be suited by two and a half miles.

THYME WHITE (FR) 4 b g Anodin (IRE) – Jane (GER)
A winner on the Flat in France, he had a good season over hurdles winning the Listed Scottish Triumph Hurdle at Musselburgh in February. Rated 130, he is eligible for novice hurdles until the beginning of December and then we will aim him at handicaps thereafter.

TIME TO TINKER (IRE) 5 br g Stowaway – Zuzka (IRE)
Runner-up in a bumper at Exeter in December, he disappointed next time at Wincanton three months later. We have operated on his wind since and I hope he will develop into a nice novice hurdler.

TOPOFTHEGAME (IRE) 8 ch g Flemensfirth (USA) – Derry Vale (IRE)
He is in very good form having missed last season. He had his first canter on the 1st August having done roadwork for a month and, all being well, he will be aimed at the Ladbrokes Trophy at Newbury (28th November). We will also give him an entry in the *Betfair* Chase at Haydock (21st November). He doesn't want a lot of racing so we may give him another run over Christmas before his ultimate target the Cheltenham Gold Cup in March.

TREVELYN'S CORN (IRE) 7 b g Oscar (IRE) – Present Venture (IRE)
Incurred a leg injury when pulling up in Persian War Novices' Hurdle at Chepstow last Autumn hence he missed the remainder of the season. He is back in work now though and will go novice chasing over two and a half miles plus.

TRUCKERS LODGE (IRE) 8 b g Westerner – Galeacord (IRE)
Developed into an awesome chaser last season with the progress he made nothing short of astonishing. Runner-up in the Welsh National, I wish we had ridden him more positively, but it was only his fourth run over fences and he lacked experience, so we rode him with a bit of restraint. However, he was very good in the Midlands National at Uttoxeter winning by eighteen lengths. Raised fourteen pounds since to a mark of 155, I am not sure what we are going to do with him now but he will be given entries in the Welsh and English Nationals.

TULIN 3 b g Gleneagles (IRE) – Talawat
Arrived during the summer having won the second of his two starts on the Flat in France. A winner of a twelve furlongs maiden at Lignieres in June, he will go juvenile hurdling.

VIROFLAY (FR) 3 b g Air Chief Marshal (IRE) – Red Vixen (IRE)
Raced three times on the Flat in France winning at Pau in December. Fourth at the same track in January, we bought him soon afterwards and he was gelded. Given time since, he is another for juvenile hurdles.

WHISKEY LULLABY (IRE) 5 b m Stowaway – Joie De Cotte (FR)
Half-sister to Grade 2 winning chaser Petit Robin, she is a very promising mare who finished runner-up in her only Irish point for Colin Bowe last Autumn. She ran well on her debut for us in a bumper at Newbury in February and we may try and win a similar event before going hurdling. She is a lovely mare.

WILD MAX (GER) 5 b g Maxios – Wildfahrte (GER)
Useful on the Flat in Germany, he took well to hurdling winning his first two starts at Taunton. Fourth at Musselburgh last time, he is another who has undergone wind surgery since and I think there is lots of improvement to come from him. Rated 133, he will be handicap hurdling this season.

WORTHY FARM (IRE) 7 b g Beneficial – Muckle Flugga (IRE)
Had a good season over fences winning twice at Wincanton. He always needs his first run but he stays well and loves soft ground. Staying handicap chases will be on his agenda and we will almost certainly give him an entry in the Welsh National at Chepstow (27th December). Despite the fact all five of his career wins, including his point-to-point, have been gained on right-handed tracks, I don't see any reason why he won't be as effective going left-handed.

YALA ENKI (FR) 10 bb g Nickname (FR) – Cadiane (FR)

A lovely horse who joined us last season and did well. Third in the Welsh National and Grand National Trial at Chepstow and Haydock respectively, he won the Portman Cup at Taunton in between. He was due to contest the Grand National at Aintree but sadly that never materialised. He loves soft ground and we will aim him at the Welsh National once again and there is every chance he will go back to Taunton in January for the same race he won last season.

YOUNG BUCK (IRE) 6 b g Yeats (IRE) – Pepsi Starlet (IRE)

Purchased at the Cheltenham Festival Sale last year, he was third on his only run over hurdles at Exeter in March. He will have another run or two in staying novice hurdles before going chasing. He reminds me of Truckers Lodge and I think there is plenty of improvement to come.

> **TRAINER'S HORSE TO FOLLOW: PIC D'ORHY**
> **TRAINER'S ASSISTANT'S (HARRY DERHAM) HORSE TO FOLLOW: ENRILO**

Jonjo O'NEILL

Stables: Jackdaws Castle, Temple Guiting, Cheltenham, Gloucestershire.
2019/2020: 61 Winners / 434 Runners 14% Prize-Money £532,918
www.jonjooneillracing.com

A DISTANT PLACE (IRE) 5 b g Sunday Break (JPN) – South Africa (FR)

A grand horse who arrived during the summer having run in three Irish point-to-points. A winner last time, he was ridden by Derek O'Connor who recommended him to us. He looks a nice horse who will make a chaser but will spend this season in novice hurdles.

ADICCI (IRE) 5 b g Shirocco (GER) – Lughnasa (IRE)

Ran well in his bumpers before winning over hurdles at Plumpton in December. Runner-up at Wetherby next time, we have always thought he was a very nice horse but he came back from his summer break and made a noise. We have therefore operated on his wind, so he won't be in action until around Christmas time. I would imagine he will stay over hurdles for the time being. Two and a half miles is probably going to be his trip.

ANNIE MC (IRE) 6 b m Mahler – Classic Mari (IRE)

She is in great form at home and is a lovely mare who has provided us with a lot of fun. She took well to chasing and really enjoys her jumping. Three times a winner last season, we tried her in the Grade 1 JLT Novices' Chase at Cheltenham in March but she came up short. She is rated 144 and, while she is probably high enough in the ratings, there is a good mares' programme nowadays and we will aim to get some black type with her. Two and a half miles on easy ground is ideal.

ARRIVEDERCI (FR) 5 gr g Martaline – Etoile D'Ainay (FR)

A bumper winner, he was progressive over hurdles last season. Third at Warwick and runner-up at Sandown, he won at Wincanton on his latest start. Rated 128, he is capable of being competitive off such a mark and, while we will start him off over two miles, he will stay further. He is a nice horse and I like him.

ASHFIELD PADDY (IRE) 6 b g Publisher (USA) – Thats Grace (IRE)
He won an Irish point-to-point before we bought him and I was pleased with him last season. A dual winner over hurdles at Haydock and Exeter, he has schooled well over fences and is set to go novice chasing. Two and a half to three miles with some cut in the ground are his optimum conditions. He will hopefully develop into a nice chaser.

BEAN IN TROUBLE 6 gr g Sulamani (IRE) – Bouncing Bean
A nice horse who surprised us when winning over two miles at Ludlow because we always thought he wanted further. His future lies over fences but we will keep him over hurdles for the time being because he remains a novice until the end of November. Still lightly, I hope there is more to come from him and we will step him back up in trip at some stage.

CARYS' COMMODITY 5 b g Fame And Glory – Native Sunrise (IRE)
Won over hurdles at Catterick at the end of January but didn't get home in the soft ground over three miles at Cartmel in August. He prefers better ground and will be suited by a drop back to two and a half miles.

CLONDAW PROMISE (IRE) 6 b g Gold Well – Present Promise (IRE)
Placed in one of his two Irish point-to-points, he had three runs over hurdles for us last season. Runner-up over two miles at Uttoxeter last time, it won't be long before he goes over fences and we will look for a suitable novices' handicap chase.

CLOTH CAP (IRE) 8 b g Beneficial – Cloth Fair (IRE)
He is a lovely horse and we are looking to him again this season. Placed at Ascot and Doncaster, he was only narrowly beaten at the latter before finishing eighth in the Kim Muir at the Cheltenham Festival. He will follow a similar programme and it would be nice to think he could reach a higher enough mark to have a crack at the Grand National. He stays well and appreciates better ground.

DARSI IN THE PARK (IRE) 7 b g Darsi (FR) – Rock In The Park (IRE)
Hasn't been the easiest to keep right, but he has ability as he demonstrated when winning over hurdles at Uttoxeter in February. Third at Wincanton last time, he may go straight over fences having already won an Irish point. I think two and a half miles is probably his trip.

DJANGO DJANGO (FR) 7 gr g Voix Du Nord (FR) – Lady Jannina
A grand horse with plenty of ability, he finished third on his chasing debut at Uttoxeter and won well at Newbury in January. Rated 137 over fences, we are hoping he will continue to improve and develop into a Grand National contender one day. He stays well and is still lightly raced over fences.

DYNAMO BOY (IRE) 5 b g Jeremy (USA) – Mary's Little Vic (IRE)
A fine big horse who had a run in a bumper at Kempton in February finishing sixth. Very much a chaser in the making, he will go hurdling this season and needs more experience. I like him.

FAST GETAWAY (IRE) 4 b g Getaway (GER) – Maddy's Supreme (IRE)
He is a nice unraced four year old who I like and one to look forward to. A half-brother to Imperial Alcazar and Jessber's Dream, he was bought at the Tattersalls Derby Sale last year and we will start him off in a bumper.

FILE ILLICO (FR) 5 b g Cokoriko (FR) – Noryane (FR)
We bought him at the Cheltenham February Sale having won his only point-to-point in Ireland for Michael Goff a few days earlier. A big raw horse, he will improve with time and is a nice prospect for novice hurdles this season. His future lies over fences though.

FLAMES OF PASSION (IRE) 4 b f Flemensfirth (USA) – Night of Passion (IRE)
Only arrived in September, so we are still getting to know her. Two lengths runner-up in an Irish point in March, she belongs to Deva Racing and, while we haven't made any plans, I would expect her to contest a mares' bumper before going hurdling. I think she is going to want a trip over jumps.

FLIGHT DECK (IRE) 6 b g Getaway (GER) – Rate of Knots (IRE)
He is a nice horse who will go over fences and we will aim him at a novices' handicap chase off his mark of 121. He looked good when winning at Newbury, although I am not convinced it was much of a race and he had been disappointing beforehand. However, he is going the right way and is a nice big horse who should be better over fences. His mother stayed well, so he should have no trouble stepping up to three miles later on.

FOLKS ON THE HILL 5 b g Black Sam Bellamy (IRE) – Any Pearl
Bought at the Derby Sales in Ireland as a three year old, he is a big backward horse who has taken time to come to hand. We gave him a run in a bumper at Warwick in January and, while he ran OK, he has started to fill his frame since. Long-term, he is very much a chaser in the making but will go novice hurdling this season.

FRISCO BAY (IRE) 5 b g Yeats (IRE) – Heath Heaven
Runner-up in one of his two point-to-points in Ireland, he had a few runs over hurdles last season but didn't appreciate heavy ground. We will be looking to step him up in trip and hopefully find some better ground this season.

GARRY CLERMONT (FR) 5 b g Maresca Sorrento (FR) – Kalidria Beauchene (FR)
Won an English point-to-point before we bought him and then he won a bumper at Aintree in the spring of last year. He had a good season over hurdles winning twice at Ludlow and showed plenty of speed in the process. Fifth in the Grade 2 Dovecote Novices' Hurdle at Kempton last time, he has schooled over fences and will go novice chasing over two miles.

GASTON PHEBUS (FR) 4 b g Coastal Path – Quarte (FR)
Trained in Ireland by Denis Murphy, he finished third in a point-to-point in March before we bought him at the Cheltenham Festival sale the following week. A big chasing type, he is only four and still raw. This season will be a learning curve over hurdles.

GENERATION GAP (IRE) 6 b g Olden Times – Kerso (IRE)
Like Garry Clermont, he won an English point for Francesca Nimmo and Charlie Poste before we bought him. Third a couple of times last season at Chepstow and Wetherby, I am still not sure what his trip is because he stayed on at the former over two miles, but didn't appear to get home over two and a half miles at the latter. Still a novice over hurdles, we have the option of going over fences and running in a novices' handicap chase.

HENRY GONDOFF 5 b g Great Pretender (IRE) – Mi Money
He was leading when unseating his rider at the last in his only point-to-point for Pat Doyle in Ireland. Even though he was with us for some of last season, we haven't done a great deal with him. A grand big three miles chaser in the making, he will spend this season over hurdles.

KILBROOK (IRE) 5 b g Watar (IRE) – Daly Lady (IRE)
He is a grand horse who ran two good races for us last season having come over from Ireland. Narrowly beaten in a bumper at Chepstow, he shaped well on his hurdles debut at Newbury finishing third. We couldn't get him right after that hence he hasn't run since. However, he is back now and will continue over hurdles. I think he will benefit from stepping up in trip this season.

LUNAR BABY (IRE) 5 b m Fame And Glory – Fiddlededee (IRE)

Like her mother who we used to train, she can be a bit of a madam but has plenty of ability. She won over hurdles at Warwick last time having finished second a couple of times at Market Rasen and Wincanton. We will give her another run or two over hurdles, but I am tempted to send her chasing because she jumps like a buck. I could see her doing well in mares' novice chases.

MAYNE (IRE) 4 b g Dansili – Pink Damsel (IRE)

Raced three times on the Flat for Andrew Balding finishing second twice and earning a rating of 84. Quite a keen horse, A.P.(McCoy) has been schooling him over hurdles and he appears to be enjoying it. He pops nicely and will go novice hurdling.

MAYPOLE CLASS (IRE) 6 b g Gold Well – Maypole Queen (IRE)

Hasn't been the easiest horse to keep sound but he possesses an engine and ran some good races over hurdles last season. A winner at Lingfield in December, he was also second a couple of times. Suited by plenty of cut in the ground, he will go novice chasing.

MERCUTIO ROCK (FR) 4 b g Maresca Sorrento (FR) – Mondovi (FR)

Still quite babyish, he was bought at the Tattersalls Derby Sale in Ireland last year. He is a nice horse though and very likeable. We will start him off in a bumper and then decide whether to send him hurdling.

MEYER LANSKY (IRE) 5 b g Mahler – Sea Breeze Lady (IRE)

A former Irish pointer, he was runner-up in a bumper at Worcester on his first start for us and finished second over hurdles at Chepstow. Still a novice, he will continue over hurdles and has done well physically during the summer. Qualified for handicaps off a mark of 114, he will go down that route this season.

MINELLA BEAUTY (IRE) 5 b g Shirocco (GER) – Native Beauty (IRE)

Ran in a couple of Irish points before we bought him. We ran him in bumpers at Catterick and Huntingdon but he was too keen and didn't get home. He has been keen at home, too, and wears a hood but I am hoping he has turned the corner because he has ability. We will send him hurdling and he will be suited by a step up in trip, provided he settles.

MORNING SPIRIT (IRE) 5 b g Milan – Morning Legend (IRE)

Still a novice over hurdles, he was runner-up at Plumpton in January and I think he will be suited by stepping up to two and a half miles this year. Rated 118, we will run him in a novices' handicap hurdle.

ON THE BANDWAGON (IRE) 5 b g Oscar (IRE) – Deep Supreme (IRE)

Bought at the Aintree Grand National Sale last year, he finished runner-up in his only point-to-point in Ireland. Despite the fact he never raced last season, there was nothing really wrong with him, except he was still very backward and has needed time. A chaser in the making, he has grown up a lot during the summer and will go novice hurdling.

PALMERS HILL (IRE) 7 b g Gold Well – Tosca Shine (IRE)

He is a useful horse but suffered a nasty injury when winning at Cheltenham in November 2018. Runner-up at Kempton in February after a long spell on the sidelines, he is back in work and will go novice chasing. Two and a half miles is ideal and he will hopefully make a nice chaser because he has plenty of ability.

PAPA TANGO CHARLY (FR) 5 ch g No Risk At All (FR) – Chere Elenn (FR)
Ran well a couple of times over hurdles at Ascot and, in particular, Newbury before disappointing at Doncaster on his latest start. Still green and a baby, he is a chasing type who will come into his own over fences eventually. However, he will remain over hurdles for the time being and we will try and win a novice before making any plans. Two and a half to three miles is going to be his trip.

PENS MAN (IRE) 5 ch g Sholokhov (IRE) – Dudeen (IRE)
Runner-up over hurdles at Fontwell in late August, he is capable of winning races. A winning pointer, he will go chasing later on but will stay over hurdles for the time being. Yet to race beyond two and a half miles under Rules, he will stay three miles eventually.

POP THE CORK 4 b g Harbour Watch (IRE) – Gospel Music
Only a four year old, he is another who will remain over hurdles having won at Uttoxeter last Autumn. Runner-up a couple of times at Perth and Warwick, he will be campaigned in two miles handicap hurdles.

PRINCE ESCALUS (IRE) 5 b g Jeremy (USA) – So You Said (IRE)
An eight lengths winner of his only Irish point-to-point when trained by Colin Bowe, he had his first run for us in a hot bumper at Newbury in January finishing ninth. I like him and we will campaign him in two and a half miles novice hurdles.

QUARENTA (FR) 8 bb g Voix Du Nord (FR) – Negresse De Cuta (FR)
A nice horse and he is in good form at home following his summer break. He won over fences at Fontwell in December before finishing runner-up at Kempton over Christmas. Three miles handicap chases will be on his agenda once again and I hope he can pick one or two up during the season.

QUARTZ DU RHEU (FR) 5 br g Konig Turf (GER) – Lady Akara (FR)
Joined us during the summer and he is a nice horse who is rated 132 over hurdles. Twice a winner in Ireland last season, he also ran well in a Grade 2 novice over three miles at Limerick over Christmas. We haven't done a lot with him, but he will be going novice chasing.

RABSKI (IRE) 4 b g Beat Hollow – Scarlet Feather (IRE)
Bought at the Goffs Land Rover Sale last year, he is a well related unraced horse who will run in a bumper before going hurdling.

RED MAPLE (IRE) 4 b g Sholokhov (IRE) – Champagne Ruby (IRE)
Another nice unraced four year old who has pleased us at home. We will give him a run in a bumper and decide whether to send him over hurdles.

SEATON CAREW (IRE) 6 b m Getaway (GER) – Millys Gesture (IRE)
A lovely mare who won a bumper at Wetherby but then missed the whole of last season. Back in action in another bumper at Southwell in early September, she stayed on nicely in fourth and will go hurdling now. She will be suited by mares' novice hurdles over two and a half miles.

SHANTOU'S MELODY (IRE) 4 b g Shantou (USA) – Glens Melody (IRE)
Bought at the Goffs Landrover Sale last year, he is the first foal of dual Grade 1 and Cheltenham Festival winning mare Glens Melody and is a lovely horse. He goes well at home and I like him. He is another who will start in a bumper and we will go from there.

SKY PIRATE 7 b g Midnight Legend – Dancingwithbubbles (IRE)
Now belongs to Martin Tedham, who sponsors the yard, having gone through the sales ring at the Goffs UK Summer sale at Doncaster in July. He is a grand horse who was unlucky last season falling four out at Wetherby and then finishing second at both Ascot and Doncaster. I hope he has a change of luck this year because he deserves it. Two and a half miles on decent ground suits him and he could be one for those valuable middle distance handicaps at Cheltenham.

SOARING GLORY (IRE) 5 b g Fame And Glory – Hapeney (IRE)
He's in good form at home and we are looking forward to him over hurdles this season. A horse with a big engine and loads of gears, he won his first two bumpers at Warwick and Ascot before finishing runner-up in a Listed event at the latter track over Christmas. From the family of Direct Route, his form is strong and we will campaign him in two miles novice hurdles.

SPANISH JUMP 4 b g Brave Mansonnien (FR) – Spanish Delight
A grand horse, he is unraced and a chaser in the making. However, he will spend this season in novice hurdles and I think two and a half miles will suit him.

STEADY THE SHIP (IRE) 4 ch g Ocovango – Vinnie's Princess (IRE)
Another nice unraced four year old who I like. A.P.(McCoy) has been schooling him over hurdles but we are likely to give him a run in a bumper first.

TEDHAM 6 b g Shirocco (GER) – Alegralil
We have been schooling him over fences and he loves it. We are therefore looking forward to sending him novice chasing. All being well, he will be running in October and, while he stays further, we will start him off over two or two and a half miles because he isn't slow. Rated 131, he ran well at Haydock in November finishing third in a Grade 3 handicap hurdle over three miles.

THE COMPOSEUR (IRE) 5 b g Mahler – Oscar's Reprieve (IRE)
A winning English pointer, his future is over fences but we will keep him hurdling for now. He benefited from stepping up to three miles when winning at Huntingdon in February and was also suited by the better ground. Long-term, he is a two and a half to three miles chaser in the making but I hope he can win over hurdles again before then.

THE TEXAN (IRE) 4 ch g Ocovango – Buzy Lizzie (IRE)
From the family of Highland Lodge and Closing Ceremony, he only arrived recently so we don't know much about him yet. Still quite weak, he is a chasing type but will have a run in a bumper.

THEME TUNE (IRE) 5 b g Fame And Glory – Supreme Melody (IRE)
From a good family, he shaped well on his debut in a bumper at Warwick finishing sixth. Still weak last year, he is a nice horse for novice hurdles this season. We may start him off over two miles but will be suited by further later on. I like him.

UPTOWN LADY (IRE) 5 b m Milan – Lady Zephyr (IRE)
A fine big mare who finished second in an Irish point-to-point for Denis Murphy in October before we bought her the following month at the Cheltenham Sales. She had a couple of runs in mares' bumpers at Doncaster and Exeter and will go hurdling this season. A chasing type, she is a grand filly with time on her side.

WASDELL DUNDALK (FR) 5 ch g Spirit One (FR) – Linda Queen (FR)
Fourth at Fontwell in August, he isstill a maiden over hurdles. He will be suited by stepping up to two and a half miles and is capable of winning races. Rated 111, we will look for a novices' handicap hurdle.

WHEN YOU'RE READY (IRE) 6 gr g Malinas (GER) – Royale Wheeler (FR)
Ran well when finishing third in a Bumper at Warwick on his first start for us. He has had a couple of runs over hurdles since and we may give him one more before going chasing. Runner-up in an Irish point before joining us, his future is over fences.

TRAINER'S HORSE TO FOLLOW: TEDHAM

David PIPE
Stables: Pond House, Nicholashayne, Wellington, Somerset.
2019/2020: 64 Winners / 341 Runners 19% Prize-Money £734,090
www.davidpipe.com

ADAGIO (GER) 3 b g Wiener Walzer (GER) – Aspidistra (GER)
Trained on the Flat in Germany, he has only raced three times being placed on both occasions as a two year old, including at Deauville in December. An eight lengths winner of a twelve furlongs claimer at Clairefontaine in August, he has been gelded since arriving and is an interesting prospect for juvenile hurdles.

BRINKLEY (FR) 5 gr g Martaline – Royale Majesty (FR)
Joined us two thirds of the way through last season having shown a good level of form when trained by Liz Doyle in Ireland. Third behind Blue Sari at Punchestown in November, he produced a good performance on his first run for us winning a two and a half miles novice hurdle at Newbury in February by fifteen lengths. A strong galloper who handles soft ground, it was an impressive win and we are hoping he can build on that this season. Rated 130, but eligible for novice hurdles until the end of November, he has strengthened up during the summer and is a real winter horse who should stay three miles eventually. We will campaign him over two and a half miles for the time being and hopefully he is an exciting horse for the future.

BUMPY JOHNSON (IRE) 4 ch g Imperial Monarch (IRE) – Country Flora
A new arrival, we don't know a great deal about him yet but he is a nice big horse with a good stride. A faller in his only Irish point-to-point, he appeared to do a bit too much early on during his race. Two and a half miles is likely to suit him over hurdles, but we may run him in a bumper beforehand.

BUSTER EDWARDS (IRE) 7 b g Kalanisi (IRE) – Hot Oscar (IRE)
Won three times over hurdles last season, including a remarkable performance at Haydock when leading close home. Placed in an Irish point, he finished third on his chasing debut at Fontwell in September. He stays all day and handles most types of ground and I envisage him running in those regional Nationals at some stage.

CATCH THE SWALLOWS (IRE) 6 b g Masterofthehorse (IRE) – Nafrah (USA)
Missed the whole of last season but will be back in action this winter and he will be going novice hurdling. Runner-up behind the subsequent Cheltenham Festival bumper second (Appreciate It) in his sole point-to-point in Ireland, he won a bumper at Bangor in January last year on his first start for us. We liked him beforehand and he produced a good performance. He will start off over two miles but will stay further.

CLOVIS DE TEILLEE (FR) 4 gr g No Risk At All (FR) – Sissi De Teille (FR)
From the family of Ramses De Teille, he is a very nice unraced four year old. In training with Colin Bowe last winter, he was due to run in an Irish point-to-point but the season was cut short. Colin reportedly liked him a lot and he has been bought by the Angove Family. He will start off in a bumper and is hopefully a nice youngster to look forward to.

CROSSING LINES (IRE) 6 b g Jeremy (USA) – Coco Opera (IRE)
An impressive winner of two of his three starts in Irish point-to-points, he suffered an injury during the second half of last season and therefore won't be running until after Christmas. A strong galloper, he likes soft ground and stays well.

DUC DE BEAUCHENE (FR) 7 b g Saddler Maker (IRE) – Quatia D'Angron (FR)
A fine big horse, he didn't surprise us when winning at Cheltenham's November meeting on his reappearance. However, we were disappointed with him in his two subsequent starts because we thought he would continue to progress. Given a break since his run at Wincanton in March, I hope he will improve this season, but it hasn't been decided whether he will continue over hurdles or go chasing. Two and a half miles suits him, but I will be surprised if he doesn't stay three miles.

EAMON AN CNOIC (IRE) 9 b g Westerner – Nutmeg Tune (IRE)
A five times winner, he has been a good horse for us, but I thought he may have scaled even greater heights. His wind has caught him out over the years, but he still ran some decent races in defeat last season, including when finishing runner-up at Cheltenham in December. Two or two and a half miles on soft ground is ideal and, given his age, he could be contesting veterans' chases at some stage in the near future, although they tend to be over longer distances.

EDEN DU HOUX (FR) 6 b g Irish Wells (FR) – Maralypha (FR)
Unbeaten in bumpers, including a Listed event at Ascot the previous season, he didn't quite progress as much as we hoped over hurdles last winter. We operated on his wind after his run at Cheltenham in November and he won narrowly at Chepstow next time. He then contested a valuable handicap hurdle at Ascot but ran a strange race. He looked like dropping away but then stayed on at the finish. Fourth in the rescheduled EBF Final at Kempton last time, we are hoping there is more to come from him, especially over fences. I think he wants two and a half miles plus.

ELAN DE BALME (FR) 6 b g Cachet Noir (USA) – Jebarde Rederie (FR)
Twice a winner over fences in France, he was disappointing in both his runs for us at Wincanton and Huntingdon. It is often the case when horses from France arrive in the UK halfway through the season it takes a while for them to acclimatise. We have operated on his wind since his last run and given him a summer break. His work at home has been decent, so hopefully he can reproduce it on the track this season. The handicapper has dropped him a few pounds, which is a help. In terms of trip, his two runs came over two and a half and three miles, but he wasn't seeing out his races.

EXTRA MAG (FR) 6 b g Kapgarde (FR) – Qrystale Mag (FR)
Back in work having missed last season, he has done nothing wrong during his short career. A winner on the Flat in France, he has only raced three times over hurdles winning at Exeter and finishing runner-up behind Precious Cargo at Kempton conceding seven pounds. He was due to contest the Imperial Cup before he suffered an injury, hence he missed last year. The time off won't have done him any harm and he is still only six years old. We will start him off over hurdles and, while he will stay further in due course, two miles on slow ground suits him.

FIRST LORD DE CUET (FR) 6 gr g Lord Du Sud (FR) – Alyce (FR)

A winning Irish pointer, he is a light framed horse who doesn't eat a lot. Fourth in a decent race at Wincanton on his hurdles debut, he then won at Southwell. Narrowly beaten at Haydock over Christmas, he appears to be on a workable mark and will have another run in a handicap hurdle before we decide whether to go over fences. I think two and a half miles is his trip.

GABRIELLE DU SEUIL (FR) 4 b f Cokoriko (FR) – Marie Du Seuil (FR)

Fourth on both her starts over hurdles in France, she was in training with us last season but never raced. Owned by Nick Shutts, the summer off has done her the world of good, strengthening up in the process. She has been given a mark in the mid-120s but is still a novice, so we have plenty of options. Quite keen when she first arrived, she has settled down since and I like her. We will start her off over two miles.

GERICAULT ROQUE (FR) 4 b g Montmartre (FR) – Nijinska Delaroque (FR)

Fourth in his only Irish point, he was very unlucky having been nearly brought down at the third last. He did well to finish as close as he did and is a nice big horse who moves well. Bought in the spring, he is likely to run in a bumper in the Autumn.

GLEN VINE 6 ch g Robin Des Champs (FR) – Gaspara (FR)

From a family we know very well being out of Gaspara who completed the Imperial Cup/ Cheltenham Festival double in 2007, he is another who missed last season but is back in work. Runner-up in a bumper at Worcester, he didn't perform as well as we hoped in two starts over hurdles subsequently. He has had his issues but hopefully the time off will have helped him. He will resume in novice hurdles over two and a half miles.

GRANGECLARE GLORY (IRE) 5 b g Fame And Glory – Annies Joy (IRE)

Trained in Ireland by Denis Murphy, he finished fourth in a point-to-point before joining us halfway through last season. He ran in a bumper at Wincanton in March but we were not sure about his wind beforehand. Having run disappointingly, we decided to give him a breathing operation and hopefully he can show what he is capable of. He is a lovely big strong horse, who may have another run in a bumper before going hurdling.

HOME FARM HOUSE (IRE) 5 bl m Winged Love (IRE) – Recession Lass (IRE)

Bought on behalf of Wayne Clifford at the Cheltenham February Sale, she battled on well to win her only point-to-point in Ireland a few weeks earlier. She has summered well and we may give her a run in a bumper before going hurdling. She looks a stayer.

HUGO N'TAZ 9 b g Kayf Tara – Ryde To Arms

An old fashioned chasing type, he came from Ireland in the Autumn and has only raced twice for us. We operated on his wind and he was only just ready to run when winning the Lincolnshire National at Market Rasen on Boxing Day. It was therefore a decent effort and he proved he is an out and out galloper who stays all day. He didn't run his race next time at Exeter but we will be aiming him at the regional Nationals throughout the season.

INDUNO (IRE) 6 b g Flemensfirth (USA) – Vast Consumption (IRE)

He has always worked like a good horse at home and I am hoping he is on a decent mark. An impressive winner of a bumper at Ffos Las on his reappearance, he then won over hurdles at Sedgefield. Only third at the same track last time, we have treated him for ulcers since and given him plenty of time off. There is room for improvement with his jumping because he tended to look about a bit. He is in good form at home and we will look to start him off in a two and a half miles handicap hurdle.

ISRAEL CHAMP (IRE) 5 b g Milan – La Dariska (FR)

A high-class bumper horse last season, he produced two very good performances to win Listed events at Cheltenham and Ascot. Only sixth on his debut for us at Worcester, we were hoping he would win that day but I may have left him a bit short. However, he made amends next time at Cheltenham and it wasn't a surprise. I thought he produced an even better effort at Ascot beating six previous winners and conceding weight all round. Things didn't happen for him in the Cheltenham Festival bumper but we thought he had an underlying issue with his breathing, which has been corrected with surgery during the summer. He is in great form at home and he ought to develop into an exciting novice hurdler. A big strong horse who is very much a chaser in the making, he has always been a good work horse since arriving from Ireland. We will start him off over two miles.

KEPAGGE (IRE) 6 b g Getaway (GER) – Miracle Lady

Unbeaten in three runs for us since coming over from Ireland, where he fell in a point-to-point. I thought it was a good performance to win his bumper at Chepstow in November making all the running. Switched to hurdles, he made heavy weather of winning when odds on at Leicester but produced a much better effort at Doncaster last time winning by nine lengths. He is another who has undergone surgery on his wind and we will run him in a handicap hurdle and then decide whether to go over fences. His mark looks workable but he is a future chaser.

KING'S SOCKS (FR) 8 b g King's Best (USA) – Alexandrina (GER)

Absent since running in the BetVictor Gold Cup at Cheltenham a couple of years ago, he is a talented horse who had some smart form in France but has been plagued with leg problems. Runner-up in a Grade 1 hurdle at Auteuil behind Footpad, he is OK at the moment but is due to have his leg scanned again. If we can keep him sound and he stands training, it would be nice to think he could start to make up for lost time.

LADYKILLER (GER) 4 ch g Kamsin (GER) – Lady Jacamira (GER)

Rated 106 on the Flat in Germany, he won four of his eight starts, including Listed and Group 3 events. He joined us in the spring and we have gelded him and he has had a long break. We have schooled him over hurdles and he finished third at Southwell in early September. A stayer on the Flat, he is quite keen and free going but we are teaching him to settle.

LEGAL HISTORY (IRE) 5 b g Lawman (FR) – Nina Celebre (IRE)

Did well a couple of seasons ago winning twice and finishing runner-up in a Listed handicap hurdle at Market Rasen. He is back in work following a spell on the sidelines and, while we may give him a run on the Flat, he will continue in the decent two miles handicap hurdles, although he doesn't want the ground too soft.

LE GRAND ROCHER (FR) 4 b g Saint Des Saints (FR) – Belle Du Roi (FR)

A lovely big four year old, he is a brute of a horse who joined us during the summer. A full-brother to Grade 1 winning former stablemate Le Rocher, we have operated on his wind and he goes nicely at home. Third behind Goshen at Fontwell in November, he was beaten a long way but is lightly raced and open to improvement. Yet to race beyond two miles, he is bred to stay further and will make a lovely chaser eventually. He wants some cut in the ground because he is such a big horse.

LEONCAVALLO (IRE) 8 br g Cape Cross (IRE) – Nafura

He joined us earlier this year and is a cracking horse who is versatile in terms of trip. Unlucky not to win on the Flat at Sandown in June on his first start for us, he was beaten a nose. Switched to fences at Stratford the following month, he appreciated the step up in trip and won well. Not the biggest, he has his own way of jumping but it was effective and he won by thirteen lengths. He has won on the Flat at Haydock since. There are plenty of options for him both on the Flat and over fences and we are delighted to be training him.

MAGGIES MOGUL (IRE) 4 b f Valirann (FR) – Grangeclare Gold (IRE)
By a new sire, she produced a nice performance to win her only Irish point-to-point in March for Colin Bowe. She isn't over big, but I like her and she has summered well. Only four, she will run in a mares' bumper in the Autumn.

MAIN FACT (USA) 7 b g Blame (USA) – Reflections
Bought for £6,000 a couple of years ago, he was a revelation last season winning five times with his official rating rising from 104 to 147. He has formed a great alliance with Fergus Gillard and he belongs to first time owners. His first three victories were gained over two miles and then we decided to step him up to two and a half miles in a valuable handicap hurdle at Uttoxeter in March and he bolted up by fifteen lengths. Raised fifteen pounds since, he loves soft ground and, while he is quirky and it is going to be much tougher this season, he could improve again. We will aim him at the good two and two and a half miles handicap hurdles with the Welsh Champion Hurdle at Ffos Las (18th October) a possibility. We also have the option of reverting to the Flat, for which he is rated 60.

MAJOR ROBINSON (IRE) 4 b g Kalanisi (IRE) – Annalore (IRE)
From the family of Granville Again and Morley Street, he battled on well to win a bumper at Thurles in March for Stuart Crawford. The trainer's brother Steven previously worked for us and he recommended we buy him. Not the biggest, he has settled in well and will either run in a bumper or straight over hurdles.

MAKE ME A BELIEVER (IRE) 5 br g Presenting – Kiltiernan Robin (IRE)
A half-brother to King Roland, he fell in his only Irish point but produced a good effort to win a bumper at Chepstow in October on his first run for us. Unfortunately, he incurred an injury which has been sorted out and we were planning to run him again at the end of the season, but it was cut short. A big lean horse, he has strengthened during the summer and will be suited by going hurdling because I never considered him a bumper horse. Long-term, he will make a smashing chaser. Two and a half miles plus over jumps will be ideal.

MARTINHAL (IRE) 5 b g Westerner – Gweedara (IRE)
Still in contention when falling in his Irish point-to-point when handled by Aidan Fitzgerald, he won well in a bumper at Huntingdon at the beginning of March. A workmanlike type, he isn't flashy but is a nice horse. He will go straight over hurdles with two miles being his trip to start with.

MEEP MEEP MAG (IRE) 6 b m Getaway (GER) – Deadly Pursuit (IRE)
A winning pointer in Ireland, she isn't overbig but very tough and genuine. Placed in a couple of mares' bumpers at Warwick and Wetherby, she chased home subsequent Grade 2 winner Clondaw Caitlin at the latter track. She then went one better in another mares' bumper at Sedgefield on Boxing Day. Unfortunately, she incurred an injury during the race and therefore missed the remainder of the season. The time off has benefited her though and I hope she will make her mark in mares' novice hurdles this winter. We may start her off over two miles on soft ground, but she is a staying type who will go up in trip later on.

NEW AGE DAWNING (IRE) 6 ch g Stowaway – Captain Supreme (IRE)
A nice old fashioned chasing type for the future, he was runner-up in his only Irish point and has done nothing wrong in three starts for us. A bumper winner at Exeter, he also won over hurdles at Chepstow but suffered a leg injury and missed the whole of last season. If we can keep him in one piece, he could develop into a decent staying novice chaser who handles soft ground.

NIGHT EDITION (FR) 4 b g Authorized (IRE) – Night Serenade (IRE)
Successful on the Flat in France, we bought him cheaply at the Arqana Sale in July last year. He didn't make his hurdles debut until December, due to a few minor hold ups, but he progressed with each run. Runner-up in a Grade 2 juvenile hurdle at Cheltenham in January, he then won snugly at Ludlow. I thought he ran a stormer to finish a length second in the Boodles Juvenile Hurdle at the Festival. We may give him a run on the Flat because he is only rated 70 before aiming him at the top two mile handicap hurdles. The valuable handicap at Ascot (formerly the Ladbrokes Hurdle) before Christmas (19th December) is a likely target.

NORDIC COMBINED (IRE) 6 b g Haafhd – Chilly Filly (IRE)
It took him a while to get his head in front but he deserved his first win over hurdles at Taunton in March. Talented but quirky, he likes soft ground and two miles appears to suit him, although I hope he will stay further. Rated 131, he has run some good races in defeat and we are hoping he can build on his victory last time.

PANIC ATTACK (IRE) 4 b f Canford Cliffs (IRE) – Toto Corde Meo (IRE)
A fine big mare who won a Listed mares' bumper at Market Rasen in January on her debut for Willie Mullins. Bought privately, she contested the Festival bumper in March on her first run for us. She hadn't been with us long and never ran her race at Cheltenham. Given a break since, she has summered well and strengthened up and her schooling has gone to plan. We may try her in a novice/maiden on the Flat before going hurdling.

POKER PLAY (FR) 7 ch g Martaline – Becquarette (FR)
Produced a good performance to win over fences at Ffos Las on his reappearance. However, he failed to progress in three subsequent starts, although he was highly tried. A horse with a high knee action, he loves soft ground and we will be aiming him at two and a half miles handicap chases. There is also a strong possibility we will take him to France at some stage because of the better prize-money.

QUEENS CAVE (IRE) 7 b m Court Cave (IRE) – Shuilan (IRE)
A decent mare who won over hurdles at Exeter in November before finishing fifth behind the subsequent Coral Cup winner (Dame De Compagnie) at Cheltenham in December. She wasn't quite seeing out her races, so we decided to operate on her wind and hopefully there is more to come. We may give her another run over hurdles before going chasing. Effective over two or two and a half miles, I think she would stay any trip.

RAMSES DE TEILLEE (FR) 8 gr g Martaline – Princesse D'Orton (FR)
A cracking horse and one of our flagbearers. Still only eight, he won three times over hurdles last season, including a couple of Grade 2 events at Doncaster and Haydock. Rated 149 over hurdles and fences, it will be tougher this time around but we may take him to France because there could be more opportunities over there. We could also consider the Becher Chase at Aintree (5th December) and it wouldn't surprise me if he got an entry in the Grand National once again.

REMASTERED 7 ch g Network (GER) – Cathodine Cayras (FR)
Placed three times over hurdles, it was frustrating that he failed to get his head in front last season. Third behind Main Fact at Uttoxeter last time, he is a fine big horse who loves soft ground. The plan is to send him over fences and I could see him lining up in the National Hunt Chase at the Cheltenham Festival in March.

SEXY LOT (GER) 4 b f Camelot – Saldennahe (GER)
She is a nice filly who has strengthened up during the summer. Fourth on her first start over hurdles at Exeter in January, she was runner-up at Newton Abbot in August. Rated 94, we have the option of running her in mares' novice hurdles or a novices' handicap hurdle.

SIRUH DU LAC (FR) 7 b g Turgeon (USA) – Margerie (FR)
He is a very nice addition to the team at Pond House. A former Cheltenham Festival winner, he was in the process of running well in the same race (Brown Advisory & Merriebelle Stable Plate) when falling at the second last in March. He joined us in the summer and, having operated on his wind, it is a case of starting from scratch but we know he is a good horse with some excellent form. We will consider races such as the Haldon Gold Cup at Exeter (3rd November) or BetVictor Gold Cup at Cheltenham (14th November). Yet to race beyond two and a half miles, there is a possibility he will stay further, too.

THINKING (IRE) 5 b g So You Think (NZ) – Laetoli (ITY)
Yet to run for us, his owner Nick Shutts has been very patient. He won his only start over hurdles during the summer of 2018, but had a leg injury soon afterwards. He was due to run last season but then the coronavirus intervened. However, he is a horse with a lot of potential and has a high knee action suggesting he will be suited by slow ground. Rated 132, he will start off in a handicap hurdle.

UMBRIGADO (IRE) 6 br g Stowaway – Dame O'Neill (IRE)
A dual winner over hurdles as a novice, he didn't achieve what we hoped last season. Fifth in a valuable handicap hurdle at Haydock, he travelled strongly but didn't appear to stay three miles and then he ran well in the Martin Pipe Conditional Jockeys' Handicap Hurdle at the Festival. Not beaten far, he may go novice chasing and I would like to run him on better ground. A good traveller, he may prove at his best over two and a half miles.

TRAINER'S HORSE TO FOLLOW: GERICAULT ROQUE

Nicky RICHARDS
Stables: Rectory Farm, Greystoke, Penrith, Cumbria.
2019/2020: 34 Winners / 183 Runners 19% Prize-Money £352,789
www.nickyrichardsracing.com

AMBEROSE 7 ch m Sulamani (IRE) – Miss Nellie (IRE)
She won a mares' handicap hurdle at Carlisle in November and finished second a couple of times at Newcastle and Doncaster. We will probably keep her over hurdles this season and aim her at some of the bonus races, which have been introduced for British bred mares. Despite the fact she won over two miles one at Carlisle, I think two and a half miles is ideal.

BIG BAD BEAR (IRE) 6 br g Jeremy (USA) – Our Polly (IRE)
Had a decent year over hurdles finishing third at Aintree in October before winning twice at Wetherby and Carlisle. His only disappointing run came at Wetherby in a handicap hurdle in January and we don't know why. It was terrible ground and he was never going at any stage. A few of our horses weren't at their best around that time, which may explain his run, but it was too bad to be true. We were waiting for some better ground in the spring and the plan was to run him again in April but we didn't get the opportunity. We are going to school him over fences and, if that goes to plan, he will go novice chasing. Not the biggest, he has always jumped hurdles well and, while we may start him off over two miles, we know he stays further.

BLAKERIGG (IRE) 9 b g Presenting – Azalea (IRE)
Runner-up at Ayr in November, he suffered a tendon injury and hasn't raced since. Back in work, he will hopefully be running around December time and will continue in two and a half miles plus handicap chases. He seems to be on a competitive mark, although I don't think he wants it too soft.

CAIUS MARCIUS (IRE) 9 b g King's Theatre (IRE) – Ain't Misbehavin (IRE)
He's been a grand horse for us winning a bumper, six times over hurdles and he took well to chasing winning four last season. The key to him is decent ground but he isn't the easiest to place now with his ratings. Fourth over fences at Cheltenham in October, it wasn't a bad run considering he made two bad mistakes early on and the ground was soft enough. We switch him back to hurdles this summer and he was placed three times in competitive handicaps at Market Rasen, Southwell and Perth. Not the biggest, he has been very consistent and we will mix and match between hurdles and fences until he has his usual winter break before returning in the spring.

CASTLE RUSHEN (IRE) 5 b g Fame And Glory – Rosie Suspect (IRE)
A half-brother to Marown, he is a very nice horse who did everything we expected on his debut in a bumper at Ayr in January. Gordon Elliott trained the second and third and I know the runner-up was well fancied. He won in good style and we thought he would do the same under a penalty a couple of months later. Unfortunately, it turned out to be a messy race, which developed into a sprint in the homestraight and he finished second. He has returned from his summer break looking very well and will go straight over hurdles. We will probably start him off in a National Hunt novices' hurdle over two miles before stepping up in trip later on.

CATHEL'S STAR 7 ch g Malinas (GER) – Hand Inn Glove
Has only raced twice for us having spent along time on the sidelines. Fourth at Doncaster over two and a half miles in December, I thought he ran well considering he hadn't raced for so long. He ran on at the finish so we stepped him up to three miles next time at the same track, but I am not convinced he stayed. Still a maiden over hurdles, he appears to be on a workable mark, so will find a suitable novices' handicap hurdle over two and a half miles. He is a big horse and will jump fences in time.

CHAPEL STILE (IRE) 8 b g Scorpion (IRE) – Peggy Cullen (IRE)
A horse with a lot of ability, he stays well with stamina being his strong suit. He ran well on his first two starts over fences finishing third at Carlisle in November before winning at the same venue next time. His stamina really came into play that day, leading close home. We then stepped him up in class and distance in the Grade 2 Towton Novices' Chase at Wetherby, but he never lifted a leg and didn't appear to be enjoying it. Pulled early on, he hasn't raced since and we might switch him back to hurdles. He has had a long break and seems to be in good form at home.

CHIDSWELL (IRE) 11 b g Gold Well – Manacured (IRE)
He is a grand horse who ran two cracking races last season. Runner-up at Kelso in December, I was delighted with his run in the Listed *Skybet* Chase at Doncaster the following month finishing third. He was being primed for another crack at the Scottish National in the spring but that never materialised. Despite his age, he retains plenty of ability and I am sure he will continue to be competitive in good staying handicaps. We have the option of running him in veterans' chases, too, and we will consider races like the *Skybet* Chase once again, plus the Grimthorpe Handicap Chase (withdrawn from last season due to heavy ground) at Doncaster.

DUKE OF NAVAN (IRE) 12 bb g Presenting – Greenfieldflyer (IRE)
Has been a smashing horse for us over the years winning six races and earning over £125,000 in prize-money. Placed a couple of times at Doncaster and Musselburgh last season, he appreciates tidy ground nowadays and wants a strongly run two miles. A big powerful horse who can take a strong hold in his races, he takes a bit of getting fit, but the handicapper has dropped him a few pounds and it would be nice if we can get another good day out of him.

FLY BY MILAN (IRE) 5 b g Milan – So Proper (IRE)
Bought at the Tattersalls Ireland August Sale as a three year old, he is a lovely unraced horse from the family of Island Chief and Chomba Womba. Owned by Langdale Bloodstock, he would have made his debut last spring but never got the chance. He has been given plenty of time and is a grand horse to look forward to in bumpers this Autumn.

GEGE VILLE (FR) 4 b g Protektor (GER) – Auvloo Ville (FR)
Another nice unraced four year old by a sire I like. We bought him at the Goffs Landrover Sale in Ireland last year and, in normal circumstances, he would have had a racecourse gallop last spring. However, he is all schooled up ready to run in a bumper in the Autumn. I like him.

GLENDUFF (IRE) 6 b g Gold Well – Last of The Bunch
From the family of Better Times Ahead and a half-brother to Cheltenham Festival bumper winner Relegate, he is a lovely big horse owned by Mr Hemmings. Having shown plenty of promise in his two bumpers, he won well on his hurdles debut at Carlisle in November. We then ran him in The French Furze Novices' Hurdle at Newcastle later the same month but he got stuck in the mud. Given a break, I was pleased with his run at Doncaster in March staying on well in third and I don't think it was a bad race either. We had waited for the better ground and the intention was to run him again during the spring. A great big long striding horse, he will be schooled over fences with a view to going novice chasing. He is bred to stay well but isn't slow either. I would think he will start off over two and a half miles.

GLINGER FLAME (IRE) 8 ro g Daylami (IRE) – Titian Flame (IRE)
Did well over hurdles the previous season winning three successive races. We sent him chasing last winter and I thought he looked good when winning at Ayr in January. Admittedly, his task was made easier when two horses fell at the fourth last, but I think he would have won in any case. We then took him at Haydock but his jumping was a bit deliberate and I am not sure he was enjoying it. Rather like Chapel Stile, we may bring him back over hurdles because he looked useful as a novice and they may suit him better. Trips around two or two and a half miles suit him, although he may get further, if necessary.

GLITTERING LOVE (IRE) 8 b g Winged Love (IRE) – Glittering Image (IRE)
Now belongs to The Fife Boys having been bought from Clare and Paul Rooney, who are sadly no longer having National Hunt horses in training. Consistent, he fell at Newcastle on his reappearance when going well before finishing third at the same track in January. The plan was to go back there for the Eider Chase the following month but that was abandoned. We gave him a spin over hurdles at Carlisle in March and, while he ran well in second, he isn't a hurdler. Still only eight, he stays well and loves soft ground and we will aim him at races such as the Borders National at Kelso (6th December) and Eider Chase in February.

GLORIOUS SPIRIT 5 b m Fame And Glory – Mrs Dempsey (IRE)
A nice unraced mare who is a half-sister to Innisfree Spirit, who has sadly been retired. Still a bit weak last year, we have given her time to mature and she is one to look forward to in mares' bumpers this Autumn.

GUITAR PETE (IRE) 10 gr g Dark Angel (IRE) – Innishmore (IRE)
He has been a grand horse for us and his owners Mr and Mrs Sloan. We were delighted with his second win in the Listed handicap chase at Wetherby in November when he beat the subsequent BetVictor Gold Cup winner (Happy Diva). His form tailed off thereafter though and I suspect he was still feeling the effects of his hard race at Wetherby. We have given him a long break since his last run at the Cheltenham Festival and he could be one for the veterans' chases but he owes us nothing.

HOME FIRE 4 b g Frankel – Hot Snap
Bought unraced as a Juddmonte cast off at the Goffs UK Spring Sale at Doncaster last year, he is very well bred and is a big strapping horse who has never stopped growing. We have operated on his wind and he is cantering at the moment. He will run in a bumper in the Autumn and is a nice horse.

KAJAKI (IRE) 7 gr g Mastercraftsman (IRE) – No Quest (IRE)
Joined us last season and is a grand little horse who was placed in both his races. Runner-up behind a well handicapped horse of Jonjo's (Pagero) at Doncaster in December, he was raised six pounds as a result, which was harsh. Third next time at Musselburgh, Brian (Hughes) thought he would prefer better ground so we were waiting to run him in the spring. He will continue in handicap hurdles and I hope he will win one.

KITTY HALL (IRE) 6 b m Fame And Glory – Set In Her Ways (IRE)
She is a decent mare who I like. Third on her debut at Kelso, she looked good when winning next time at Carlisle before finishing sixth at Doncaster on her latest start. Brian (Hughes) came back in afterwards and was disappointed with the ride he gave her. She has grown a lot since and has developed into a big strong mare. For sale, we might give her another run in a bumper before aiming her at mares' novice hurdles. Trips around two or two and a half miles will suit her. She is a nice mare.

LANTY SLEA (IRE) 5 b g Beat Hollow – Catleen (IRE)
A nice youngster who we thought would win first time out at Carlisle in March and he duly did so, although it was a lot closer than we were expecting. Owned by Langdale Bloodstock, he is for sale and is a real National Hunt horse. He jumps like a buck and will go novice hurdling.

LEGAL BEAGLE (IRE) 5 b g Rule of Law (USA) – Knockamullen Girl (IRE)
Half-brother to Carefully Selected, he ran OK on his debut at Ayr last Autumn and Brian (Hughes) thinks he will win races. Given time since, he may run in another bumper and then go hurdling. Two or two and a half miles will be his trip to begin with.

LOOKING WELL (IRE) 11 b g Gold Well – Different Level (IRE)
Missed last season but he is back in work and we are looking forward to seeing him run again. He is a good horse but hasn't had much luck over the years. He was all set to win the Edinburgh National at Musselburgh a couple of years ago when running through the wing at the last and he was going strongly when falling three out in the Borders National at Kelso the same year. We will campaign him in staying handicaps such as the Borders National (6th December) once again and also have a look at the veterans' chases, which are always very competitive.

MAROWN (IRE) 6 b g Milan – Rosie Suspect (IRE)
A lovely big strapping horse who has done nothing wrong winning all three of his starts. Twice a winner over hurdles at Ayr last season, the plan was to run him in the Grade 1 Sefton Novices' Hurdle at Aintree in April. Brian (Hughes) likes him a lot and I think he is a proper one. A great big horse, we might see if they will put on a few intermediate hurdles during the Autumn because he lacks experience. Otherwise, we will school him over fences and go novice chasing. Like all of Mr Hemmings' horses, he was bought to be a chaser.

MAYO STAR (IRE) 8 b Stowaway – Western Whisper (IRE)
Arrived here with an injury and was off the track prior to making a winning return over hurdles at Ayr in January. He then followed up at Newcastle and we were going to run him again in the spring. A half-brother to Grade 1 winner Outlander, he handles desperate ground very well but Brian (Hughes) thinks he will cope with good ground, too. He is another who is likely to go novice chasing.

MISS MILANO (IRE) 5 b m Milan – Dewasentah (IRE)
Still a bit weak last year, she is a nice unraced filly who we purposely have given time. She has worked nicely at home and we will find a mares' bumper for her in October/November.

MURVAGH BEACH (IRE) 5 ch g Doyen (IRE) – Magic Park (IRE)
From the family of Kicking King, I was disappointed with him on his debut at Newcastle because he had shown a fair bit of ability at home. Green before and during the race, he didn't take the preliminaries very well and needs to grow up. We might run him in another bumper.

MY OLD GOLD (IRE) 10 b m Gold Well – Tenbo (IRE)
A good mare who didn't start racing until she was a seven year old. She has won four times for us, including a decent staying handicap chase at Doncaster in December. Fourth and second in veterans' chases at Doncaster and Carlisle respectively since, she will follow a similar campaign and we will have a look at some of the Listed mares' chases, too. A consistent mare, she stays well and handles soft ground.

NELLS SON 5 b g Trans Island – Miss Nellie (IRE)
Half-brother to Amberose and Rubytwo, he ran very well on his only start in a bumper at Doncaster. Beaten a nose, the first two pulled a long way clear of the rest and I would say they are two nice horses. It was a proper race. It won't do his breeding any harm, if he can win a bumper, so I would imagine that's what we will try and do and then go novice hurdling.

NO REGRETS (IRE) 6 b g Presenting – E Mac (IRE)
He wasn't the easiest horse to break in but has ability as he showed when finishing fourth in a bumper at Ayr's Scottish National meeting a couple of seasons ago. Sent hurdling last winter, he wasn't settling in his races and raced too keenly. Returning at Perth in July, I was a bit disappointed he didn't win but he has won twice since at Southwell and Stratford. Raised eleven pounds, he will hopefully continue to progress. He doesn't want the ground too soft and he will stay three miles once he learns to settle properly.

ON A PROMISE (IRE) 8 gr g Definite Article – Silvers Promise (IRE)
Had a good season over hurdles a few years ago but was then off the track for nearly two years. He made his chasing debut at Catterick in February and I thought he ran well considering the trip was on the short side. He kept on in the closing stages and will be suited by a return to longer distances because he stays well.

PADDOCK COTTAGE (IRE) 4 b g Pour Moi (IRE) – Blend
Owned by David Wesley Yates, the plan was for him to make his debut in the Goffs UK Doncaster Sales bumper at Newbury in March but the race never took place. I think he is a nice horse who will make a lovely hurdler. He has done well during the summer and will have a run in an Autumn bumper and then go hurdling.

PARISENCORE (FR) 4 b g Walk In The Park (IRE) – Folk Dancing (FR)
Another nice unraced four year old who we bought at the Tattersalls Ireland August Sale last year. He would have had a racecourse gallop last spring in preparation for a bumper but we were unable to do that. However, he is schooled up and ready to run in the Autumn.

REIVERS LAD 9 b g Alflora (IRE) – Reivers Moon
Has not run since winning on his chasing debut at Newcastle in December 2018, but is back in work. He sustained an injury that day, which is a real shame, because I have always thought he was a good horse. He glided round that day at Newcastle. Two miles is his trip and he wants some dig in the ground.

RIBBLE VALLEY (IRE) 7 b g Westerner – Miss Greinton (GER)
Has done nothing wrong during his career winning two of his three races in bumpers before going hurdling last season. An easy winner at Hexham in November, I thought he was impressive at Wetherby under a penalty next time. We then ran him a Grade 2 novice hurdle at Ascot before Christmas but he spoilt his chance by getting lit up and pulling hard during the race. He fell in a hole after the second last and the race took a lot out of him, both mentally and physically. We were going to bring him back in the spring and either run in the Grade 1 novice hurdle at Aintree or aim him at the Scottish Champion Hurdle at Ayr. We gave him a racecourse gallop after his run at Ascot and he worked like a dream. I would therefore put a line through that run. We were thinking of sending him chasing but he lacks jumping experience. Therefore we will give him another run over hurdles and then go for the Grade 1 Fighting Fifth Hurdle at Newcastle (28th November).

SAUCE OF LIFE (IRE) 5 b g Califet (FR) – Salsaparilla (FR)
Purchased at Tattersalls Ireland August Sale as a three year old, he is a nice horse who would have run in a bumper in the spring. He will be ready to go in the Autumn.

SHE'S A ROCCA (IRE) 5 b m Shirocco (GER) – Hannigan's Lodger (IRE)
Won on her debut in a mares' bumper at Ayr in November, but I made the mistake of running her back too quick next time at Huntingdon. I thought she ran well on her hurdles bow at Perth during the summer because another horse kicked a hurdle down and it swung back into her and nearly knocked Brian (Hughes) out of the saddle. It took her a while to get back into the race before running on at the finish. She will have no trouble staying two and a half miles.

SIMPLY NED (IRE) 13 b g Fruits of Love (USA) – Bishop Lass (IRE)
He has been a wonderful horse for us and owes us nothing. Very consistent and durable, we will take it race by race but I would expect he will follow a similar programme starting at Kelso (4th October) followed by the Shloer Chase at Cheltenham (15th November). Third in the latter event last year, he has run in the last six renewals, which is some achievement. Fourth in the Grade 1 at Leopardstown over Christmas, which he has won twice already, his jockey Mark Walsh felt the ground was too soft for him. He was also fourth in the Game Spirit Chase at Newbury in February behind Altior and ran a cracker. He received a great reception afterwards, too, which was very nice.

SKIDDAW TARA 6 b g Kayf Tara – Bob Back's Lady (IRE)
Consistent last season, he was placed a couple of times at Ayr and Carlisle before beating Glittering Love at the latter track in March. A proper old fashioned chasing type, he isn't the quickest but stays well. He will go over fences and we will campaign him over three miles.

SOFT RISK (FR) 4 b g My Risk (FR) – Douce Ambiance (FR)
Unraced, he is a great big four year old who belongs to James Westoll. We bought him last year at the Goffs UK Spring Sale at Doncaster and he will tell us when he is ready to start. He is a smashing horse who will probably run in a bumper after Christmas.

TAKINGRISKS (IRE) 11 b g Golden Tornado (IRE) – Downtown Rosie (IRE)
Another lovely horse who owes us nothing winning the Scottish National a couple of years ago and the Listed Rehearsal Chase at Newcastle in November. We were aiming him at the Grand National last spring and I fear he may have missed his chance now. We may be better aiming him at veterans' chases and the Scottish National once again, but we will see what his owner wants to do.

TFOU (FR) b g Authorized (IRE) – Fire Moon Julie (FR)
A fantastic looking horse who we bought at the Goffs Land Rover Sale as a three year old. If looks are anything to go by, he will have no trouble winning races. Every jockey who has ridden him at home loves him and we will start him off in a bumper in the Autumn. He is a grand horse.

UNCLE ALASTAIR 8 b g Midnight Legend – Cyd Charisse
Now owned by Eddie Melville and Partners, he hasn't run since finishing second behind Vinndication in a novices' chase at Carlisle nearly two years ago. We may have got him back at the end of last season but the time off won't have done him any harm. All being well, he will be back in action around December time and we will educate him in novice chases and hope he retains all his ability.

UNIVERSAL FOLLY 5 b g Universal (IRE) – Madam Jolie (IRE)
Ran well on his first start in a bumper at Sedgefield in December finishing a close second. He went back there a month later but got stuck in the mud. He still ran respectably in fourth and is ready to go novice hurdling now. His schooling has gone well and we will campaign him over two and two and a half miles.

WETLANDS (IRE) 5 b g Westerner – Un Jour D Ete (FR)
Another lovely young horse owned by Mr Hemmings, he is very much a chaser in the making. He did nothing wrong in two bumpers last season finishing fourth on his debut at Newcastle in November before winning at the same track in March. We have schooled him over hurdles and he jumps very well. We will educate him over hurdles this season before he goes chasing in twelve months time. Although he may start off over two miles, he will have no trouble staying two and a half miles. He is a nice horse.

Unnamed 4 b g Shantou (USA) – Guydus (IRE)
Bought at the Goffs Land Rover Sale last year, he is another who will start in a bumper in October/November. A nice horse owned by Jimmy Fyffe, he would have had a racecourse gallop in the spring in a normal year.

TRAINER'S HORSE TO FOLLOW: WETLANDS

AHEAD ON THE FLAT 2021

Please see page 195

The *Top 40 Prospects* in the 2020 version included
AL AASY (Group 3 Bahrain Trophy),
FAR ABOVE (Group 3 Palace House Stakes),
NAZEEF (3 wins including the Group 1 Falmouth Stakes), ORBAAN (25/1),
PALACE PIER (Group 1 St James's Palace Stakes& Prix Jacques Le Marois),
PATRICK SARSFIELD (3 wins)
TOP RANK (Group 3 Superior Mile)

"Nazeef is another four year old filly who resides at Clarehaven Stables and, while she has yet to tackle a Listed or Group race, it is only a matter of time before the daughter of Invincible Spirit heads down that route. Indeed, she looks tailormade for the Group 2 Duke of Cambridge Stakes at Royal Ascot (17th June)." **WON the Duke of Cambridge Stakes @ 100/30**

"Located at Owning Hill near Piltown in County Kilkenny, O'Brien, who rode six Irish Classic winners and four in the UK, has a strong team of older horses for 2020. With an official rating of 86, the lightly raced Patrick Sarsfield is by no means the highest rated older horse in the yard but he looks one of the best handicapped inmates, especially having only raced twice for his current connections." **PATRICK SARSFIELD won this first three races in 2020 with his official rating climbing from 86 to 109.**

Talking Trainers

"A beautifully bred filly, she is a half-sister to Breeders' Cup winner Juvenile winner Line of Duty. Her homework has always been very good but it has taken her along time for the penny to drop. She was unlucky at Kempton one day and then ran well at Newmarket before getting her head in front at Newcastle last time. She won nicely and I am hoping she might develop into a Sandringham Handicap contender at Royal Ascot (17th June)." **Charlie FELLOWES – ONASSIS – WON the Sandringham Handicap @ 33/1**

"A lovely kind horse who won at Windsor in April before finishing a short head second in the London Gold Cup behind subsequent dual Group 2 winner Headman. Drawn wide at Royal Ascot in the King George V Handicap, he never got involved before being placed at Goodwood and Haydock. We have gelded him during the winter and he is moving great. He doesn't want firm ground and a mile and a quarter is his trip. Races such as the John Smith's Cup at York (11th July) will be on his agenda." **William HAGGAS discussing SINJAARI – WON the John Smith's Cup at York @ 11/1**

"He is delicate hence he has only raced half a dozen times but he is very talented, too, and has a lot of ability. A comfortable winner at Doncaster on his reappearance, he was then narrowly beaten in the Jorvik Handicap at York's Dante meeting. Third in the Duke of Edinburgh Stakes at Royal Ascot, I thought he was unlucky because he didn't get the clearest of runs and wasn't beaten far. I think he will stay beyond a mile and a half and we are hoping he could develop into a Skybet Eborhorse (22nd August)." **Roger VARIAN discussing FUJAIRA PRINCE – WON the Skybet Ebor @ 11/2**

www.mhpublications.co.uk

CHANGING CODES

The following feature highlights a selection of Flat horses set to go jumping for the first time this winter who will, hopefully, prove profitable to follow.

Joseph O'Brien looks to have a strong team of juvenile hurdlers for the winter and I am hoping he is going to take charge of his father's **DAWN RISING**. A three year old by Galileo and a full-brother to last year's Irish Derby winner Sovereign, he is also a younger sibling of Triplicate, who Joseph trained to win twice over timber. He has only raced four times on the Flat winning a twelve furlongs maiden at Limerick (Good) in June by a dozen lengths. His jockey Wayne Lordan commented afterwards: **"He's a lovely, big, staying horse who had a very good run at the Curragh the last day. He was very idle in front and I know we won by 12 lengths, but you never know when there's something coming from behind you and the way he was rolling around, I just wanted to keep the revs up. He won with plenty in hand at the end."** Stepping up in class ten days later, he was an excellent second behind the highly regarded Al Aasy in the Group 3 Bahrain Trophy at Newmarket (1m 5f : Good/Soft). Attempting to make all, he got warm beforehand and, while he couldn't match the winner's turn of foot late on, he stayed on and had the subsequent Group 1 German Oaks winner Miss Yoda six and a half lengths behind him. Significantly, he has been gelded since suggesting a career over obstacles could be in the offing. If sent jumping, he could be a similar type to the ill-fated Grade 1 winning former stablemate Sir Erec and develop into a Triumph Hurdle contender.

DRUID'S ALTAR is another O'Brien inmate set to go juvenile hurdling. A half-brother to five times winning hurdler Waterlord, the gelded son of Mastercraftsman has also only raced four times on the Flat earning an official rating of 84. Four lengths behind *Top 40 Prospects* entry Zanahiyr at Fairyhouse (1m 4f : Good/Yielding) in July, he was then sixth to 142 rated hurdler Mt Leinster in another twelve furlongs maiden at the Galway Festival (Soft). Half a length runner-up behind Golddragon Reef at Bellewstown (1m 4f : Heavy) in late August, he handles cut in the ground and should have no trouble staying two miles over hurdles.

Stablemate **FLYING SCOTSMAN** has unfinished business on the Flat to attend to this Autumn, but it is hoped a jumping career is on his agenda, too. Owned by J.P.McManus, he raced three times for Aidan O'Brien as a juvenile (in the space of three weeks) before being transferred to his son Joseph during the winter/spring. Well held over seven furlongs on his handicap debut at Leopardstown in June, he has improved markedly since winning twice within twenty four hours at the Galway Festival. Stepped up to a mile and a half off a mark of 73, he appreciated the longer trip and slow ground (Soft) to beat Dark Voyager by three lengths. Dropped back to a mile the following day and fitted with cheekpieces for the first time, he led inside the final furlong to win going away by half a length (third has won since) under a six pounds penalty. Rated 88, he will make a cracking hurdler.

DARK VOYAGER may have proved no match for Flying Scotsman at Galway but he returned to the same track five days later and won a 50 – 70 handicap (1m 4f : Soft) by three lengths. Willie Mullins' charge was always going well before running on strongly inside the final furlong. Raised ten pounds since to a mark of 80, he is a progressive type who has come into his own over middle distances. A three year old by Raven's Pass, he is a half-brother to Grade 1 winning juvenile hurdler A Wave of The Sea. Previously owned by the trainer's wife Jackie, he has been subsequently bought by Joe Donnelly with a view to going juvenile hurdling.

His stablemate **MICRO MANAGE** seemingly hasn't been easy to train having only raced four times but there is no mistaking the four year old's ability. The son of Rip Van Winkle beat subsequent Royal Ascot winner South Pacific as a two year old at Tipperary (Soft) and then ran out a twelve lengths winner in a twelve furlongs handicap at the Curragh (Good/Yielding) off a mark of 91 in June last year. Unfortunately, a stress fracture cut short his three year old career and he was gelded, but he returned to action in the Group 3 Irish St Leger Trial at the same track (1m 6f : Good) in August. Absent for 434 days, he was only two and a half lengths in third behind Delphi. He then finished seventh in the Irish St. Leger. Rated 107, he reportedly schooled over hurdles as a two year old and jumps 'brilliantly' according to assistant David Casey. Suited by cut in the ground, he could be a top-class hurdler.

LAYFAYETTE finished a close third behind the aforementioned Flying Scotsman over an extended mile at the Galway Festival (Yielding) in late July. Noel Meade's son of French Navy then stepped up to ten furlongs for the first time at Naas (Soft) in August and stayed on strongly to lead close home off a mark of 84. The 147 rated Galway Hurdle winner Tudor City was a length back in third. Despite the fact he won over five and a half furlongs as a juvenile, he gives the impression he will stay two miles over jumps. Owner Patricia Hunt has had plenty of decent jumpers with Meade, including Graded winners Apache Stronghold, Monksland and Snow Falcon. Related to winning hurdler Praeceps, he was bought for €54,000 at the Goresbridge breeze-ups in May last year.

METIER raced eight times on the Flat for Andy Slattery in Ireland and is rated 88. A six lengths winner of a nine furlongs maiden at Gowran (Yielding/Soft) in August last year, he was runner-up in a ten furlongs handicap at Fairyhouse next time. He rounded off his three year old career by finishing fifth in a premier handicap at Leopardstown (1m 4f : Soft/Heavy) in October before going through the sales ring two days later. Sold for 150,000gns, he joined Harry Fry and was gelded. Entered in the Triumph Hurdle last season, his new connections were unable to get a prep run into him so his jumping debut was delayed until this season. Reported to have schooled very well, he is an exciting prospect.

Alan King has few peers when it comes to juvenile hurdlers and the head of Barbury Castle is understandably relishing the prospect of unleashing **MIDNIGHTS LEGACY** over timber this Autumn. From a family his trainer knows well, the son of Midnight Legend is a full-brother to Giving Back (2 wins) and Midnights' Gift (2), plus a half-brother to Giveaway Glance (4) and Giving Glances (2). Rated 90, he has won three of his five races, including twice at Haydock (10f & 12f) in June. Below par in the Melrose Stakes at York in August, the ground was very testing and he never landed a blow. Good or good to soft ground is ideal and he has schooled proficiently at home.

Owner Michael Ryan will always be associated with the top-class hurdler Al Eile, who won the Aintree Hurdle three times for trainer John Queally. His green and blue silks are currently being carried by the John Oxx trained three year old **MONA'S STAR**. A big strong gelding by Sea The Stars, he has the size for jumping and ploughed through the mud to win a twelve furlongs maiden at Roscommon (Heavy) in August. A two lengths winner, he had been third at Leopardstown (1m 4f : Good) on his previous start. Having only raced a handful of times, he has plenty more to offer, especially if sent hurdling.

It will be interesting to see what Henry De Bromhead can achieve with the former Sir Michael Stoute trained **NASHY**. Rated 75 on the Flat, the son of Camelot remains a maiden but was runner-up over ten furlongs at Kempton in early June. A fine big three year old, his dam was second behind The Fugue in the Group 1 Yorkshire Oaks for Aidan O'Brien. Well bred, he has been gelded and will go juvenile hurdling.

Gary Moore bought **TAMARIS** for 60,000gns at the Tattersalls August Horses in Training Sale this summer. A half-brother to the John Smith's Cup winner Pivoine, he raced four times for Roger Charlton and improved when stepped up in trip. Fourth behind Almighwar (rated 94) and Melrose Stakes winner Coltrane (97) at Kempton (1m 4f) in June, he was a six and a half lengths winner on his handicap debut at Wolverhampton (1m 6f) the following month off a mark of 64. Raised nine pounds since, he has only run once on turf. The West Sussex based handler indicated that the Dansili colt had been bought with a dual purpose career in mind.

ENGLISH POINTERS

My *Racing TV* colleague Jonathan Neesom, one of the finest judges of the English point-to-point scene in the business, has unearthed the likes of **KING ROLAND, SANTINI** and **TEA CLIPPER** amongst others in this feature over recent years. The following is a list of horses who caught his eye last winter and are set to race under Rules for the first time

ADJOURNMENT (IRE) 4 b g Court Cave (IRE) – Cherry Eile (IRE)
British pointing came to an abrupt end in mid March, along with everything else, and Adjournment made his debut on the last weekend of action. A €42,000 three year old, he was beaten less than a length by fellow newcomer Grizzman over two and a half miles at Larkhill, the pair finishing a long way clear of the rest. He was always just inferior to the winner but stayed on stoutly after a final fence mistake. Trained by **Francesca Nimmo**, this four year old should have a future under Rules, if all goes well.

FEDELTA (IRE) 6 b g Flemensfirth (USA) – Old Moon (IRE)
Not the usual precocious type often seen on these pages, this Trevor Hemmings-owned gelding didn't appear until after his sixth birthday, at Larkhill in January from the Francesca Nimmo yard. Having made an efficient winning debut, he was transferred to **Emma Lavelle** and ran well when third in a Ludlow novice hurdle the following month, With a pedigree that is all about stamina, he should be able to repay some of the £115,000 he cost as a three year old in due course.

FREEZING POINT (IRE) 4 b g Arctic Cosmos (USA) – Maisey Down
It's easy to pick holes in the winning debut performance of this four year old at Buckfastleigh in January, over two and a half miles. He won by less than a length, the placed horses failed to win next time and the time was relatively slow. However, he had matters under control in the straight and showed enough for **Dan Skelton** to buy him for £65,000 the following week at the Cheltenham Sales. Out of a half-sister to Grand National winner Earth Summit, Freezing Point looks a potential stayer for racing under Rules.

GOLD CLERMONT (FR) 4 b f Balko (FR) – Une Dame D'Or (FR)
It is difficult to know what to make of this four year old's winning debut at Brocklesby Park in February, where she faced just two rivals in very testing conditions, but she was well on top at the finish. Unsold at £28,000 the following week, this **Tom Lacey**trained filly, a half-sister to a winning hurdler, could well be seen to better effect when tackling stronger opposition.

GRAND KNIGHT (FR) 4 b g Slickly (FR) – La Grande Dame (FR)
A new name in the point training ranks appeared in 2020, with **Ger Costelloe**, the former partner of Rebecca Curtis, making an immediate impact. Grand Knight was heavily supported ahead of his debut in a Larkhill bumper (2 miles), in January, and once he had swept past his rivals to lead three furlongs out, the gamble was in no danger. Bought for €90,000 as a three year old and a half-brother to a French chase winner, Grand Knight's future under Rules should be fascinating to monitor.

Based at Maizey Manor Farm just outside Marlborough, Costelloe commented in late January: **"He is a very nice horse with a very good pedigree. He's a proper horse with Graded potential and everything comes easy to him."**

INDIGO BREEZE (FR) 4 bb g Martaline – Miss Poutine (FR)
This four year old was another to make a winning debut in a point bumper for **Ger Costelloe**. Sent on the long journey to Alnwick in Northumberland in March, he made all and won by a wide margin, although it is doubtful if a coup was landed as the betting market in the Northern pointing area has sadly collapsed in recent seasons. His next appearance was at the Cheltenham sales four days later but he was led out unsold at £140,000. Related to several winners, including the very smart ill-fated Cheltenham Festival winner Brindisi Breeze, this Martaline gelding is one to watch out for when he races under Rules.

KAPHUMOR (FR) 4 b g Kapgarde (FR) – Money Humor (IRE)
The four year old won at Larkhill (3m) on the same day as stable companion Grizzman, and eventually did so with a degree of comfort. Outjumped over the last few fences by a heavily-backed favourite, he still powered away in the final hundred yards to win by four lengths. He cost €60,000 as a three year old and, while this debut win didn't suggest potential greatness, he should be capable of paying his way under Rules for **Tom Lacey**.

KENYAN COWBOY (IRE) 4 b g Sholokhov (IRE) – Joleen (IRE)
The two and a half miles maiden at Charing in February often throws up a useful prospect and this year's winner, Kenyan Cowboy, could add his name to the list. Despite being outjumped for much of the final circuit by his market rival, he still held the upper hand before producing a good leap at the last to seal the deal (first pair long way clear). Sold out of the Nimmo academy soon after to **Neil King** for £45,000, this half-brother to useful chaser Mind's Eye should be capable of winning under Rules.

RED BUCCANEER 5 ch g Black Sam Bellamy (IRE) - Florarossa
This five year old was beaten on his Larkhill debut in January but the form of the race couldn't have worked out better with the winner, third and fourth all subsequently producing solid winning performances. Red Buccaneer went down fighting and, although probably not out of the top drawer, could well pay his way in future. He was sold for £35,000 later that month.

REVELS HILL (IRE) 5 b g Mahler – Chlolo Supreme (IRE)
The Mahler gelding was up with the pace when unseating in the race won by Velascoon his debut at Milborne St Andrew but made no mistake in quite a competitive event at Badbury Rings three weeks later, having matters firmly in control on the final circuit, despite a mistake three out. Evidently held in some regard, Revels Hill should definitely find opportunities under rules for **Harry Fry**.

STRIKING A POSE (IRE) 4 b g Getaway (GER) – Clonsingle Native (IRE)
It would be surprising if there wasn't at least one representative in this list trained by Tom Ellis and this Getaway gelding fits the bill. Making his debut at Brocklesby Park in February, he jumped better as the race progressed and made light of desperate conditions to draw right away in the closing stages. A half-brother to useful chaser Ackertac, Striking A Pose was bought for £95,000 purchase the following week by **Colin Tizzard** and his future under Rules will be watched with interest.

TAKE YOUR TIME (IRE) 5 b g Dubai Destination (USA) – Don't Be Bleu (IRE)
It's always good to include one from a less familiar source and Take Your Time fits the bill perfectly. Making his debut at Alnwick last December for owner/trainer Anthony Ross, he was patiently ridden and still full of running when leading in the home straight. He won by 30 lengths, the time was solid and the form has been upheld. Sold the following month to Anthony Bromley for £55,000, he could be a useful recruit to racing under rules for **Paul Nicholls**.

VELASCO (IRE) 4 b g Sholokhov (IRE) – Bilboa (FR)
The four year old didn't jump with any great fluency on his debut at Milborne St Andrew in February but still ran out an easy winner by 40 lengths in testing conditions (2m4f). In doing so, he recorded a time significantly quicker than the other division of the race and looks another potentially promising recruit from the **Tom Lacey** yard. This well-bred type was led out unsold at £95,000 later in the month.

JONATHAN'S HORSES TO FOLLOW: INDIGO BREEZE

Please see pages 182-194
for details of the
One Jump Ahead Updates

Don't forget to read my Diary @
www.mhpublications.couk

FRENCH REVOLUTION

Last year's article produced **12 winners** from 52 runners (23%) yielding a £10 level stakes **PROFIT** of **£115.30**. The selections included Cheltenham Festival winners **ARAMAX** (Boodles Juvenile Handicap Hurdle @ 15/2), **BURNING VICTORY** (Triumph Hurdle @ 12/1) and **SAINT ROI** (County Hurdle @ 11/2). The feature has also unearthed other Cheltenham Festival winners over the years, namely **A PLUS TARD, DEFI DU SEUIL**, the ill-fated Champion Hurdle winner **ESPOIR D'ALLEN** and **KLASSICAL DREAM**.

As discussed, it is fair to say, due to the enforced lockdown during the spring/summer, I was able to watch more French racing and research the horses than ever before. Therefore the followingwill hopefully prove exciting recruits for their new connections, none of which have yet raced in either Britain or Ireland. Largely unknown, some of them may develop into household names in years to come.

Similar to last year, a number of the write-ups have been accompanied by comments from former French champion jockey **James Reveley**. Son of former trainer Keith, James has ridden 11 Grade 1 winners in France, including the Grand Steeple-Chase de Paris in three successive years (2016, 2017, 2018), plus the Grande Course de Haies d'Auteuil aboard the David Pipe trained Un Temps Pour Tout in 2015.

FUTURE STAR

HUBRISKO (FR) 3 b g Doctor Dino (FR) – Ubriska (FR)
In normal circumstances, the Doctor Dino gelding would have featured in the *Top 40 Prospects* but **Willie Mullins** invariably saves the three year olds he purchases from France until the following season before making their Irish debuts. Regardless of whether this **Rich and Susannah Ricci** owned three year old runs this season or next, he is likely to prove well worth the wait. Having watched his eight lengths victory in an AQPS Flat race at Le Lion D'Angers (1m 4f : Good/Soft) in August, the former Alain Couetil trained gelding looked star material. Contesting a small field (5 runners) of debutants, Hubrisko raced in fourth position for much of the contest but was produced on the outside in the home straight before streaking clear. It was a performance which oozed class and the fourth, who was beaten nearly ten lengths, has won by six and a half lengths since. The Ricci's best horses over the years all began their careers in France and it is possible they have recruited another superstar. If he does run this season, it is likely to be in juveniles hurdles during the second half of the campaign.

AIME DESJY (FR) 5 b g No Risk At All (FR) – Kassadame (FR)
Yet to run for **Willie Mullins**, the No Risk At All gelding was bought on behalf of the **Roaringwater syndicate** after he finished fourth on his debut in a Listed hurdle at Auteuil (2m 2f : Very Soft) in September last year for Robert Collet. Beaten four and a half lengths, the winner (Autocrat) has won two out of three since, plus the runner-up won next time. The form looks sound and the five year old ought to be hard to beat in a maiden hurdle before hopefully going on to better things.

ALL IN LOVE (FR) 4 b g No Risk At All (FR) – Ot Love (FR)

The first of a number of new recruits for owners **Simon Munir** and **Isaac Souede**, the No Risk At All gelding has joined **Nigel Twiston-Davies**. Trained in France by Jean-Philippe Dubois, he was fourth on his sole start on the Flat before switching to obstacles. Fifth a couple of times at Compiegne and Auteuil, the four year old then finished three parts of a length runner-up at the former track (2m 2f : Very Soft) in May. Switched to fences, All In Love was three lengths runner-up behind the Lord Daresbury owned Gesskille at Dieppe (Right-Handed – 2m 1f : Soft) the following month. The winner finished runner-up at Auteuil next time, while the third has won at the Parisian track since. A novice over both hurdles and fences, it will be disappointing if he isn't placed to win races in the UK.

BLUE LORD (FR) 5 b g Blue Bresil (FR) – Lorette (FR)

Raced three times on the Flat last year, finishing fourth behind stablemate Elton Des Ongrais at Dieppe (Soft) in July before filling the same position at Craon (Good/Soft) at the beginning of September. Beaten six lengths, the Blue Bresil gelding got off the mark at the third time of asking when winning narrowly at Morlaix (2m : Good) a fortnight later. Purchased soon afterwards by Anthony Bromley for **Simon Munir** and **Isaac Souede**, the five year old joined **Willie Mullins** last season and has been given plenty of time.

BUSSELTON (IRE) 3 b g Mastercraftsman (IRE) – Blessed Luck (IRE)

Sixth on his only start on the Flat at Angers in November last year when trained by Louis Baudron, he was switched to David Cottin and made a successful start to his jumping career at Auteuil (1m 7f : Very Soft) in May. A two lengths winner of the Prix Wild Monarch, the fourth (Hades) has won impressively over fences since. The Mastercraftsman gelding has joined **Joseph O'Brien** since and was in full training for his new handler in September. He could take high rank amongst Ireland's juvenile hurdlers this winter.

CAPODANNO (FR) 4 ch g Manduro (GER) – Day Gets Up (FR)

News broke during the summer that triple Group 1 winner Manduro had died at the age of 18 having suffered a heart attack at Haras du Logis in Normandy on the 27th June. The former Andre Fabre trained son of Monsun was responsible for this once raced four year old, who is owned by **J.P.McManus**. Purchased for €185,000 at the Arqana November Sale last year, he was trained in France by Daniela Mele and made his debut over hurdles at Compiegne (2m 1f : Heavy) in November. Leading over the last, he was headed on the run-in and beaten two lengths by Fire Dancer. The fourth, Baxter Du Berlais, who was eleven lengths behind Capodanno, has won three times since and finished fourth in a Grade 1 chase. **"He is a lovely big horse who jumps very well. He is a horse for next year,"** commented Charlie Swan at the Arqana Sales. Sent into training with **Willie Mullins**, he could be a high-class novice hurdler.

FILS D'OUDAIRIES (FR) 5 b g Saint Des Saints (FR) – Pythie D'Oudairies (FR)

Entered at the Cheltenham Festival last spring, the former David Cottin trained gelding finished fourth on his debut in an AQPS Flat race at Fontainebleau (1m 7f : Good/Soft) in September last year before switching to hurdles. Only eighth on his jumping debut at Compiegne nearly three weeks later, he improved markedly on that effort when winning at Auteuil (2m 1f : Heavy) in November. A big strapping chasing type, he raced prominently but was taken wide by Kevin Nabet. Leading on the run-in, he appeared to catch the jockey on the runner-up napping as he stayed on strongly. Bought by Henrietta Knight on behalf of **Mike Grech**, the Saint Des Saints gelding is trained by **Joseph O'Brien** and will appreciate a step up in trip this winter. Likely to chasing, he is built for fences.
Reveley's remarks: **"I like him. He's a big horse with plenty of scope and should make a nice chaser."**

FULGURIX (FR) 5 b g Maresca Sorrento (FR) – Union De Sevres (FR)
Bought**by Simon Munir** and **Isaac Souede,** he joined **Colin Tizzard** during the summer having finished runner-up on his only start over hurdles at Pau (2m 1f : Soft) in December. Handled in France by David Cottin, he was ironically beaten by a Munir/Souede owned runner, namely Fors Fortuna. Always to the fore, he had every chance and pulled eight lengths clear of the third. Fences will bring out the best in the five year old, who appears to have plenty of size and scope, but he is expected to more than pay his way over hurdles this season.

GAILLARD DU MESNIL (FR) 4 gr g Saint Des Saints (FR) – Athena Du Mesnil (FR)
Trained in France by Isabelle Gallorini, the four year old ran in six AQPS Flat races in 2019 with form figures of 621222. A five lengths winner at Saint-Jean-De-Monts (Right Handed – 1m 5f : Good/Soft) in August, the Saint Des Saints gelding finished runner-up in his next three outings. A length and three quarters behind Gant De Velours in a Grade 2 event at Saint-Cloud (1m 4f : Very Soft) in September, the winner has subsequently won at hurdles at Auteuil and finished second in a Grade 2 hurdle at the same track. A month later, he was beaten three and a half lengths in a Grade 3 bumper at Nantes (Left-Handed - 1m 4f). He was then sold at the Arqana November Sale for **€250,000** to owner **Joe Donnelly**. Agent Pierre Boulard, who was bidding on behalf of **Willie Mullins**, said afterwards: **"He's a lovely horse by a very good sire. He wasn't cheap, but nothing is. He looks like he could make into a nice chaser one day."** It is worth nothing the four year old wore cheekpieces.

GANAPATHI (FR) 4 b g Samum (GER) – Une Dame D'Avril (FR)
By the same sire as dual Grade 1 winning novice chaser Notebook, he is another new recruit for dual Cheltenham Gold Cup winning owner **Joe Donnelly**. A length winner of his only AQPS Flat race at Paray- Le-Monial (Right-Handed – 1m 4f) in November when trained by Emmanuel Clayeux, he was snapped up by **Willie Mullins** shortly afterwards. Novice hurdling will be on his agenda this season.

GANZO D'AIRY (FR) 4 b g Legolas (JPN) – Panzara D'Airy (FR)
Cheltenham Festival winning owner **Barry Connell** took out a training licence recently and he is responsible for this once raced four year old. A half-brother to the Venetia Williams' trained Enzo D'Airy, he was a close second on his debut in an AQPS Flat race at Nancy (Right-Handed – 1m 4f: Soft) in October. Agent Toby Jones bought the Legolas gelding for Connell for **€300,000** at the Maisons-Laffitte National Hunt Sale later the same month and remarked. **"He's a very correct, good-moving horse. He's a real easy, laid-back, relaxed horse and lovely to see. He's got all the options. He could stick to bumpers or go straight over hurdles. He's already been schooled and goes very well over obstacles. He's a horse with a lot of speed."**

GARS EN NOIR (FR) 4 b g Masked Marvel – Touche Noire (FR)
Another exciting recruit for **Willie Mullins**, the four year old is only a novice until the end of November but looks a horse with a big future. The Masked Marvel gelding was in behind the leaders but going well when falling at the second last at Pau (2m 1f : Heavy) on his debut in in January. Daniela Mele's charge made amends next time though when beating eleven rivals by upwards of three lengths at Auteuil (2m 1f : Heavy) a couple of months later. Not always the most fluent of jumpers, his future lies over fences but it will be disappointing if he doesn't win a good prize over hurdles in the meantime. He could be top notch over fences when the time comes.
Reveley's remarks: **"I rode the fourth at Auteuil and was impressed with the winner. He is a chaser in the making and should do well for his new connections."**

GAULOISE (FR) 4 br f Samum (GER) – Sans Histoire (FR)
This daughter of Samum was trained by Nicolas De Lageneste when winning a twelve furlongs maiden at Lignieres (Soft) in late April 2019 by two and a half lengths. The second and third have won since. The form therefore looks solid and she is an interesting proposition for mares' novice hurdles in Ireland. Trained by **Willie Mullins**, she could be another useful mare for her owner**Kenny Alexander**.

GIN COCO (FR) 4 b g Cokoriko (FR) – Qlementine (FR)
Snapped up for €80,000 at the Arqana summer sale in July, the four year old has joined **Charlie Mann**. Previously trained by Augustin Adeline De Boisbrunet, he was four lengths runner-up on his only start over hurdles at Pau (2m 1f : Very Soft) in May. The sixth has won over hurdles since and being placed over fences at Auteuil. He will go novice hurdling. Reveley's remarks: **"I rode him at Pau and quite liked him. He won't be a star but will be suited by racing in the UK and should win races."**

GINGEMBRE MENTHE (FR) 4 ch g Barastraight – Jolie Menthe (FR)
Trained by **Nick Williams**, the four year old has raced three times over hurdles and will be eligible for handicaps in the UK. Well held on his first couple of runs at Compiegne and Fontainebleau, he produced a much improved effort in a conditions hurdle at Auteuil (2m 1f : Heavy) in March. Beaten three lengths by the aforementioned Gars En Noir, he was thirty lengths clear of the third.

GINGER DU VAL (FR) 4 b f Rail Link – Ahkel Vie (FR)
The Rail Link filly ran in four AQPS Flat races for Gabriel Leenders finishing 3121. A four and a half lengths winner at Saumur (Left-Handed – 2m) in October, she was then two lengths runner-up in a Grade 3 event at Durtal (Right-Handed – 1m 3f) the following month. Back to winning ways last time at Pornichet (Left-Handed – 1m 4f: Standard) on the all-weather in December, she scored by six lengths. Now trained by **Nigel Twiston-Davies** for **Simon Munir** and **Isaac Souede**, she is one for mares' novice hurdles.

GLOIRE D'ATHON (FR) 4 b g Doctor Dino (FR) – Aster D'Athon (FR)
A potentially exciting recruit for **Cheveley Park Stud** who is in training with **Henry De Bromhead** in Ireland. A two lengths winner of an AQPS Flat race at Cholet (Right-Handed – 1m 6f: Very Heavy) in October last year when trained by Alain Couetil, bloodstockagent Alex Elliott bought him for **€200,000** at the Arqana Sale the following month and said: **"I was alerted to him three weeks ago by Nicky Bertran de Balanda and Sebastien Desmontils, who are my eyes and ears in France and who have helped me buy some nice horses. He's by Doctor Dino, who is a sire who has all before him and he was very impressive when he won despite being very green."**

GOLD LINK (FR) 4 b g Rail Link – Une De Montot (FR)
Leading agent Anthony Bromley bought this twice raced gelding on behalf of the **Owners Group** and he has joined **Emma Lavelle**. Previously trained by Adrien Lacombe, he was runner-up on both starts, including on his debut at Senonnes (Right-Handed – 1m 3f : Very Soft) in June last year. Beaten a length and a half by Grand Bornand (joined Willie Mullins since), he was then two and a half lengths behind Grand D'Espagne at Le Mans (Left-Handed - 1m 3f : Heavy) in November. He is another for novice hurdles.

GORKI D'AIRY (FR) 4 b g Legolas (JPN) – Norsa D'Airy (FR)
Purchased for £60,000 at the Cheltenham November Sale, he joined **Willie Mullins** last season but has yet to race for Ireland's champion trainer. Owned by **Jackie Mullins**, he was trained in France by Hugo Merienne and was beaten five and a half lengths by the aforementioned Gloire D'Athon on his only start at Cholet (1m 6f : Very Heavy) in October.

HACKER DES PLACES (FR) 3 b g Great Pretender (IRE) – Plaisance (FR)
Paul Nicholls has been very active during the spring/summer acquiring new talent from France, particularly in the juvenile hurdle department. This gelded son of Great Pretender raced twice for Francois Nicolle finishing well in third on his debut at Dieppe (Right-Handed – Very Soft) in May. Five and a half lengths behind the winner Paros (now with Nicky Henderson), the runner-up has won since and finished second in a Grade 3 hurdle at Auteuil. He confirmed the promise when winning by three and a half lengths at Dax (2m 1f : Soft) the following month (the runner-up has won since). Bought on behalf of the **Owners Group**, he is a nice prospect for three year old hurdles.

HA D'OR (FR) 3 b g Nidor (FR) – Rosewort (FR)
As discussed, **Rich and Susannah Ricci** made two potentially top-class purchases from France during the summer and this was the second one. Like Hubrisko, it is very possible **Willie Mullins** will give the three year old plenty of time and he won't make his Irish debut for another twelve months. A half-brother to a Listed hurdle winner at Auteuil, he was trained by Laurent Viel and was an impressive six and a half lengths winner of his AQPS Flat race at Senonnes (Right-Handed – 1m 3f : Soft) in early July. A strong looking gelding, he was held up during the early stages but once hitting the front in the homestraight, he readily pulled clear looking a smart prospect in the process. The second, third and fourth have all been beaten since but the Nidor gelding looked in a different league to his rivals.

HARRISBURG (IRE) 3 b f Authorized (IRE) – Hyde (FR)
Currently still in France, it is hoped this full-sister to potentially top-class hurdler Goshen is bought to run in the UK or Ireland later this year. Handled by Francois Nicolle, she has run twice over hurdles finishing ten lengths third behind Hystery Belle (sold since) on her debut at Le Lion D'Angers (Good/Soft) in late July. Reappearing at Vichy (Right-Handed – 2m 1f : Very Soft), the Authorized filly bolted up by sixteen lengths.
Reveley's remarks: **"I rode the fourth at Vichy and was very impressed with the winner. She has a great pedigree and could be smart."**

HEIA (FR) 3 b f No Risk At All (FR) – Ulla De Montot (FR)
Unfortunately, I have failed to locate the destination of this unbeaten three year old filly but she has been sold to race in Ireland and is one to watch out for in juvenile hurdles this season. By the increasingly popular sire, No Risk At All, she was a two lengths winner of her only appearance in an AQPS Flat race at Le Lion D'Angers (Left-Handed – 1m 4f : Good/Soft) in late July. Trained by Isabelle Gallorini, the runner-up (Hedilla) finished fourth in a Grade 3 event next time.

HELL RED (FR) 3 gr g Martaline – Queen Margot (FR)
Team Ditcheat have taken charge of the first two home in the Prix Rush, a conditions hurdle at Auteuil (1m 7f : Heavy) in March. This grey gelding finished two and a half lengths runner-up behind his new stablemate Monmiral. Trained by Guillaume Macaire, he couldn't match the winner for speed but stayed on well after the last and looks a useful sort. A half-brother to dual Grade 3 winner Hell Boy, Paul Nicholls has indicated the son of Martaline gelding, who is now owned by **Martin Broughton**, could make his UK debut at Chepstow (10th October) – the former champion has won the juvenile hurdle at that meeting five times in the last ten years.
Reveley's remarks: **"I finished seventh in the Prix Rush and it rode like a good race. I thought Hell Red should have won that day and he is a very nice horse who will do well in juvenile hurdles in the UK."**

HEROSS DU SEUIL (FR) 3 b g Rail Link – Tulipe Du Seuil (FR)
Another potential star who made a striking impression when winning his only AQPS Flat race at Moulins (Right-Handed - 1m 4f : Good/Soft) in late August. Trained by Mickael Seror, he was positioned towards the rear during the early stages before making ground down the back straight. Leading with around two furlongs to run, he quickened away to win hard held by three lengths. There was a lot to like about the performance and he was subsequently sold. He has got a big future.

HOPE YOU DO (FR) 3 b g Boris De Deauville (IRE) – Un Tournee (FR)
Philip Hobbs' seven times Grade 1 winner Defi Du Seuil began his career by contesting AQPS Flat races in France and he has been sent a similar type owned by **J.P.McManus** during the summer. A gelded son of Boris De Deauville, Hope You Do is a half-brother to the Tom Lacey trained Ginflix and he was handled in his home country by Isabelle Pacault. Sent off favourite on his debut at Angers (Right-Handed – 1m 3f : Soft), he made virtually all before staying on well to score by a couple of lengths. The runner-up has won since to give the form some substance. Juvenile hurdles will be on his agenda this season and he looks a fine prospect for his new connections.

HORN CAPE (FR) 3 gr g Fame And Glory – Capstone (FR)
Previously owned by M.L.Bloodstock and trained by Erwan Grall, he is a fine big grey three year old who ought to progress with time and has been acquired by **J.P.McManus**, but had't been allocated a new handler, at the time of writing. Sixth on his debut in an AQPS Flat race at Moulins (1m 4f : Soft) in June, he was beaten around eighteen lengths behind the Lord Daresbury owned Herbiers. However, he took a marked step forward next time when winning by a length and three quarters at Argentan (Right-Handed – 1m 4f : Very Soft). Sporting a noseband, the Fame And Glory ran on strongly and is a progressive type.

IDOLES DES JAUNES (FR) 4 b f Helmet (AUS) – Akka
Miss M.A.Masterson, of Carefully Selected fame, is the new owner of this lightly raced four year old filly. Purchased for €110,000 at the Arqana Sale in October, she raced four times on the Flat for Fabrice Chappet. Fourth on her debut at Fontainebleau (1m 3f : Good/Soft) in May, she won by three lengths at Compiegne (1m 6f : Good/Soft), pulling away inside the final furlong. Beaten less than a length in a conditions event at Deauville (1m 7f) on her final start, she is a half-sister to a dual hurdles winner and is a big powerful looking filly with plenty of scope. Given time since her sale by **Willie Mullins**, she looks a cracking prospect for mares' novice hurdles.

INDIANA JONES (FR) 4 b g Blue Bresil (FR) – Matnie (FR)
Brian Acheson (**Robcour**) has invested heavily into bloodstock during the last couple of years and he purchased this once raced gelded son of Blue Bresil for **€280,000** at the Osarus Maisons-Laffitte National Hunt Sale at the end of October. Trained in France by David Cottin, he finished two and a half lengths second on his hurdles debut (Prix Pride of Kildare) at Auteuil (2m 2f : Very Soft) in September. The winner Onestepforward has won again since and both the third (General En Chef) and fourth (Moises Has) won their next two outings. Therefore the form looks particularly strong. One note of caution is the fact he wore cheekpieces that day. Otherwise, he could prove a potentially high-class novice hurdler for **Mouse Morris**, who also trains his 135 rated half-brother French Dynamite for the same owner.
Reveley's remarks: **"He finished second at Auteuil behind a horse I know from Macaire's, Onestepforward. He is well regarded, so the form is strong and he should make a useful novice hurdler."**

JAMES DU BERLAIS (FR) 4 ch g Muhtathir – King's Daughter (FR)
Only four, this **Simon Munir** and **Isaac Souede** owned gelding looks a tremendous long-term prospect and it would be no surprise to see him racing in the UK in the spring. A half-brother to Grade 1 winning chaser Goliath Du Berlais, he has won 3 of his 10 races and is already a dual Listed and Grade 3 winner over hurdles. Trained in France by Robert Collet, he won a Listed hurdle at Auteuil (2m 2f : Very Soft) by seven lengths in May before finishing a short neck runner-up in a Grade 1 hurdle at Compiegne (2m 3f : Very Soft) in June. Back to winning ways last time, he beat the previously unbeaten Galleo Conti (won over fences since) by two and a half lengths in the Grade 3 Prix Questarabad (2m 3f : Very Soft) at Auteuil in mid July. Previous winners of the race include Hurricane Fly (2008), Footpad (2016) and Master Dino (2018). He will reportedly stay in France for the major winter races, but it will be interesting to see if he is aimed at something like the Stayers' Hurdle at Cheltenham or Aintree Hurdle next spring. Long-term, he is likely to develop into a top-class chaser.
Reveley's remarks: **"He is a very good horse who was unlucky not to win a Grade 1 hurdle at Compiegne during the summer. Still improving, he won well at Auteuil last time and would be a very interesting horse, if he came over to Britain."**

LA DOMANIALE (FR) 4 b f No Risk At All (FR) – La Pinede
Trained in France by Gab Leenders, she won her only start over hurdles at Vichy (2m : Very Soft) in late September. A length and three quarters scorer, the daughter of No Risk At All was purchased by **J.P.McManus** and has been sent to Jackdaws Castle and will be trained by **Jonjo O'Neill**. The third and fourth have won subsequently and she will presumably be aimed at mares' hurdles because she is no longer a novice over timber.

MANITOPARK AA (FR) 4 b f Walk In The Park (IRE) – Manitoba (FR)
Willie Mullins has enjoyed plenty of success from the progeny of Walk In The Park, most notably with multiple Grade 1 winners Douvan and Min. Ireland's champion trainer has taken charge of this five times Flat winner, who is owned by **Simon Munir** and **Isaac Souede**. Handled in France by Didier Guillemin, her form figures on the level were 112111 and she was unbeaten over trips from ten to eleven furlongs. Unraced at two, she gained victories at Mont-De- Marsan twice (Good), Tarbes twice (Very Soft) by five and a half lengths in April and four lengths in October, and La Teste De Buch (Good) in August. She is another for mares' novice hurdles.

MICA MALPIC (FR) 3 ch g Hunter's Light (IRE) – Moon Malpic (FR)
A big flashy chestnut with white markings on his face and feet, he made virtually all when winning by nine lengths on his hurdles debut at Compiegne (Left-Handed – Very Soft) in June. Trained by David Cottin, he pulled away after the second last and looked a relentless galloper. Subsequently bought by **J.P.McManus**, he remains in Francebut could be aimed at the Triumph Hurdle in March – the same owner/trainer successfully combined with Easysland at the Festival last spring. The runner-up Prunay finished third in a Grade 3 at Auteuil next time before being sold for €240,000 in July.
Reveley's remarks: **"I finished sixth in the race at Compiegne and was very impressed with the winner. Set to stay in France with David Cottin, he would be really interesting if coming over to the UK for the top juvenile hurdles."**

MONMIRAL (FR) 3 bl g Saint Des Saints (FR) – Achere (FR)
As discussed, **Paul Nicholls** has taken charge of the first two home in the Prix Rush at Auteuil (1m 7f : Heavy), which was run in mid March. This striking looking black gelding was purchased by Anthony Bromley on behalf of **John Hales, Sir Alex Ferguson** and **Ged Mason** soon after his two and a half lengths victory (the eleventh has won since). Held up early on, the Francois Nicolle trained three year old crept into contention down the back straight before hitting the front jumping the third last. Staying on strongly, he is a chaser in

the making, but is expected to make a big impact in juvenile hurdles this winter. He looks a smashing long-term prospect for the top connections.

Reveley's remarks: **"Won the race in which Hell Red was second at Auteuil, I think it was a decent event and Paul Nicholls has bought a couple of potentially very good juvenile hurdlers."**

NASSALAM (FR) 3 ch g Dream Well (FR) – Ramina (GER)

A half-brother to Msassa, who won twice over hurdles for Willie Mullins, James (Reveley) rode him on his only start over jumps for Guillaume Macaire at Clairefontaine (2m : Soft) in late June. Contesting a debutants event, he was beaten two lengths by Hemevoici (sixth in a Listed hurdle next time) filling the runners-up berth. The fourth has scored since. A big flashy chestnut with white markings of his feet, he has joined **Gary Moore** since and will be running in juvenile hurdles in the UK.

Reveley's remarks: **"He is a nice horse who I rode at Clairefontaine. He is very tough and it wouldn't surprise me if he developed into a Boodles Juvenile Hurdle contender at Cheltenham next March."**

NIGHT AND DAY 3 b f Sea The Moon (GER) – Distinctive Look (IRE)

Concertista provided owners **Simon Munir** and **Isaac Souede** and trainer **Willie Mullins** with Cheltenham Festival glory in March and the Nathaniel mare previously belonged to the Wertheimer family in France. The same connections have returned to the same source to acquire this three year old daughter of Sea The Moon. A half-sister to triple Grade 1 winning hurdler Supasundae, she was bought for €90,000 at the Arqana summer sale in July. Trained by Yan Durepaire, she raced four times on the Flat earlier this year and, while she failed to get her head in front, she was placed three times. Beaten a short head at Angers (Right-Handed - 1m 6f : Good/Soft) in June, she filled the same position in a handicap at Clairefontaine (Right-Handed – 1m 6f : Good) the following month.

OBEONE (FR) b f Muhtathir – My Fair Lady (FR)

A length and a half winner of the Listed Prix Finot (2m 2f : Very Soft) on her racecourse debut at Auteuil in September, the Mikael Mescam trained filly ran on strongly after the last. A daughter of Muhtathir, she got the better of Yannick Fouin's Riviere D'Etel on the run-in with the pair pulling twenty lengths clear of the third. The first two home looked above average juvenile hurdle fillies. Her victory will inevitably have attracted the agents and her progress is worth monitoring.

PAROS (FR) 3 ch g Masterstroke (USA) – Soft Blue (FR)

Champion trainer **Nicky Henderson** has won the Triumph Hurdle on seven occasions and the Seven Barrows team will be hoping this unbeaten gelding will develop into a contender for the 2021 version. A two lengths winner on his jumping debut at Dieppe (Right-Handed – 2m : Soft) when trained by Gabriel Leenders, he jumped well, racing handily throughout before staying on strongly. Both the second (Jeu De Paume) and third (Hacker Des Places) have won since. The Masterstroke gelding is now owned by **Middleham Park Racing**.

Reveley's remarks: **"I rode the fourth at Dieppe and the form has worked out well. The runner-up has won and finished second in a Grade 3 at Auteuil, plus the third won next time and the fifth (Nobody Knows) is well regarded at Macaire's. He looks a good addition to Nicky Henderson's yard."**

PONT DU GARD (FR) 4 b g Kapgarde (FR) – Panzella (FR)

Half-brother to Willie Mullins' ill-fated Grade 1 winning hurdler Pont Alexandre, the Kapgarde gelding raced once for Guillaume Macaire finishing third of nine at Compiegne (Left-Handed – 2m 1f : Heavy) in November. Having jumped to his right early on, he was still nearly last at the penultimate flight before making good headway. Holding every chance on the run-in, he was beaten two and three quarters of a length by Gary Du Chenet (both the winner and runner-up have won over fences since). Bought soon afterwards by **J.P.McManus**, he is in training with **Joseph O'Brien** and is one to watch out for in a maiden hurdle in the Autumn. Reveley's remarks: **"I remember him at Guillaume Macaire's, he was a big backward horse who should improve with time. He ought to make a very nice chaser one day."**

QUILIXIOS 3 b g Maxios – Quilita (GER)

Another exciting prospect for **Cheveley Park Stud**, he was a twelve lengths winner on his debut at Compiegne (Left-Handed – 2m : Heavy) in March for Francois Nicolle. Revelling in the testing conditions, he pulled away after the last to score impressively from the well regarded Yes Indeed (the fourth who was beaten 40 lengths has finished runner-up in a Listed hurdle at Auteuil since). **Gordon Elliott** has won the Triumph Hurdle twice and may have another leading contender by next March.
Reveley's remarks: **"I was impressed with him because I rode the runner-up (Yes Indeed), who we thought was very good beforehand. Despite the fact my horse has turned out to be disappointing (beaten three times since), it was still a really good performance by the winner, who handled the testing ground well."**

RAMBRANLT'JAC (FR) 4 b g Masterstroke (USA) - Gastibellzza (FR)

Grade 1 runner-up Cash Back provided the **Watch This Space syndicate** with plenty of enjoyment over fences last season and they are responsible for this four year old who has joined **Willie Mullins**. The Masterstroke gelding raced twice for Hector Lageneste finishing fifth on the Flat at Royan (Right-Handed – 1m 6f) in August last year. Beaten around ten lengths, he switched to hurdles the following month. Seven lengths third at Bordeaux (Right-Handed – 2m : Very Soft), he raced prominently on the inside but made a mistake at the third. Staying on at the death, he gives the impression a step up in trip will suit.

ROAD SENAM (FR) 4 b g Saint Des Saints (FR) – Madison Road (IRE)

Another tremendous young prospect for **Simon Munir** and **Isaac Souede**, the four year old has joined **Colin Tizzard** and is a maiden over hurdles and fences. A full-brother to Grade 3 winning chaser Buddy Banks, he raced seven times for Francois Nicolle, including twice over hurdles finishing third at Compiegne (2m) and fourth at Auteuil (1m 7f) last year. Switched to fences, he was runner-up twice at the latter venue, including in a Listed chase (2m 1f) in October. A length third in a Grade 2 chase next time at the same track (2m 2f), he produced a career best last time. Three and a half lengths runner-up in a Grade 2 chase at Auteuil (2m 6f : Very Soft) in May, the winner Gardons Le Sourire won the Grade 1 Prix Ferdinand Dufaure at Compiegne next time. Given his age, it wouldn't be a surprise to see him run in novice hurdles this season before reverting back to fences in twelve months time. Stamina looks his strong suit and he could develop into an Albert Bartlett Novices' Hurdle contender this time around.
Reveley's remarks: **"His form is strong and the fact he is a maiden over hurdles and fences gives his connections plenty of options. He should do well in the UK."**

RONDE DE NUIT (FR) 3 b f Doctor Dino (FR) – Nuit De Guerre (FR)

A length and three quarters fourth on her only start on the Flat at Angers (1m 6f : Soft) in early June when trained by Etienne Leenders, she took on the colts that day. The runner-up was the aforementioned Night And Day and the daughter of Doctor Dino stayed on well on the outside. Subsequently bought by **J.P.McManus**, she has joined **Philip Hobbs** and will go juvenile hurdling.

SAINT SAM (FR) 3 b g Saint Des Saints (FR) – Ladeka (FR)

Successful in two of his three races over hurdles for Jean-Philippe Dubois, the Saint Des Saints gelding only finished ninth on his debut at Dieppe in early June. Returning to the same track later that month, he produced a much improved display to win by a length and a quarter (2m 1f : Soft). The runner-up (Shentri) has won twice since. An even better display at Clairefontaine (2m 1f : Soft) in July followed when beating Piriac by two lengths (third and fifth have won subsequently). Acquired by **Willie Mullins** in August, he is likely to be aimed at the leading juvenile hurdles, culminating in the Triumph Hurdle at Cheltenham in March. He is a fast improving horse who is bred to jump fences eventually.

SIROCO JO (FR) 3 ch g Hurricane Cat (USA) – Diana Vertica (FR)

Mickael Seror trained this chestnut (has a white face) to finish a neck second on his debut over hurdles at Clairefontaine (Right-Handed – 2m : Very Soft) in early August. The winner (Blackiron) had raced four times beforehand and the third (Yes Indeed), who was four lengths behind Siroco Jo, had chased home the aforementioned Quilixios earlier in the year. Leading early on, he jumped better once getting a lead and rallied well after the last flight. He has joined **Paul Nicholls** and is owned by **Paul Vogt**, who is also responsible for Frodon at Ditcheat.

Reveley's remarks: **"I rode the third and, while the form is only modest, it was a good run by the second because he was making his debut and both the winner and my horse had plenty of experience over hurdles beforehand."**

STATE MAN (FR) 3 ch g Doctor Dino (FR) – Arret Station (FR)

Made his debut in the Prix Wild Monarch at Auteuil (1m 7f : Very Soft) in May and finished second to the aforementioned Busselton. Owned by M.L.Bloodstock and trained by Daniela Mele, he was beaten a couple of lengths but was staying on strongly at the finish. A big powerful looking chestnut, he has been sold since and is a horse with a bright future over hurdles and fences.

One for the long-term.....

T'ARAISON (FR) 3 b g Buck's Boum (FR) – Al Gane (FR)

It remains to be seen whether he runs this season or who will be training him (no decision had been made at the beginning of September), but it will be interesting to monitor the progress of this unraced three year old. A full-brother to dual Cheltenham Gold Cup winner Al Boum Photo, he was bought for €150,000 as a two year old at Arqana Summer Sale in July last year by **J.P.McManus**. Like his older sibling, the Buck's Boum was in training with Emmanuel Clayeux who commented earlier this year: **"He worked with a three year old of mine and jumped better than him. He was incredible, so Charlie (Swan) bought him. At the same age he felt stronger than Al Boum Photo and I think he could be a very good horse."**

www.mhpublications.co.uk

IRISH POINTERS

Once again, point-to-point expert **Declan Phelan** has written his invaluable article regarding those horses who caught his eye 'between the flags' in the Emerald Isle last winter/spring. Last year's feature yielded **37 winners** at an impressive **strike-rate of 27%** and produced a £10 level stakes **PROFIT** of **£274.60** (following on from his **40 winners** and **PROFIT** of **£462.90** the previous year). The latest success stories included **ADRIMEL** (2 wins), **BIG BRESIL** (10/1), **CILL ANNA** (3 wins), **CLONDAW CAITLIN** (4 wins – 12/1, plus Grade 2 success), **FRENCH DYNAMITE** (6/1, 5/1), **KEARNEY HILL** (20/1), **MINELLA MELODY** (3 wins), **MOSSY FEN** (3 wins) and **SPRINGFIELD FOX** (7/1).

ACROSS THE CHANNEL (FR) 5 b g Dunkerque (FR) – Aulne River (FR)
Trainer: Philip HOBBS   Form Figures: F1

Over recent decades, Philip Hobbs has illustrated his ability to maximise the potential of his occasional big money point recruits. In the past year, he continued that trend as he conditioned leading 2019 four year old, Sporting John, into a most promising young jumper. The Minehead yard acquired Across The Channel at the Cheltenham December Sales for £150,000, and the stable has already had a positive experience with another member of the same French family. Wait For Me, a half brother to Across The Channel, has won five times for Hobbs and attained a mark in the 136-140 range as a hurdler and chaser.Colin Bowe handled Across The Channel for a couple of autumn Irish points in 2019: dispatched as favourite for his Lisronagh debut, he looked likely to oblige when striding to the lead at the third last: engaged in battle away from the second last, he was two lengths down when falling at the final fence when second place looked to be his lot. Three weeks later he pitched up for one of the three divisions of a four year old maiden staged at Mainstown (Soft) on the first Sunday of December. In a steadily run affair, no more than seven lengths covered the field as they left the backstraight and raced towards the second last fence. Ridden prominently throughout, Across The Channel was coaxed home to win by Barry O'Neill without said jockey having to resort to his whip. The time of the race was modest and the field no more than average: one positive is that the fifth home, One More King, moved to the UK and won a point and Ludlow bumper, prior to a commendable tenth place finish in the Cheltenham Festival bumper. Across The Channel is an elegant athletic bay gelding: both his performances between the flags recommend that he is a smooth fluid traveller and has gears. He seems to be the sort of horse who can muster one run, judged on Lisronagh, his ability to rally is unproven. He raced on easy/flat Irish point tracks and this aspect may drop clues to his future preferences: I fancy he may be more effective at two miles to two and a half miles trips as opposed to stamina tests, and less taxing circuits like Wincanton, Kempton and Ludlow may favour his style. To date he has only raced with dig in the ground, though given his action and speed, he could also be potent on good ground. One can imagine him becoming a fair to decent 135+ hurdler/chaser and competing at Graded level over jumps is a possibility, if new connections can unlock extra improvement.

BOOTHILL (IRE) 5 bb g Presenting – Oyster Pipit (IRE)
Trainer: Harry FRY   Form Figures: 221

Elegant, lengthy bay gelding, raced twice between the flags in the autumn for Wilson Dennison collecting two silver medals. Initially he failed to match the winner Mr Josiey Wales from the second last when eventually beaten three lengths at Castletown (Soft) on his debut. Two weeks later, on the Dennison home farm at Loughanmore (Yielding) he failed to justify short odds when succumbing to another talented Colin Bowe victor in Fiston Des Issards, again outmuscled in the final hundred yards. Snapped up by the Fry yard for £125,000 at the November Sales, he began to repay the investment by posting a classy track winning debut in a Kempton (Good/Soft) bumper in February. The family tree includes notable jumps horses such as Frantic Tan, Warne, Gaye Brief, Gaye Chance and Black Humour. My read on his form is that he is likely to require an easy three miles and he may perform best when hurdling over the middle distances. I doubt if he is capable of winning at Grade 1 level over hurdles or fences, though it is highly possibly that he can achieve a hurdles and chase rating north of 140. In two or three years time, he may be poised to win a premier handicap and he may prefer easy flat circuits rather than stiff finishes. He has operated to effect on good and soft and is therefore versatile in that range, heavy ground may be troublesome for him.

CARRIG COPPER (IRE) 6 b g Presenting – Copper Dusht (IRE)
Trainer: Terence O'BRIEN   Form Figures: 2
Punted with confidence for a competitive five year old maiden at Dromahane (Yielding/ Soft) in November. Consented to settle and arrived to get involved at the third last travelling sweetly. From there to the finish he locked horns with Eklat De Rire and came out the wrong side of a photo finish. From the well known "Copper" jumps clan with includes the likes of Copper Bleu, Presenting Copper and Give Me A Copper, he is a strong bay gelding with scope to develop and progress. Absent since that debut appearance in November, I would imagine connections will switch to track racing and although now a six year old, he could make up for lost time this coming winter and should be capable of winning a two and a half miles and upwards maiden hurdle and could even be competitive in the three mile Graded novice hurdles. The horse who defeated him at Dromahane, Eklat De Rire having won on the track himself has boosted the form line and Carrig Copper would slot into the category of an above average maiden pointer. A fine crisp jumper of point fences.

CHOSEN PORT (IRE) 4 b f Well Chosen – Despute
Trainer: Olly MURPHY   Form Figures: 1
Tom Meagher stands the stallion Well Chosen at his stud farm in Tipperary and this mare by that stallion raced in his red and blue silks, as breeder/owner in a four year old mares point at Ballycahane (Yielding/Soft) in March. Trained by Colin Bowe, a medium bay mare with a white face, she was always in her comfort zone and moved to wrestle the lead between the last two fences and scored by a snug two lengths. She has an appetite for racing and revelled in the testing conditions and on the evidence of this one race, she will be effective in two and a half miles and upwards mares' novice hurdles and chases. Definitely capable of grabbing either a win or black type placing in Listed/Graded races for mares. Her dam has thrown six winners from ten matings: siblings of this mare include former Reynoldstown winner Burton Port and 130s rated staying chaser Burtons Well. Tom Meagher cashed in at Cheltenham March Sales with Olly Murphy paying £115,000 for a mare who can be ranked amongst the top three of her sex from the shortened four year old campaign in 2020.

CLONDAW BERTIE (IRE) 5 b g Thewayyouare (USA) – Female (IRE)
Trainer: Mouse MORRIS   Form Figures: 1
A big powerful bay gelding with a broad white face: clocked the fastest time of the day on the eight race card at Dromahane (Soft/Heavy) in late December. The Mick Goff yard were expecting big things from this youngster and he lived up to expectations with a spectacular triumph. Buried towards mid to rear of a fifteen runner field, Shane Fitzgerald injected him into proceedings with a big move soon after the fourth last: in a matter of a few hundred yards, he took the race by the scruff of the neck and flew over the three homestraight fences to score by a dozen lengths. That move from the fourth to third last was one of the memorable moments of the 2019/20 pointing campaign and identified this horse as one with a discernible change of gear. He was bred by Christy Roche: the sire (now deceased) has little stock on the ground, however the dam line of this gelding catches the eye: his mother, Female, was an above average bumper mare, a dual winner on the track, and this lady was a sibling of Joe Mac, Penny A Day and the top class Direct Route. In terms of appearance and racing style, Clondaw Bertie is a ringer for his uncle Direct Route. Certainly one of the

classiest pointers of the past shortened campaign, he may be most effective as an elite chaser in the two miles to two and a half miles distance range. Bought privately by Robcour, he unfortunately contracted an infection in a hock, due to an embedded thorn in February and nearly lost his life. The intervention of the vets saved him. If that near life threatening illness has not left physical or psychological scars and he makes a complete recovery, then he may be the horse to get Mouse Morris back into the big time.Track debuted in early September and folded tamely inside the last quarter mile having led over the second last. He may require time, patience and some more medical aid to assist in recapturing his exciting mo-jo.

CLONDAW SECRET (IRE) 5 b g Court Cave (IRE) – Secret Can't Say (IRE)
Trainer: Gordon ELLIOTT   Form Figures: 1
In 2014, Just Cause won the four year old geldings maiden at the Boulta/Dungorney December fixture and, by a quirk of fate, in 2019 his full brother Clondaw Secret repeated the feat for handler Mick Goff. Not alone is this five year related to Just Cause, the most talented full brother in the family was the high class bumper horse Clondaw Court, a talent whose career was cut short due to injury. The market spoke in favour of Clondaw Secret at Boulta (Soft/Heavy) and patiently ridden, he arrived with a menacing effort at the second last and got the better of a late tussle with Champagne Gold to win by two lengths, a hard fought success. He did carry his head a little high at the climax, it may be habit or greenness. He turned up at the Cheltenham January sales, declared a windsucker, that vice did not deter Gordon Elliott as he took control of this bay gelding at a price of £135,000. This is a horse who is impossible to evaluate on the basis of the one outing: he did not strike me as star material: he enjoy getting his toe into the ground and therefore he may become a winter operator for his new handler.

COQOLINO (FR) 5 b g French Fifteen (FR) – Classical Angel (GER)
Trainer: Gordon ELLIOTT   Form Figures: 12
Eugene O'Sullivan found this French bred at the 2018 Derby Sale and secured him for €24,000. Ballindenisk held their December 2019 fixture on soft ground and the four year old maiden was divided. Coqolino appeared in the ten runner second division. Partnered by Maxi O'Sullivan, he settled in a close third/fourth until moving to the front at the fourth last fence. The intended final fence was omitted, resulting in a near two furlongs extended run in. Coqolino jumped the effective final fence (intended second last) with a two length advantage and bypassing the omitted fence Maxi gave him a squeeze and he settled the issue with a decisive turn of foot to account for subsequent Wincanton bumper winner Smurphy Enki by a dozen lengths. Visually quite appealing, and he recorded the fastest time on the card, nine seconds faster than the preceding first division. J.P. McManus signed a significant six figure cheque and posted him to Gordon Elliott. In early 2020, he delighted new connections when winning a schooling bumper and he became a warm order to score on his track debut at Gowran (Soft/Heavy) in the pointers' bumper in March. I think he failed to fire on the day as he struggled home a moderate second to Bob Olinger. Whilst tagged a French bred, the dam side of his family are German horses: the dam was a dual purpose winner and the pedigree relates a stream of prolific winners across the continent. He is a medium sized bay gelding with one white front sock, and he struck me as more racy and athletic than one blessed with massive scope. Given the change of gears on display at Ballindenisk, it could be the case that the heavy soil at Gowran blunted his speed. He could be a slow handicapping project for team McManus, and conceivably one that will be frustrating for punters to get right. One item to remember is that this horse has an engine and it may propel him to a valuable handicap in due course.

DOCPICKEDME (IRE) 4 ch g Getaway (GER) – Hard Luck (IRE)
Trainer: Harry WHITTINGTON   Form Figures: 1
Medium sized chestnut gelding: Ellen Marie Holden travelled him to the Limerick track of Ballycahane (Yielding/Soft) in March and he collected the gold medal following a hard fought win in a competitive four year old maiden. Derek O'Connor partnered him and, with four to jump, he was held up seventh of the eight runners. A closing fourth at the second last, he careered down the wide outside to get involved in a three way battle at the final fence, under a strong Derek steer, he squeezed home in front. The first three from this race all turned up for the same Cheltenham March sale, the runner up, Patroclus (£150,000) and the third, Gaston Phebus (£140,000) made far higher prices than Docpickedme, who Harry Whittington picked up for £75,000. This anomaly was possibly down to physical appearance as of the trio, Docpickedme had the least apparent scope. He may not be a superstar and may have limitations, nonetheless, he displayed the application and desire to win under the cosh, and he will win a handful of races for his new owners, operating in the 120-135 range, and he is one I expect to find no difficulty in winning a modest two and a half miles maiden hurdle on soft terrain. His half-brother Another Venture is a 130 chaser and he may become a jumper of similar calibre.

EKLAT DE RIRE (FR) 6 b g Saddex (FR) – Rochdale (FR)
Trainer: Henry DE BROMHEAD   Form Figures: 121
Athletic bay gelding: an aggressive front runner: on his one run within the pointing discipline, racing for Liz Doyle, at Dromahane (Yielding/Soft) in November, he jumped slickly and led the field on the run to the third last: tackled soon after by market fancy Carrig Copper, he withstood a sustained challenge to score by a neck. Sold to Henry De Bromhead for £110,000 at Cheltenham November sales, the horse has already made his mark for new connections. He lost out by less than two lengths to a vastly more experienced rival on his hurdles debut at Punchestown, and then went one better in terrific style when making all to win a two miles seven maiden hurdle at Thurles (Soft/Heavy), always travelling smoothly. His dam, a five times winner in France, was a dual purpose operator and the family page is littered with black type French jump winners. From two and a half miles and upwards he will become a very effective pace setting chaser, and if given too much rope on any given day, would have aspirations of winning a Graded chase, and he could be a surprise packet in the novice chase ranks in 2020/21: he is an uncomplicated ride and this characteristic may result in positive results.

FOLCANO (FR) 5 b g Falco (USA) – Floriana (GER)
Trainer: Gordon ELLIOTT   Form Figures: FF1
A light framed bay gelding with a white star on his forehead: half-brother to 2018 Triumph Hurdle winner Farclas, the majority of the dam line are Flat racers. Represented Wilson Dennison in three winter points. He raced twice before Christmas, falling at the final fence each time. On his debut at Turtulla (Yielding) he was ten lengths down on Bob Olinger and a clear second best when crumbling at the last. A fortnight later at Mainstown (Soft) he ran a little flat, arguably due to the quick turnaround, and he folded at the second last and was weakening in fourth when falling again at the final fence. His luck turned in 2020, at Tinahely (Soft) in January, exaggerated waiting tactics were employed. A close third at the second last, with the leader Kilbeg King blundering at the last, Folcano pounced to take over and lead where it counted to record a win by a length and a half. He has a bad habit of getting in low to his fences and this trait needs addressing. Bought by the Gordon Elliott yard for £110,000 at Cheltenham January Auctions, this horse could prosper for a drop to two miles or two and a half miles, and may be capable of reaching a 130+ mark and be on the fringes of Grade 3 level. May possess more in the way of speed than stamina and therefore he could improve when racing on a sound surface, to date all his runs have been on soft or testing terrain.

GARTERS LANE (IRE) 5 ch m Getaway (GER) – Tariana (IRE)
Trainer: Barry CONNELL   Form Figures: 1
Robust barrelled chestnut mare: landed some bets when triumphing in the 14 runners four year old mares maiden at Lisronagh(Soft) in November. Then in the care of Philip Fenton, she was sited fourth ten lengths down at the third last fence. She made steady headway to challenge for the lead at the second last. Given a few reminders, she asserted and then survived an awkward leap at the last to win by a snug four lengths. She has scope and it was no surprise she made a price of £100,000 at the Cheltenham November Sales as she has genuine aspirations of competing at Listed/Graded level in mares' races. Her dam line originated in Germany and contains plenty with Flat wins to their name, so this lady having proven she has stamina and guts, may also possess some toe. She clocked the fastest time at Lisronagh on a card that included two maidens for the four year old geldings.

GARS DE SCEAUX (FR) 4 gr g Saddler Maker (IRE) – Replique (FR)
Trainer: Gordon ELLIOTT   Form Figures: 1
Wexford point handler Denis Murphy purchased this French bred for a sum of €40,000 euros at the 2019 Derby Store Sale. A tall steel grey gelding, still a shell of a horse, he made a winning debut in the second division of the four year olds maiden staged at Borris (Yielding/ Soft) in March. Partnered by Jamie Codd, he was held up towards the rear for two circuits until moving into a closing fourth by the third last fence. Heading towards the homestraight and penultimate fence, he challenged for the lead. He survived a clumsy leap at that fence, quickly getting back into rhythm and galloping on with purpose to score by six lengths. He clocked a time (6.28) which was three seconds faster than the first division (won by Amarillo Sky). An interesting comparative is that Sporting John won the 2019 maiden at this Borris track in a time of 6.31, albeit on slightly softer terrain. His pedigree page is rather light, in fact if you delve deep the name of Bristol De Mai crops up as a distant relative. J.P. McManus privately recruited this youngster and has sent him to Gordon Elliott. It may take a year or two to cultivate him and hone him physically. He stays the three mile trip as his ease, and long term he may be a green and gold owned project for valuable handicaps rather than a top end Graded entertainer. He has a pounding knee action in his movement style which may suggest he will prefer soft/heavy ground during his future career.

GERRI COLOMBE (FR) 4 b g Saddler Maker (IRE) – Ruse De Guerre (FR)
Trainer: Gordon ELLIOTT   Form Figures: 1
A physically imposing bay gelding with a white star on his head: Colin Bowe paid a premium price of €85,000 for him at the 2019 Derby Store Sale: the produce of a French dam who has bred a four times French winner, with the third line of the page crowded with French black type jump winners. Scored at the first time of asking when lifting the top prize in the four year old maiden held at Lingstown (Soft) in March. With six participants, this was a slowly run event, with the half dozen still covered by a couple of lengths at the third last. Heading for home, with an injection of pace, Gerri Colombe and Lakota Warrior knuckled down for a shoot out: the latter held sway on landing over the last, but Gerri Colombe responded to the urgings of Barry O'Neill and won in a bob of heads: first and second hitting the line with running left, probably down to the late burn up. The time of 6.50 was rather slow and a consequent of the early pedestrian proceedings. Gerri Colombe jumped crisply when the chips were down and proved he was up for a battle. This victory earned him a visit to the Tattersalls March sales and he was bought by Gordon Elliott for Robcour for a price of £240,000. He looks to have scope and can win an ordinary bumper this winter and be competitive in winners' bumpers. Over hurdles, two and a half miles plus can be his cup of tea, and time will tell if soft/heavy are crucial for optimum returns.

GLENGLASS (IRE) 4 ch g Ocovango – Funny Times
Trainer: Gordon ELLIOTT   Form Figures: 1
Tall well toned chestnut gelding. Bought by Colin Bowe for €42,000 at the 2019 Derby Sale, he provided a tidy profit inside the space of nine months, as he sold to Gordon Elliott for £155,000 at Cheltenham February Sales on the back of a debut point win earlier that month. He lined up for the competitive four year old maiden at Tallow (Soft/Heavy) with the market speaking in his favour. In a true run three miles race, his position fluctuated as he made several jumping errors. To his credit, he was still in contention racing to the second last and his superior stamina counted in the end as he saw off the attentions of rivals Poppa Poutine and Bebraveforglory. He did plenty wrong during the race, yet managed to win. He handled the testing underfoot conditions and stayed the trip. His dam won the mares' Listed bumper at Sandown in 2005 for Nicky Richards, and possessed speed: called Funny Times, she failed to add to this victory and tasted defeat on all three of her runs over hurdles: she was either precocious and failed to train on, or had injury problems. Prior to producing Glenglass, her early offspring include bumper winners Flementime and Mrs Hyde - a feature of the current line of the family is that they seem to produce their best in their first few runs and don't enhance it later. Glenglass will try to write a different script. He should be in the mix to win a bumper, though I don't think he is one that would be under consideration for premier bumpers. He could figure in Grade 2 or 3 company as a two and a half miles and upwards novice hurdler, though his new trainer will have to address his shoddy jumping when he eventually enters the discipline of novice chasing.

GUARDINO (FR) 4 br g Authorized (IRE) – Monicker
Trainer: Ben PAULING   Form Figures: 2
A towering bay physical unit: tight track, trip and the way the race developed contributed to his defeat on his one point appearance. That race run over an easy 2m4f at Oldtown (Soft/Heavy) in February, witnessed the nippy front runner Supreme Jet poach a handy advantage and Guardino struggled to reel that leader back in, failing by over three lengths and forced to accept the runner up spot on the day for the Denis Murphy/Jamie Codd partnership. He raced greenly but gained an education about racing that day. His family is predominantly Flat biased, his dam a dual Flat winner, and current leading jumps stallion Getaway is a progeny of his granddam. Therefore he may unlock some gears as he fills his frame over time. He cost Ben Pauling £170,000 at the Cheltenham February sales: based on performance that looked a steep outlay, however as a horse who fills the eye, an extra six to twelve months of maturity and careful cultivation could render an individual producing a level of talent to match his looks.

HOLLOW GAMES (IRE) 4 b g Beat Hollow – I'm Grand (IRE)
Trainer: Gordon ELLIOTT   Form Figures: 1
In 2019, James Doyle produced one of the smartest four year old pointers of that spring in Israel Champ. In 2020, he prepared another talented youngster to grace the winners enclosure in Hollow Games. A physically imposing bay gelding, in an eight runner maiden at Turtulla (Soft/Heavy) in March, he tracked the leader until taking over at the second last and he maintained a relentless gallop to the line to win by a distance. The first half of this race was slowly run, however, Hollow Games clocked the fastest closing half mile fractional on the day. He was the fourth highest lot sold at the Cheltenham Festival sales, moving to Gordon Elliott for a sum of £255,0000. If one examines his pedigree, one is left with mixed feelings, his dam showed nil in two track runs for Arthur Moore and, prior to Hollow Games, cut no ice as a broodmare. If you delve deep into the roots of the family tree, at the third generation, up pops the name of Champion Chaser Remittance Man. Inferred from this victory at Turtulla, Hollow Games should win a bumper on a stiff track and could even figure in black type bumper races and he will be competitive in staying Graded novice hurdles. Until tested by classier opponents, we will not know his limitations or the range of his talent.

KILBREE WARRIOR (IRE) 5 bb m Mahler – Tukawhile (IRE)
Trainer: Oliver McKiernan   Form Figures: F1
One of the more impressive mares' maiden winners of 2019/20 between the flags. A rangy bay mare, she raced for Waterford handler James Collender. She enjoyed galloping along in the lead and on her Boulta (Soft/Heavy) in December, she held the call and still had juice in her tank, when she clipped the second last fence and came a cropper. She returned to action at Tallow (Soft/Heavy) in February and jockey Tom Feeney committed her from the start, soon twenty lengths clear, she maintained a relentless gallop, pinging her fences and came home without a glove laid on her to win by a dozen lengths. Given that it was in effect, a solo run, her time was very commendable compared to other races on that card. That point fixture was run on the lands of Jimmy Mangan and he advised Oliver McKiernan to purchase this mare and a private deal was brokered. She has a positive racing attitude, to date has only raced on soft/heavy and her lengthy stride will knock rivals out of their comfort zone. We do not know how she will react, if pestered for a lead. A talented mare, her dam won a point and a three mile maiden hurdle (both heavy/soft) and she looks a certainty to bag some track wins, probably at two and a half miles and upwards in winter conditions over hurdles and fences.

LAKOTA WARRIOR (IRE) 4 br g Valirann (FR) – Talkin Madam (IRE)
Trainer: Dan SKELTON   Form Figures: 2
Contested a six runner maiden on his sole start for Denis Murphy at Lingstown (Soft) in March. It was a steadily run race with all six runners bunched at the third last, on the descent to the second last the wheat separated from the chaff with Lakota and Gerri Colombe asserting and engaging in a fantastic duel. In a bob of heads, Gerri Colombe gained the day, though Lakota Warrior earned plaudits in his narrow defeat. He displayed speed at Lingstown and he may be effective as a two to two and a half miles novice hurdler this winter. His dam won a point and he is a half brother to 2020 Grade 3 hurdle winner Run Wild Fred. He failed to sell through the ring at Cheltenham March Sales (£145k n/s), however Dan Skelton struck a deal to recruit him for a price in the same ballpark soon afterwards. He can develop into a 130+ hurdler/chaser and could be up to Grade 2 or 3 class as a novice hurdler,and may be versatile groundwise because he has a nice fluid galloping action.

LARGY DEBUT (IRE) 5 b g Shirocco (GER) – Debut (IRE)
Trainer: Henry DE BROMHEAD   Form Figures: 13
Subject to a certain degree of hype on the back of an impressive point win at Oldtown (Soft/ Heavy) in February. Racing for the Crawford brothers, he was anchored at the back of the six runner field for the first half of the race, and as they came down the hill into the homestraight for the final time, he came through swinging on the bridle and toyed with his rivals, pulling away for a thirteen lengths triumph. He was then purchased privately by owner Chris Jones for a six figure sum. He was heavily punted for a bumper at Navan in March, and his fans were most likely on good terms when he loomed up to take the lead entering the final quarter mile: his two threats rallied and in the end he was found wanting as he did not find when pressurised, forced to take a disappointing third. The Navan performance would hint he does have a high cruising speed, though may have suspect battling qualities. His owner may elect to move the horse to some of his other retained trainers into the future. A well defined muscular deep bay gelding, his dam won a Fontwell bumper for Nicky Henderson, and he is a half brother to A Little Magic, a 140 rated five times winner for Jonjo O'Neill and J.P. McManus: the family seem to prefer a sound surface and trips in the two to two and a half miles range. Given that Largy Debut has raced exclusively in mud and muck, he may have more to offer on better ground and perhaps, given his style of racing, he may perform to his optimum at shorter distances.

MAGGIES MOGUL (IRE) 4 b f Valirann (FR) – Grangeclare Gold (IRE)
Trainer: David PIPE   **Form Figures: 1**

Athletic bay mare with a physical presence: her dam won six times for the late Dessie Hughes and loved a sound surface. Therefore, it was arguably an extra feather in the cap of Maggies Mogul when she won her only point at Ballyarthur (Heavy) in March on very testing terrain. Another of the Colin Bowe team of four year olds to win a maiden in the spring of 2020: in a nine runners mares' maiden, Barry O'Neill made all the running and coaxed her home to a two lengths win without asking her any serious questions. Her half sister, Little Nugget has proved effective on the track (3 wins), and this mare can develop into a candidate for black type over jumps on the track proper, she may have best prospects when competing in mares' novices chases of gaining Graded class wins. She handled the conditions at Ballyarthur (one of the stiffest circuits in Ireland) and, if she replicates the trend of her mother, then she may become ultra versatile in terms of trip and ground (dam won all races up to 2m4f maximum). She was bought privately during the summer by the Pipe yard.

MAGIC TRICKS (FR) 4 b g Davidoff (GER) – Cadoubelle Des As (FR)
Trainer: Gordon ELLIOTT   **Form Figures: 2**

Medium sized bay gelding and not in the same pristine league as his full brother Abacadabras. Arguably performed best of the virus stricken Monbeg four year olds when he claimed second place in a maiden at Borris (Yielding/Soft) in March. Jumping cleanly, he forced the pace from the start, and by the penultimate fence, along with Gars Des Sceaux had put daylight to the rest of the field. In the last quarter mile, Magic Tricks gave best and lost by six lengths. A racy type, this Borris race may supply clues that he had stamina limitations and he may be best served racing between two and two and a half miles in track races. Bought in a private deal by Gordon Elliott on behalf of J.P.McManus, I think this horse may improve for racing on a sounder surface and he can pick up a bumper and construct what could be a money spinning career as a hurdler and chaser.

MINELLA ESCAPE (IRE) 5 b g Beat Hollow – Be My Leader (IRE)
Trainer: Henry DE BROMHEAD   **Form Figures: 41**

A big barrel of a bay gelding and powerful unit: carried the Nallen silks for a couple of points either side of Christmas: on his Boulta (Soft/Heavy) debut in December, he got tightened approaching the cross fence (3 out) and he was knocked out of his stride and thereafter not punished, he ambled home a remote fourth. Next time at Bellharbour (Yielding) in February, Nallen saddled two for the five year old maiden. The second string, Minella Away, set honest fractions at the head of affairs: racing to the third last Minella Escape jumped to the lead: he quickened up off the home turn to open up a five lengths advantage and coasted home as he liked to score by six lengths. He is a half brother to the five time track winner, Dashing Oscar, and in the third line of the family trace you locate One Man and Bellshill. His dam, Be My Leader, completed the full set of wins as a track mare, landing a bumper, hurdle and chase and closed her career as a 125 rated chaser. She had size and stature and has passed on those characteristics to this son of hers. In 2018, Henry de Bromhead purchased Minella Indo from John Nallen after his point victory at Dromahane and that decision has matured to effect. It was no surprise then that Henry was prepared to pay £100,000 for Minella Escape, another son of Beat Hollow from the Nallen academy at Cheltenham February Sales. I rated the win at Bellharbour as an above average performance in a five year old maiden category: he did clock the fastest time on the card and he is suited to a proper gallop. Examining his dam, she preferred ground with ease in it, soft or heavy and perhaps this offspring will follow suit. He can develop into a competitive Grade 3 or more staying novice chaser.

MUCKAMORE (IRE) 6 b g Sholokhov (IRE) – Gales Return (IRE)
Trainer: Nigel TWISTON-DAVIES   Form Figures: 2 – 1221
A product from the Dennison pointing camp: he debuted on his owner's track at Loughanmore (Good/Yielding) in the autumn of 2018 and following a promising second place finish, he became a sought after commodity at a subsequent Tattersalls Cheltenham Sale. Paul Nicholls signed for him at a price of £190,000. Some problem arose and a few weeks later the sale was cancelled and the horse returned to Dennison. He disappeared until surfacing for a modest five year old maiden at Mainstown (Soft) in December: ignorant at some fences, he had the class to make light work of limited opposition and win untroubled. He then had another date at Tattersalls Cheltenham sales, in December 2019, this time the tariff dropped to £50,000 with the combination of Nigel Twiston Davies and Noel Fehily picking him up. This sturdy bay gelding was purchased for the Noel Fehily Racing club and he gave them fair sport at the start of 2020, placing second in a pair of hurdle races, before romping away with a poor maiden hurdle at Taunton in March. Already rated 125 over timber, that mark gives him a few pounds to play with, and although from a family which includes Jezki, a case can be made he may achieve more over fences. He will continue to give his club owners some bang for their buck and may nick a valuable two and a half to three miles handicap chase, if placed to effect.

ONLY THE BOLD (IRE) 5 b g Jeremy (USA) – Cloghoge Lady (IRE)
Trainer: Evan WILLIAMS   Form Figures: U1
A bay gelding with a prominent white stripe down his face: limited stature. His dam won a bumper and his half sister Westerner Lady was a prolific (ten times) winner. Racing for Warren Ewing, he unseated his rider on his Borris debut in December. Closer to Ewing's Antrim base was his second port of call, namely the Tyrella (Good) track in February. He relished the sound surface at this coastal circuit and he nipped around the tight bends and readily quickened away from his rivals in the last half mile to post a smart win, in a slick time(two seconds faster than a quality Open later on the card). Evan Williams probably took a risk stumping up £215,000 for such a small horse at the February Tattersalls auction. The Borris unseat hinted that jumping fences could be an issue in time at a high level. However, all National Hunt racing does not revolve around chasing, and there is plenty of prize money to be scooped up with a speedy hurdler. This five year old has more natural gears than most of the pointers from the 2019/2020 campaign, and he could develop into a highly competitive two to two and a half miles hurdler. The pedigree is a positive for supplying bumper winners, so he could succeed initially in that arena. He looks like one of the pointing graduates who will prosper on a sound surface.

ORBYS LEGEND (IRE) 4 b g Milan – Morning Legend (IRE)
Trainer: Philip HOBBS   Form Figures: 2
Amateur jockey Harley Dunne has dabbled in horse ownership for the past few years and been relatively successful: he had a significant share in Israel Champ in 2019. Harley is planning to become a trainer/jockey in 2020/21 pointing, as he has acquired a training premises. He owned and rode Orbys Legend for his sole point at Knockmullen (Soft) in February. Harley decided to front run in the ten runner field and he gradually upped the ante as the race entered the last half mile of a 2m 4f contest. As they climbed uphill to the second last, Orbys Legend and danger Brooksway Fair asserted and had the race to themselves. It appeared from the final fence that the latter worried Orbys Legend out of the verdict, as Harley and his charge were obliged to settle for the runner up spot. Nonetheless, it was a promising debut and the horse was looked after rather than punished. Secured in 2019 for a price of €32,000 as a store, Harley trousered a profit when Hobbs paid £80,000 for this lanky bay gelding at Cheltenham February Sales. He has size and scope and Hobbs may be capable of building him into a 130 handicapper over time.

PATROCLUS (IRE) 4 b g Shirocco (GER) – Kings'andqueen's (IRE)
Trainer: Nicky HENDERSON   Form Figures: 2
An elegant lengthy bay gelding: subject of positive vibes prior to his first start for Mick Goff in the competitive looking four year old maiden at Ballycahane (Yielding/Soft) in March: he left the start a warm order odds on favourite and his punters were relatively happy when he was poised a close second and ready to roll as they raced between the last two fences. Upsides two rivals at the final fence, in light of the market optimism, it was then a shade disappointing that he failed to cope with Docpickedme, losing out by a length in a driving finish. At the Cheltenham Tattersalls festival sale Nicky Henderson secured him for a price of £150,000 (Walters Plant Hire) and forthwith has the task of moulding his natural talent into track triumphs. His dam won a Kilbeggan bumper in 2010 for Colin Bowe, and raced exclusively on a sound surface, and perhaps that may be a clue that this youngster could reveal more on better terrain. More than capable of winning a bumper as he has a decent cruising speed and a relaxed manner of racing. To date the stallion Shirocco is best known for the mare Annie Power and we are waiting for the sire to unearth a top National Hunt gelding: Patroclus may not be the one, nonetheless he has the makings of a competitive Grade 3 jumper and might be happiest racing at trips in the two to two and a half miles range.

PETIBONOME (FR) 4 gr g Al Namix (FR) – Olafane (FR)
Trainer: Henry DE BROMHEAD   Form Figures: F1D
A robust well toned steel grey French bred: he was led out of the 2019 Goffs Land Rover Sale unsold at €24,000 euros and then consignor Peter Vaughan sent him to Pat Doyle to prepare for pointing. He debuted at Bellharbour (Yielding) and he led the seven runner field for just over two miles before he thumped the fifth last and somersaulted taking a crunching fall. Given that backdrop, he was the standout pick of the parade ring for his second run at Lismore (Soft) four weeks later. This time in an eight runner affair, he was tucked in third or fourth until given the office to take over approaching the second last. To most present, he then asserted and drew clear for a smooth twelve lengths victory. A key rule in point to point races is that you must race between the appointed flags. Unfortunately, the jockey on Petibonome, Pa King, somehow got his bearings wrong on the approach to the final fence and went outside a flag (in effect taking a longer route). The acting stewards studied the video footage and it resulted in an instant disqualification for this four year old.There was no mistaking his superiority on the day and whilst he retains his maiden pointing tag due to the disqualification, the performance was above average. He was snapped up by Robcour and joins Henry de Bromhead. A concern would be that he has a full brother called Ataguiseamix, another ex-Irish pointer, has been a bitter disappointment on the track, in fact already dumped by Paul Nicholls.On the plus side, with a bad experience on his first day out, this horse displayed character to cast that memory aside and produce a polished "first past the post" at Lismore. He is a budding chaser and should progress into at least a Grade 3 novice chaser, and he may be capable of scoring over a variety of distances.

POPPA POUTINE (IRE) 4 b g Sholokhov (IRE) – Sherchanceit (IRE)
Trainer: Nigel TWISTON-DAVIES   Form Figures: 2
Angular bay gelding: represented Denis Murphy in the true run four year old maiden held at Tallow (Heavy) in February (fastest run race on the card). He sat midfield and was pushed along four out as the tempo increased. He kept on resolutely and was positioned a close third when tightened for room at the second last fence, an incident which cost him momentum. Nonetheless, he managed to rally to effect and bagged a fine second, beaten a length by Glenglass. He illustrated a fine racing attitude and this characteristic will lend itself to track success as he will be a doughty battler in tight finishes. His dam won a couple of two mile hurdle races and was ordinary at best: this offspring may give the pedigree a shot in the arm, as joining Twiston Davies via £100,000 sale at Cheltenham February auctions, he may develop into a competitive staying novice hurdler and handicap chaser, stamina looks his trump card.

REALITY CHEQUE (IRE) 5 b g Getaway (GER) – Coolaghmore Yeats (IRE)
Trainer: Willie MULLINS   Form Figures: F1
Well proportioned bay gelding: headed the market at Dromahane on his debut in December, alas his supporters had a short lived interest, as he tipped up when leading at the third fence. Pat Doyle pulled him out three weeks later, in the new year, at Kilfeacle (Soft/Heavy): with veteran Damian Skehan at the steering wheel this time, he was settled in midfield: gradually inching closer inside the closing mile, he loomed up travelling best at the second last, and settled the issue with a swagger from the final fence, recording a five lengths win from nine rivals. He clocked the fastest time on the card, though it was significant that he raced on the freshest ground in race one, and conditions deteriorated later in the afternoon. Willie Mullins struck a private deal, and he will be hopeful of developing this grand model into a talented track horse: past acquisitions from Pat Doyle, have scaled serious heights for the Closutton handler. Undoubtedly a candidate one can anticipate comfortably winning a bumper and even a winners' event in that discipline. He has only run on testing ground, given his galloping movement, he should not be inconvenienced by a sounder surface. The pedigree is rather light, so for now, he would be considered a good prospect as opposed to a great one.

RED LION LAD (IRE) 4 b g Flemensfirth (USA) – Hotline (FR)
Trainer: David PIPE   Form Figures: 1
One of the top lots from the 2019 Land Rover store sale and no surprise as his dam (a winner over jumps) is a half-sister to former Champion Chaser Master Minded: in looks and confirmation he is of similar mould to that illustrious relative. Colin Bowe took him home last summer with a successful bid of €155,000 Euros and waited until Ballyarthur (Soft/Heavy) to introduce him to the pointing game. Reigning champion point jockey, Barry O'Neill partnered and he was happy to sit off the leaders and during the closing mile, he nudged closer and without ever getting too serious, he moved between the two leaders as they faced the final fence and showed gears to settle the issue in a few strides, posting a comfortable ten length win. Those that chased him home may be limited, a remark that does not apply to this gelding as he is rich in potential. He will not be inconvenienced dropping back in distance. He failed to sell through the Goffs sales ring in July (led out unsold at £135,000): he remained in the UK as David Pipe secured him via a private deal.

SHIROCCO'S DREAM (IRE) 5 b m Shirocco (GER) – Dream Function (IRE)
Trainer: Colin TIZZARD   Form Figures: 21
The most expensive mare sold from the 2019/20 pointing season. Racing for team Monbeg, she was favourite for her debut at Tattersalls (Soft/Heavy) in December. She sat off pacesetter, Rose Of Arcadia, around fifteen to twenty lengths adrift for two thirds of the race: she began to close from the second last, and although beaten into second by two lengths, she never troubled that impressive winner on the day. Three months in later in March at Borris (Yielding/Soft), this stout bay mare (with a masculine appearance) lost her maiden tag in an eleven runner five years and upwards mares' maiden. She enjoyed the run of that race, slipstreaming the long time leader until taking over rounding the home turn. Victorias Peak emerged from the pack and posted a serious challenge and in fact led over the final fence. Shirocco's Dream rallied to great effect, and won by half a length. The winning margin arguably flattered the runner up, as it may have been a case of the winner idling when in front at the second last. On the bare bones of her two point runs, the form certainly does not justify the price of £260,000 which the Tizzards stumped up at Tattersalls Cheltenham Festival sale. Much of the investment would rest on her size and potential scope, plus the fact that her dam was a decent three time winner at 2m 3f (2 hurdles and a chase) and that dam (Dream Function) was a full sister to 2011 Arkle winner and multiple Grade 1 winning chaser Captain Chris. As the Monbeg string were riddled with a virus in the spring, winning in the circumstances may suggest that she is a hardy mare who likes the racing game.

She could be the sort of lady that will do ok as a hurdler, but who may reach her peak as a novice chaser: her action hints she may be effective on soft and good, replicating the versatility of her mother.

SOVEREIGN GOLD (IRE) 6 b m Gold Well – Sovereign Lass (IRE)
Trainer: Henry DE BROMHEAD   Form Figures: 211
Tough durable bay mare: raced three times between December 2019 and February 2020 for Damian Murphy: a promising second (not punished) on her Boulta (Soft/Heavy) debut, in the New Year she quickly got off the mark, landing her maiden in style at Aghabullogue (Soft/Heavy). She confirmed that she was an improving mare when making a successful transition into winners' grade: at Kildorrery (Soft) in February, she received a patient steer and powered home from the second last to land a winners of three, defeating a few benchmark geldings. In terms of mares contesting all sex winners' events, this victory performance was one of the best by any mare in the 2019/20 season. She has an ordinary pedigree, nonetheless, with scores on the board, she appealed to De Bromhead who bought her privately in the spring. All her runs to date have been on soft/heavy and she is comfortable in such conditions: moreover she has plenty in the stamina department, plus a gear or two: she will pay her way in winter mares' only hurdles/chases.

STAR GATE (IRE) 4 b g Imperial Monarch (IRE) – Supreme Judge (IRE)
Trainer: Evan WILLIAMS   Form Figures: 1
Jockey Rob James and trainer Colin Bowe in partnership purchased this youngster as a three year old store at Tattersalls Ireland May sale in 2019 for a sum of €20,000. They elected to produce this bay gelding (with a white blaze on his face) for the four year old maiden at Bellharbour (Yielding) in February and it was a decision that bore fruit. Against six opponents and with joint owner James at the steering wheel, he took a share of the lead from five out after the exit of Petibonome, and from the second last he was controlling matters and scored by a non taxing three lengths. The time recorded of 6.24 was noticeably slower than recent renewals of this race. In 2019, Fado Des Brosses won this race for Colin Bowe clocking 5.56: Evan Williams recruited that horse and, having won a maiden hurdle at Chepstow, he remains fertile raw material. In a case of déjà vu, when Star Gate came under the hammer at Cheltenham in February, he too was purchased by the Welsh handler for £140,000, suggesting Evan trusts the credentials from Bellharbour. One could be critical of the form, if taking the runner-up (Womalko) as a guide, because this mare subsequently finished a distant eighth of fourteen in a two mile maiden hurdle at Gowran. There is nothing of note in the immediate family of Star Gate, his great grand mother was the dam of Aintree Grand National winner Amberleigh House. He is a difficult four year old to pigeon hole, all the more considering his sire is trying to establish himself in the National Hunt ranks. Suffice to say that in the short term, Star Gate is capable of winning a midweek two and a half miles and upwards maiden hurdle and could earn himself a crack at a decent Graded novice hurdle in 2020/21, depending on his rate of progression.

STARVOSKI (IRE) 5 b m Aizavoski (IRE) – Telstar (IRE)
Trainer: Kim BAILEY   Form Figures: 1
Lengthy athletic bay mare with a white stripe down her face: represented little known handler John Byrne on her debut at Dungarvan (Yielding/Soft) in January. She shared the lead for most of the race, jumping smartly: when given the office after jumping the final fence, she drew right away on the way to the winning post to record a dominant ten length win. The standard of her rivals may have been low, however I rated the style of her victory as comprehensive. Her dam has produced four track winners, including 2019 winning half sister, Win My Wings (125 rated): she did not sell through the ring at Tattersalls Cheltenham sales in February: agent Aiden Murphy agreed a price of £35,000 outside the ring on behalf of Kim Bailey. Inferior pointing mares form the 2019/20 season made more money, and I

think this lady may prove to be a value addition to the Bailey yard and she is a surefire winner of a mares' novice hurdle and could be the type to progress into a serious candidate for the mares' novice hurdle final at Newbury in the spring of 2021. She is very uncomplicated, and her slick jumping will be an asset going forward. She did display a high knee action and therefore may generally prefer some degree of juice in the ground.

STELLAR MAGIC (IRE) 5 b g Arctic Cosmos (USA) – Inter Alia (IRE)
Owner: Allan STENNETT   **Form Figures: 1**

Hails from a rock solid family of recently successful chasers: his siblings include Dr Robin (125 rated), Witness In Court (145) and Heron Heights (141). Purchased at the 2018 Derby store sales by trainer Ian Williams for owner Allan Stennett: he appeared to have been posted to Jonathan Fogarty in Wexford to gain some experience as a pointer and condition him for track racing. He was easy in the market for the five year old maiden at Ballyvodock (Yielding/Soft) in early February. In a competitive race, he was sited in the first four all the way. Six counted as they rounded the bend for home and headed to the second last. Over the second last, it was still in the balance, then from the final fence Stellar Magic managed to find enough to win narrowly by half a length from Pay The Piper. That runner up failed to frank the form subsequently, though I would not knock the winner on that score. A medium sized bay gelding, he has the initial hallmarks of a 120+ 2m4f and upwards handicapper, who may be shy of Festival class credentials. Could be versatile in terms of ground preference.

VANILLIER (FR) 5 gr g Martaline – Virgata (FR)
Trainer: Gavin CROMWELL   **Form Figures: P – 1**

French bred grey gelding, medium build: bought by Timmy Hyde for €40,000 Euros at the 2018 Land Rover Sale and sent to Sam Curling to mould for pointing. Favoured in the market at Castletown Geoghegan (Yielding) in April 2019 on debut, cutting out tamely from three out as if something amiss (pulled up). Next competed at Dromahane (Soft/Heavy) in late December in one of the divisions of the four year old geldings maiden. Front running tactics employed by Pa King, with the grey jumping with relish at the head of the fifteen runner field. Coming down the home straight for the final time, he did look to be a target for the closing Fishkhov and Derek O'Connor: together over the final fence, Vanillier displayed the greater resolution, refusing to yield to his rival and taking the prize by three parts of a length. His dam won a Flat race in France, and whilst there may be concerns on scope, if replicating his determination under pressure, he will collect track races. More a 115-130 handicapper than a top ranking prospect, he is effective on winter terrain, and could be comfortable operating in the two and a half to three miles range.

YOUSAYITBEST (IRE) 5 b g Doyen (IRE) – Lady Hoover (IRE)
Trainer: Henry DE BROMHEAD   **Form Figures: 16**

An athletic bay gelding with a white spot on the top of his crown: Cian Hughes paid €25,000 for him at the 2018 Derby store sale: the produce of an unraced dam, you locate successful chasers like Sraid Padraig, Robinsfirth and Strong Promise in his clan. Cian waited until November 2019 to debut him in a maiden at Moig South (Soft/Heavy): he jumped cleanly in the hands of Jamie Codd and asserted with Gabynako from two out. He mastered that opponent in the final furlong, winning a shade cosily. He fetched a price of £220,0000 on his subsequent visit to the Cheltenham Tattersalls sales ring in November and headed to Henry de Bromhead and Robcour. He failed to give his running when a disappointing sixth in a bumper at Clonmel in March: leading past halfway and then folding and hanging left under pressure. It could be that he requires a left handed circuit (as per Moig South). Perhaps he is not a bumper horse and he may be witnessed in his element when jumping hurdles and fences. He had a wind procedure in the close season. For now, he will have to locate plenty of improvement to become a graded performer in the National Hunt game.

DECLAN PHELAN'S
NATIONAL HUNT SERVICE
2020/21

The service for the **2020/21** season includes:

(1) Full Irish Point to Point Dossier

The indexed production contains over 120 individual essays on track bound Irish pointers emerging from the 2019/20 pointing campaign. The individual essays are prepared with punting in mind: the pointer profiles are designed to offer an introduction to each horse and arm you with a vital knowledge edge. My composition is the only such source covering the past pointing season in such depth,and is scripted by someone who has been present at these fixtures and seen in the horses in close-up in action.

(2) Weekend E-Mail Preview Service

Covering 22 weekends from mid October to Aintree Grand National weekend in April 2021.

Posted via email by 8pm each Friday evening. The preview covers weekend jumping action in the UK & Ireland and generally I focus on low key races because I deem them more punter friendly than the bookmaker promoted feature races.

The weekend previews recorded a healthy profit in past seasons.

Additional preview packages included in the service : a Boxing Day preview, a special Cheltenham Festival preview, and coverage of the Punchestown Festival in the spring.

(3) **Midweek Morning late news service:** depending on the value on offer, at 11.30 midweek, once a week, more or less, depending on the betting market, you receive a late email bulletin.

If you would like to join the winter jumps service, contact via email mrdeclanphelan@hotmail.com for full details.

For Irish(only) clients, Declan's nightly views on the next day's action are available from 10pm on 1560111 112.

UNRACED BUMPER HORSES

FAMOSO (IRE) 4 b g Fame And Glory – Mucho Macabi (IRE)
Trainer: P.F.NICHOLLS. Ditcheat, Somerset.
Paul Nicholls has an enviably team of youngsters with a host of unraced talent set to contest bumpers this spring. These include this €175,000 purchase, who was acquired at the Goffs Land Rover Sale in Ireland as a three year old. Owned by **Paul Barber and Paul Vogt**, he is a half-brother to Willie Mullins' Grade 3 winning chaser Tornado Flyer, who was also placed in the Cheltenham Festival bumper a couple of years ago.

FINAL ENCORE 3 b g Dunaden (FR) – Act Three
Trainer: H.MORRISON. East Ilsley, Berkshire.
Third Wind has won four times over hurdles for Hughie Morrison and is rated 141. A former winner of the EBF Final at Sandown, he was fourth in the Pertemps Final at the Cheltenham Festival last March. The head of Summerdown is also training his half-brother Final Encore. Described as 'a nice horse' by Morrison, there is a possibility he will make his debut in a junior bumper later this year. His stable have a very good record in bumpers – 25 winners from 108 runners (23%) and the gelded son of Dunaden is one to watch on his debut.

INVESTMENT MANAGER 4 b g Nathaniel (IRE) – Two Days In Paris (FR)
Trainer: C.TIZZARD. Milborne Port, Dorset.
Owned by **Brocade Racing**, he cost €70,000 at the Tattersalls Derby Sale last year and his trainer Colin Tizzard commented in the Autumn: **"We bought him at the Derby Sale and he looks a really nice horse. He's a sharp three year old – probably the sharpest we've had in a while – and we plan on running him in a bumper. He's very athletic and works nicely at home, so we're excited to get him started."**

KNAPPERS HILL (IRE) 4 b g Valirann (FR) – Brogella (IRE)
Trainer: P.F.NICHOLLS. Ditcheat, Somerset.
Purchased for €155,000 at the Goffs Land Rover Sale as a three year old, he is owned by **Paul Barber and Paul Vogt**. A half-brother to Listed chase winner and Grade 1 runner-up Rene's Girl, he is also a younger sibling to Galway Hurdle second Swamp Fox. His sire Valirann, who was Group 2 winner on the Flat for the Aga Khan, is a name to watch out for this winter and beyond.

NO RISK DE FLOS (FR) 5 b g No Risk At All (FR) – Marie Royale (FR)
Trainer: O.MURPHY. Wilmcote, Warwickshire.
Half-brother to Grade 2 winning hurdler Vison Des Flos and three times winner Umndeni, he was purchased at the Tattersalls Derby Sale for €200,000 as a three year old. Owned by **Diana Whateley**, he has 'a big engine,' in the words of his trainer Olly Murphy, and will begin his career in a bumper in October/November.

QUALISMART (FR) 4 b g Martaline – Qualita (GER)
Trainer. H.WHITTINGTON. Sparsholt, Oxfordshire.
As discussed, Simply The Betts provided Harry Whittington with his first Cheltenham Festival winner when landing the Brown Advisory & Merriebelle Stable Plate Handicap Chase in March. The seven year old is owned by **Kate and Andrew Brooks** and they are also responsible for this highly regarded four year old by Martaline. A half-brother to a dual Listed winner on the Flat in France (Qualisaga), his homework has been good and is one to watch out for on his racecourse debut in a bumper.

TFOU (FR) 4 br g Authorized (IRE) – Fire Moon Julie (FR)
Trainer: N.G.RICHARDS. Greystoke, Cumbria.
Bought for €180,000 as a three year old at the Goffs Land Rover Sale in Ireland in June 2019, he is held in the highest regard at Greystoke and will make his debut in a bumper during the Autumn. Reported to have worked very well at home, he is likely to carry the **Tarzan Bloodstock** silks, unless sold in the meantime.

WHERE IT ALL BEGAN (IRE) 4 b g Yeats (IRE) – Peggy Cullen (IRE)
Trainer: G.ELLIOTT. Longwood, Co.Meath.
Due to contest a point-to-point last spring when trained by Donnchadh Doyle last season, he was bought for €72,000 as a store horse at the Tattersalls Derby Sale the previous summer. He is a half-brother to Cheltenham Festival winner and Grand National third Rathvinden and was subsequently bought by **Max McNeill** and has joined Gordon Elliott.

★ ★ ★ ★ ★ ★

BRIAN ELLISON is one of the best dual purpose trainers in the business and he is responsible for a handful of unraced three year olds who will contest junior bumpers later this year.The first three are all owned by **Gordon Bulloch**.

HACKBERRY was bought for 12,000gns at the Tattersalls February Sale and is by Nathaniel and is a Juddmonte cast off. From the family of Banks Hill and Intercontinental, he is impeccably bred and could develop into a useful dual purpose performer.

HUNTSMAN'S CALL was in training with Simon Crisford but didn't race. A gelded son of Golden Horn, he is a half-brother to dual Listed winner Pelerin and six times winner Road To Dubai. He was purchased for 22,000gns at the Newmarket July Sales.

NIGHT RANGER, like Hackberry, is ex-Juddmonte and is a son of Dansili out of the useful sprinter Sleep Walk. Like his dam, he was trained by Roger Charlton but didn't race before being bought for 16,000gns at the Newmarket July Sales. Reportedly the speediest of the five, he is considered a lovely prospect.

PUNXSUTAWNEY PHIL is a son of Shirocco and a half-brother to stablemate Burn Some Dust (4 wins) and Nordic Combined (3). Held in high regard, the **Dan Gilbert** owned three year old is going well at home and should be followed on his debut.

Speaking to Brian in early September, he also suggested keeping an eye out for an **unnamed three year old by Nathaniel out of Bridle Belle**. A half-brother to dual winner Major Snugfit, he is owned by Dan Gilbert, M.Lawrence and A.Bruce.

The head of Spring Cottage Stables reported his exciting novice chaser from last season **WINDSOR AVENUE** has had a wind operation and strengthened up during the summer. The Listed Colin Parker Memorial Intermediate Chase at Carlisle (1st November) is likely to be his first target. Rated 148, the eight year old's form figures at the cumbrian track are 121. The trainer believes **BARON DE MIDLETON** is one to follow over fences this season, while the pick of his novice hurdlers is expected to be **FAIR STAR, KEARNEY HILL** and **TUPELO MISSISSIPPI**.

Finally, Cheltenham Festival winning owner **SEAN MULRYAN** is believed to have a promising team of unraced bumper horses. I suggest keeping an eye on **LONESOME BOATMAN**. He is a four year old by Jukebox Jury who was bought for €65,000 at the Goffs Land Rover Sale in June last year. **WHO'S HOUDINI** cost €90,000 at the same sale and is a four year old by Beat Hollow. A half-brother to four times winner Masons Daughter, the pair are trained in Ireland by **Martin Brassil**.

APPENDIX

As in previous years, I have attempted to highlight a number of horses, in various categories, who are expected to contest the major prizes during the 2020/2021 campaign.

Two Mile Chasers

Last season's Queen Mother Champion Chase threatened to be one of the races of the Festival with dual winner **ALTIOR** set to clash with impressive Leopardstown winner **CHACUN POUR SOI** and dual Festival winner **DEFI DU SEUIL**. Unfortunately, the first two named suffered last minute setbacks, which ruled them out, while the last named performed well below par and finished a distant fourth of five. Instead, it was nine year old **POLITOLOGUE**, who had finished runner-up the previous year, who provided Paul Nicholls with his sixth win in the race when scoring by nine and a half lengths.

ALTIOR, who was lame a few days before the Festival, due to a splint problem, lost his unbeaten record over fences at Ascot in November when outstayed by Cyrname in a Grade 2 chase over two miles five. It took Nicky Henderson's ten times Grade 1 winner a long time to recover but the High Chaparral gelding was back to form when winning the Grade 2 Game Spirit Chase at Newbury in February for a third time. Following his three and a quarter lengths victory, his trainer said: **"Nico (De Boinville) said what he really liked was when he went to put it to bed, the gears were there."** At the age of ten, the former champion may be vulnerable to a younger challenger but he is likely to be kept to the minimum trip during the first half of the season, at least.

CHACUN POUR SOI was withdrawn on the morning of the race at Cheltenham having been found to have a foot abscess. The ex-French gelding is delicate having only raced four times for Willie Mullins since joining the yard in 2016. He is hugely talented though winning two Grade 1 chases and rated 171. Runner-up on his reappearance behind A Plus Tard at Leopardstown over Christmas, the Policy Maker gelding made amends in the Grade 1 Dublin Chase at Leopardstown (2m 1f : Yielding) in early February. A three and three quarters of a length winner from stablemate Min, he travelled beautifully and jumped slickly. Ireland's champion trainer, who has never won the Champion Chase at Cheltenham, enthused afterwards: **"That was a very good performance. His jumping was electric. The day I brought him here for Cheltenham's trials day last year, I let him go around with a few of ours. I said to Danny (Mullins), who rode him, to follow around but after two fences he was in front and led all the Cheltenham horses. It was absolutely eye opening. Once every two or three years you get a horse coming up the gallops who shows you something they shouldn't be able to do, and that's what he did that day. I said 'wow we could have something here' and he's turned out that way."** Granted luck, he remains an outstanding two mile prospect and is likely to head back to Leopardstown over Christmas and hopefully line up at the Festival next spring.

Sent off 2/5 favourite, **DEFI DU SEUIL** failed to shine at Cheltenham in March and was struggling from the outset. Beaten over thirteen lengths, his rider Barry Geraghty reported: **"He was never really going. I was trying to nurse him into it but I knew from the back of the third last the game was up. He's fine, but for no obvious reason, he just didn't perform. He's still a gorgeous horse."** Earlier in the campaign, the seven times Grade 1 winner had won three out of three, including a neck victory in the Tingle Creek Chase at Sandown followed by an even more convincing display in the Clarence House Chase at Ascot beating Un De Sceaux for a second consecutive time. **"It was dazzling and breathtaking. He's not the biggest in the world but he has so much scope. He's up for it and that's what you love about good two mile chasers. Moscow Flyer wasn't the** biggest or flashiest but he was up for it, and so is this lad," remarked Geraghty at the Berkshire track. Philip Hobbs added: **"He could go three miles if you wanted to."** Indeed, the seven year old looks well worth a try over further this season – I remain convinced he is tailormade for the King George. As far as March is concerned, the Ryanair Chase may prove to be his optimum target because it is possible the New course (11121) at Cheltenham suits him better than the Old course (1514). It will be interesting, too, to see who rides the Voix Du Nord gelding this season – Richard Johnson (11172) is the only jockey to have partnered him since arriving from France.

As discussed, Paul Nicholls feels there is huge improvement to come from **GREANETEEN**. Still only six, the ex-French gelding is rated 151 having won three of his four starts as a novice last term. Successful at Ascot (off 132), Musselburgh (138) and Fakenham, he was only beaten around five lengths in the Grand Annual Chase at Cheltenham having met trouble in running at the second last. The Haldon Gold Cup at Exeter (3rd November) has been earmarked for his seasonal return – he is unbeaten at the track. He could be the dark horse of the division.

PUT THE KETTLE ON became the first mare to win the Arkle Trophy since Anaglogs Daughter in 1980 when beating Fakir D'Oudairies by a length and a half. The six year old won five of her six starts over fences and is unbeaten at Cheltenham having also won the Grade 2 novice in November. Henry De Bromhead, who was winning the Arkle for a second time, said in March: **"Aidan (Coleman) said she'd handle any ground. She's lightly raced and why not think about the Champion Chase. She's won an Arkle and is a big immature mare with the heart of a lion."** Rated 155 over fences compared to 123 over hurdles, the Stowaway mare is thriving with racing, but I am not convinced last season's two mile novices were a vintage crop.

Two and a half Mile Chasers:

Willie Mullins has won three of the last five runnings of the Grade 1 Ryanair Chase at Cheltenham in March and **ALLAHO** looks the sort to emerge as a big player in the two and a half miles event next March. Third in the Albert Bartlett Novices' Hurdle at the Festival in 2019, he was a twenty one lengths winner from subsequent Kim Muir winner Milan Native in a beginners' chase at Fairyhouse (2m 5f : Yielding/Soft) in January. **"We've always looked on him as a potentially high-class staying chaser and it was great to see him put up such a good performance,"** remarked Mullins. The No Risk At All gelding then returned to three miles in the RSA Chase at the Festival and, while he ran a fine race in third, the six year old's stamina appeared to give way late on. Beaten two lengths behind Champ and Minella Indo, he races enthusiastically and may prove at his best over this shorter distance. Rated 157 and placed twice at the Festival, he is a very smart horse and it is only a matter of time before he wins at Grade 1 level over fences. His form figures over 2m 5f are 21 compared to 1323 over three miles.

Similar to Allaho, Festival winner **A PLUS TARD** is owned by Cheveley Park Stud and the six year old became only the second horse to beat Chacun Pour Soi over fences when winning the Grade 1 two miles one chase at Leopardstown (Soft) over Christmas. A three and three quarters of a length winner, the Kapgarde gelding was sent off 7/4 favourite for the Ryanair Chase in March but could only finish third. Henry De Bromhead's horse made a mistake at the second fence and never looked comfortable thereafter. A length and three quarters behind Min and Saint Calvados, his trainer remarked afterwards: **"Rachel (Blackmore) said he never seemed to be going at all. It definitely wasn't the distance as he was closer at the line than he was at the last. He just didn't seem to run his race."** With time still on his side, the 167 rated chaser remains a top-class horse and capable of adding to his Grade 1 tally over two and two and a half miles.

Compatriot **SAMCRO** silenced his doubters when returning to his best in the Grade 1 JLT Novices' Chase at Cheltenham. The eight year old, who underwent wind surgery and had a new box built for him following his defeat at Limerick over Christmas, was providing Gigginstown House Stud with their 100th Grade 1 winner when edging out Melon by a nose. The former Ballymore Novices' Hurdle winner had won impressively on his chasing debut at Down Royal in November before falling at the second last in the Grade 1 Drinmore Novice Chase at Fairyhouse. **"Jack (Kennedy) said he was absolutely cantering at the time. He just thought he slipped on landing after the fence. I thought he was travelling very well at the time and Jack did too,"** stated Gordon Elliott. Beaten ten lengths by Faugheen at Limerick on St Stephen's day, the Germany gelding cut out quickly having held every chance on the approach to the second last. Jack Kennedy, who fractured his right femur at Leopardstown's Dublin Racing Festival in early February when unseated from Dallas Des Pictons, is his regular partner (1111F225F2) but Davy Russell rode him for the first time in March. The Grade 1 John Durkan Memorial Chase at Punchestown (6th December) looks an obvious first half of the season target. The Grade 2 Skymas Chase at Down Royal (31st October) over the same distance is a possible starting point. The same connections won both races with their subsequent Cheltenham Gold Cup winner Don Cossack in 2014.

Following his agonising defeat in March, **MELON**'s form figures at the Cheltenham Festival read 2222, which typifies the eight year old's career with only 3 wins from 18 races over obstacles. Runner-up in the Champion Hurdle twice, Willie's Mullins' gelding won over fences at Leopardstown (2m 1f : Soft) over Christmas before finishing well held in fourth behind Notebook at the same track's Dublin Racing Festival in Grade 1 company. He then tackled two and a half miles for only the second time (fell at the third last when leading in the Aintree Hurdle last year) and was fitted with cheekpieces at Cheltenham. It was the first time Patrick Mullins had partnered the son of Medicean and he ran a mighty race with stablemate Faugheen a length behind him in third. **"He ran a fantastic race. The cheekpieces have definitely helped his jumping as he was gaining lengths with his jumping. Hopefully, he might race in the big one (Gold Cup) in the future as he jumps and stays,"** remarked his trainer. Unexposed over the trip, he has the ability to win a Grade 1 over fences.

Al Ferof (2012) and Caid Du Berlais (2014) provided Paul Nicholls with success in the race now known as the BetVictor Gold Cup at Cheltenham (14th November). The latter was a French bred five year old and **SAINT SONNET** is of a similar ilk. Rated 147 over fences, he won three times over hurdles and once over fences in France when trained by Augustin Adeline De Boisbrunet. Transferred to Ditcheat early in the New Year, the Saint Des Saints gelding won a novice chase at Catterick (2m 3f : Heavy) in February with Harry Cobden commenting: **"They went no pace but he's a class horse and that was a nice start."** Seventh in the Grade 1 JLT Novices' Chase at Cheltenham the following month, he was only beaten thirteen lengths by Samcro and Melon having held every chance on the approach to the hometurn. With only three runs over fences to his name, the Colm Donlon owned gelding looks tailormade for the race.

Martin Pipe won the two and a half miles event on eight occasions and his son David landed the prize in 2011 with Great Endeavour. The Pond House team may have a prime contender for this year's renewal in new arrival **SIRUH DU LAC**. The seven year old pulled up in the race last year when trained by Nick Williams, but was still in front when falling at the second last in the Brown Advisory & Merriebelle Stable Plate Handicap Chase at the Festival in March, a race he had won the previous season. Officially rated 150, he has had a wind operation since joining Pipe and his form figures at Cheltenham are 411PF. The Turgeon gelding's record first time out is 3P1P. Longer-term, he looks worth a try over further and it will be no surprise if he is given an entry in the Ladbrokes Trophy at Newbury (28th November).

Staying Chasers:

AL BOUM PHOTO became the first horse since Best Mate (2002 – 2004) to win the Cheltenham Gold Cup in successive years when beating Santini by a neck under Paul Townend (151R1211). The Buck's Boum gelding has won 6 of his 11 races over fences and is rated 175. One would imagine Willie Mullins will aim him at the Grade 3 Savills New Year's Day Chase at Tramore (2m 5f) for a third time before heading back to Cheltenham in March.

Nicky Henderson came so close to winning his third Cheltenham Gold Cup in March and, granted slower ground and a stronger gallop, **SANTINI** may well have prevailed. Sporting cheekpieces for the first time, he stayed on strongly on the run-in. Benefiting from a wind operation (had his soft palate cauterized) earlier in the year, he won the Grade 2 Cotswold Chase by three and a half lengths in receipt of two pounds from Bristol De Mai. **"He lives and thrives on work and the more you can get into him, the better he becomes – he's always been like that. He's a bit of a Bobs Worth, as he's not as flamboyant as Long Run, but he's workmanlike and those horses can win Gold Cups,"** remarked the head of Seven Barrows at Cheltenham in January. The eight year old's record at Cheltenham is 13212 and racing left-handed (111311212) and it will be interesting to see which races he contests en route to a return to Prestbury Park next spring. With only half a dozen races over fences to his name, he must have every chance of going one better in March.

CHAMP provides another string to Henderson's Gold Cup bow having won three out of four over fences as a novice, including the RSA Chase in March. From the family of Best Mate, the eight year old seemingly had a hopeless task jumping the second last but Barry Geraghty's mount stayed on strongly after the final fence to collar Minello Indo close home. The step up to three miles for the first time was undoubtedly in his favour but his jumping remains unconvincing and he needs to brush up in that department, if the King's Theatre gelding is to emerge as a major contender for steeplechasing's Blue Riband.

MINELLA INDO appeals more because there is feeling that Henry De Bromhead's runner was the best horse in the race and would have won had he been ridden with more restraint. Rachel Blackmore's partner was locked in a duel with Allaho a long way from home and paid the price when making a mistake at the last and losing his momentum. Beaten a length, it was only his third run over fences and the former Albert Bartlett Novices' Hurdle winner remains unexposed over three miles plus (21112). His form figures at Grade 1 level are 112. **"It's one race, in particular, I don't like watching back. I wish I'd got a better jump out of him at the last. I think the result might have been different, we lost a lot of momentum there. It was a bit frustrating."** The same connections were responsible for the fourth in last season's Gold Cup, namely Monalee, and this gelding looks a strong stayer. Expect him to be a big player in all the top staying chases on either side of the Irish Sea this campaign.

LOSTINTRANSLATION also had his soft palate cauterized towards the end of January having pulled up in the King George at Kempton on Boxing Day. The eight year old arguably produced a career best when a length and a half behind Al Boum Photo in the Gold Cup having led between the final two fences. Colin Tizzard's dual Grade 1 winner didn't quite see out the trip as well as the first two and may be at his best over slightly shorter trips. Colin Tizzard has won the *Betfair* Chase at Haydock (21st November) on four occasions, including with this eight year old last season, and it would appear to be his obvious target once again. Given his record on right-handed tracks (421P), a return to Kempton over Christmas may not be the most appealing mid season target. A trip to Ireland for the Grade 1 Savills Chase at Leopardstown may prove to be much more to his liking. He is a top-class chaser over three miles on left-handed tracks (113). The Grade 1 Bowl at Aintree in April will be ideal, too (course form 21).

When it comes to top flight staying chasers, Paul Nicholls is the king and, once again, Team Ditcheat has a formidable hand with dual King George winner **CLAN DES OBEAUX**, **CYRNAME** (still to prove he stays three miles) and the returning **TOPOFTHEGAME**. The last named hasn't been seen since chasing home Lostintranslation at Aintree in April 2019, having suffered an injury to his near-fore tendon last Autumn. However, the former RSA Chase winner, who has only had a handful of races over fences, is back in work and is likely to reappear in either the *Betfair* Chase at Haydock – a race Nicholls has won six times – or the Ladbrokes Trophy at Newbury the following week (28th November). A half length winner of the RSA Chase from Santini and Delta Work, it is worth recalling his trainer's comments in September last year: **"He strikes me as an ideal Gold Cup horse. He travels beautifully, jumps and stays, and those are the qualities you need."**

A new arrival to the yard this summer is last season's Gold Cup sixth **REAL STEEL**. Owned by Jared Sullivan, the seven year old has won 5 of his 11 races over fences and is rated 166. A dual Grade 2 winner last term, he travelled strongly at Cheltenham until his stamina gave way after the second last. Brian Hughes was on board and the champion jockey reported afterwards: **"I thought they went steady enough and my horse got into a nice rhythm. He jumped well throughout and when I pulled him out going to the third last, he winged it. Turning in, I thought for a second we might just get there but then his stride began to shorten and I knew that was it. He probably didn't quite get up the hill but he did well."** Despite that run, his former trainer Willie Mullins has always felt the Loup Breton gelding is more effective on right-handed tracks (1P41121141P). With that in mind, **he looks tailormade for the King George** with his new trainer seeking his twelfth win in the Christmas showpiece. **Available at 33/1 with Betfred and William Hill, at the time of writing, he is vastly overpriced** given the fact a number of the market leaders are unlikely to head to Sunbury over the Festive period.

GRAND NATIONAL

It is early days to be thinking in terms of the Grand National, plus my luck regarding ante-post selections has not been the best in recent years – Prince De Beauchene was advised at 33/1 and was favourite for the race only to be ruled out with injury a few days beforehand in 2012, and Any Second Now was selected at the same price and was set to be a leading contender last spring only for the coronavirus to intervene (the fact Ted Walsh's gelding finished third in the virtual version was no consolation). However, there are a couple who are worthy of a long-term interest.

EASYSLAND is only six but has won 8 of his 15 races over fences and is officially rated 152. Twice successful over the cross country course at Cheltenham, including in March when beating dual Grand National winner Tiger Roll by seventeen lengths, he was bought by J.P.McManus last winter and the Grand National next spring is reportedly on his agenda. Trained in France by David Cottin, the Gentlewave gelding has won his last seven starts. **"I was expecting a good run from him. He seemed really well at home. The heavy ground was also in his favour. He's extremely well balanced and, while he's only six, with a cross-country horse you have to train them when they're young over those jumps,"** remarked his young handler at the Cheltenham Festival. A seven lengths winner at the same track in December, his former owner David Futter commented: **"Easysland is not over big and it's why we bought him cheap at the sales. We stand the stallion Gentlewave at Yorton Farm and we support our stallions."** He looked every inch a Graded staying chaser in the making at the Festival and makes plenty of appeal at **25/1** (generally) for Aintree success.

It wouldn't be a major surprise if **MILAN NATIVE** developed into a leading player next spring either. Seven years old and rated 149 over fences, the Milan gelding is unexposed over staying trips (1 from 1 over three miles plus). A length and three quarters winner of the Kim Muir at the Cheltenham in March, he was providing 27 year old Rob James with his first Festival success. **"Milan Native winged the second last and he was gone, he was actually pricking his ears going to the line. I went up to Leopardstown the week before Cheltenham to sit on him. He gave me a great feel. He is a lovely big horse and Gordon (Elliott) felt that going up in trip would really suit him,"** commented his rider, who has partnered 219 point-to-point winners, including Topofthegame and Colin Tizzard's new recruit Killer Kane. Elliott has won the National three times and the Gigginstown House Stud owned gelding couldn't be in better hands. At the time of writing, **he is available at 40/1 (BetVictor, Paddy Power) for the Aintree showpiece**.

Two Mile Hurdlers:
EPATANTE provided owner J.P.McManus and trainer Nicky Henderson with their ninth and eighth victories respectively in the Champion Hurdle in March. The daughter of No Risk At All began her second season over timber with an official rating of 137 and, following three wins, she is now on a mark of 162. The ex-French trained mare was a taking winner of the Christmas Hurdle at Kempton on Boxing day brushing aside Silver Streak by five lengths. Her trainer said afterwards: **"She is much more mature now, mentally, and she travelled like a dream there."** She then became only the second mare to win the Champion Hurdle since 1994 when beating triple Grade 1 winner Sharjah by three lengths. **"I thought she would struggle on the ground. I was worried about it all week but every step of the way she was a dream. It was a brilliant performance,"** enthused Barry Geraghty afterwards. Successful in five of her six races over hurdles, she is a top-class mare who proved her effectiveness at Cheltenham, which was a concern beforehand.

It remains to be seen when stablemate and dual Champion Hurdle winner **BUVEUR D'AIR** returns to action. The nine year old was bidding to win the Grade 1 Fighting Fifth Hurdle for a third consecutive time when making a mistake at the second last before finishing a short head runner-up behind Cornerstone Lad. It transpired the eight times Grade 1 winner had a splinter of wood in his foot with Henderson stating: **"It's gone in through the top of the coronet band and underneath the hoof. It's a matter of getting the piece of wood out from under the hoof."** Having undergone surgery on Sunday 1st December, he missed the remainder of the season but will hopefully be back in action this winter and bid to become the first horse to win the Champion Hurdle as a ten year old since Sea Pigeon in 1980 and the sixth horse to win the race three times.

Ireland have won 6 of the last 10 runnings of the Champion Hurdle and both Grade 1 winners **HONEYSUCKLE** and a fully fit **SALDIER** will have their supporters. The former, who was bought by Mark O'Hare for €9,500 as a three year old before being sold after her point-to-point win for €110,000, is unbeaten in nine races, including four at the highest level. Half a length winner of the mares' hurdle at the Festival in March, she had won the Irish Champion Hurdle at Leopardstown prior to that. All being well, she will back at Cheltenham next spring to take on the 'boys' in the big one. An injury meant the latter only raced once last term. Recording his second Grade 1 victory in the Morgiana Hurdle at Punchestown in November when beating Petit Mouchoir by a length and a half, Willie Mullins said: **"We let nature take its course after his injury (shattered his nose) last year and it appears to have worked. His run at Naas last year showed us he could be Grade 1 material and he is. I think he'll improve from that and a stronger gallop will suit him."** Off since, the Soldier Hollow gelding has only raced six times over hurdles and could provide his trainer with his fifth win in the Champion Hurdle since 2011.

Rooster Booster won the County Hurdle in 2002 off a mark of 144 and, twelve months later, Philip Hobbs' grey landed hurdling's Blue Riband at the age of nine. Saldier's stablemate **SAINT ROI** won the County Hurdle in March off a rating of 137 and looked a Graded performer in the making when trouncing his twenty three opponents by upwards of four and a half lengths (runner-up and stablemate Aramon has won the Galway Hurdle since). The five year old was previously trained in France by Guy Cherel and was only having his fourth run over timber last spring. **"He's had only three runs, he's a young horse so you're sending on him, hoping he's gonna find after the last. When you have lots of horse, the stride pops up easy. He was electric. For a horse with little experience and the pace they went, he was very good. Willie (Mullins) was sweet on him and he's not a bad judge,"** commented Barry Geraghty afterwards. A chaser in the making, the 151 rated Coastal Path gelding has huge potential.

The Champion Hurdle is one of the few top races not to feature on Gordon Elliott's CV but many believe the *Skybet* Supreme Novices' Hurdle runner-up **ABACADABRAS** has the credentials to develop into a major player. The French bred six year old was denied by a head behind Shishkin with his trainer commenting afterwards: **"He ran a great race. The way the race worked out, he was left in front a bit too soon but he jumped great and didn't do anything wrong. He could be a Champion Hurdle horse. The faller definitely cost us a bit of ground. Our fella is a very speedy horse and I would think he will stay over hurdles next season."** A Grade 1 winner at Leopardstown over Christmas, he looks tailormade for the Grade 2 WKD Hurdle at Down Royal (30th October), a race Elliott won last season with Coeur Sublime. The Fighting Fifth Hurdle at Newcastle (28th November) could also entered calculations.

There is not much doubt that the unluckiest horse at the 2020 Cheltenham Festival was **GOSHEN** who had the Triumph Hurdle in safe keeping when making a mistake at the last and depositing Jamie Moore to the floor. Rated 88 on the Flat, the Authorized gelding had won his first three races over hurdles by an aggregate of 68 lengths. An eleven lengths scorer at Ascot in January, he beat subsequent winner Nordano, despite the fact he was found to be sore afterwards having lost two shoes, with Gary Moore saying: **"He's learning all the time. The one thing that really pleased me today was that he was as cool as a cucumber beforehand. He's been edgy before his other races but he was as dry as a bone today."** Sent off 5/2 favourite in March, the four year old went clear rounding the hometurn until hitting the deck at the final flight. A disconsolate Jamie Moore commented: **"The amazing thing is he was still quickening into that hurdle. I've never let the horse down before and this was the first time I pushed him and he was flying. He could be an unbelievable horse for us."** Most effective on soft/heavy ground, it remains to be seen how he copes with a quicker surface but he has every chance of emulating Katchit (2008) and Espoir D'Allen (2019) by winning the Champion Hurdle as a five year old next spring. A half-brother to two and a half miles Grade 2 winning chaser Elimay, it wouldn't be a surprise to see him return in something like the Ascot Hurdle (21st November) even though it means a step up in trip. Unbeaten at the Berkshire track, he is bred to stay further, despite the fact he possesses sufficient speed for the minimum trip.

Seven Barrows is home to another very good mare in the shape of the unbeaten **MARIE'S ROCK**. A five year old by Milan, she won a bumper at Ffos Las and both her starts over hurdles at Haydock and Taunton last season. A five lengths winner at the former track, she then followed up by taking a Listed mares' novice hurdle at the West Country track in late December. Following her eight lengths win from the 124 rated Midnights' Gift, owners Middleham Park's racing manager Tom Palin commented: **"Nico (De Boinville) said she was something out of the ordinary when she won her bumper at Ffos Las."** One of the ante-post favourites for the Dawn Run Novices' Hurdle at the Cheltenham Festival, it was announced in February she had suffered a stress fracture. Palin stated: **"It's a slight stress fracture, which means she'll have six weeks in her box and then we can resume walking and light trotting exercise. In terms of next season, it shouldn't affect her at all."** Rated 144, she ought to be very competitive in good handicaps (Greatwood Hurdle at Cheltenham (15ᵗʰ November)) and has the potential to make an impact in Pattern company, including against geldings.

Stablemate **ALLART** is rated one pound lower on a mark of 143 and his trainer has indicated the six year old has unfinished business over hurdles. From the family of useful two miles chaser William's Wishes, the Shantou gelding won twice over hurdles before finishing fifth in the *Skybet* Supreme Novices' Hurdle at the Festival. Following his nine lengths win at Ludlow in January, the champion trainer commented: **"Allart has been an unlucky horse as he should have won his bumper but he didn't and then he was knocked over on his hurdles debut at Ascot. I've been trying to get him onto the track for a while but he's come back with dirty trachea washes."** A month later, he defied a penalty to win at Doncaster (2m : Soft) by fourteen lengths with Nico De Boinville saying: **"The more racing Allart has done, the more he's settled. I was very happy with that, it was just a glorified schooling session for him. He's a smart horse. His jumping is coming together nicely and he's an exciting prospect."** Beaten around fifteen lengths in the Festival opener, there is a big prize over timber to be won with the Ronnie Bartlett owned gelding before he goes chasing.

Nicky Richards won the Grade 1 Fighting Fifth Hurdle at Newcastle (28ᵗʰ November) with The French Furze in 2003 and he is eying the two mile prize for his high-class novice from last season **RIBBLE VALLEY**. A dual bumper winner, the Westerner gelding won over hurdles at Hexham and Wetherby with Brian Hughes saying at the former track: **"I think the world of this horse and hopefully we've found one."** An eleven lengths winner at the A1 track next time, he led three out before powering clear under his penalty. His trainer believes: **"He's got everything about him as he is a good traveller with speed to burn. He has a very bright future."** Too keen in the Grade 2 Kennel Gate Novices' Hurdle at Ascot last time, he was beaten eight lengths by Master Debonair. Off since, he is a chaser in the making but his trainer feels this 141 rated hurdler has more to offer over the smaller obstacles.

Two and a half Mile plus Hurdlers:

With the last two winners of the Stayers' Hurdle, namely Paisley Park and Lisnagar Oscar, looking vulnerable, it is a wide open division. Two novices from last season who could emerge as live contenders include **THYME HILL**. Third in the Festival bumper in 2019 behind Envoi Allen, the Kayf Tara gelding won his first three starts over hurdles, including the Grade 2 Persian War Novices' Hurdle at Chepstow followed by a similar event at Cheltenham's November meeting. A length and a half winner of the Grade 1 Challow Hurdle at Newbury over Christmas, Philip Hobbs' charge stepped up to three miles for the first time in the Albert Bartlett Novices' Hurdle at Cheltenham (his only run on the New course). Sent off 4/1 favourite, Richard Johnson's mount didn't enjoy the clearest of runs approaching the last and was forced to switch. Beaten a length and a half by Monkfish, his trainer is eyeing the Grade 2 West Yorkshire Hurdle at Wetherby (31ˢᵗ October), a race his stable have won three times (Brother Joe (2002), Fair Along (2009 & 2010)). The six year old's form figures at Cheltenham are 2314.

Paul Nicholls won the Stayers' Hurdle on four occasions with the brilliant Big Buck's and, despite the fact he remains a novice over hurdles until the end of November, there is a feeling at Ditcheat that the progressive **McFABULOUS** could develop into a high-class staying hurdler. A half-brother to Grade 1 winning chaser Waiting Patiently, the Milan gelding won three of his four starts in bumper, including the Grade 2 championship event at Aintree in April last year. Sent hurdling, he didn't fire on his first couple of starts at Chepstow or Ascot, but was back to form with a bloodless win at Market Rasen (2m 4f) in February. His rider Harry Cobden commented: **"Things haven't gone right in his first two runs. He had a hurdle knocked out in front of him at Chepstow and he lost his confidence. I'm not sure what his problem was last time but he's done it very well today, he's got a big engine. We quickened up over the last two and he had loads of gears there. There's a lot more to come from him. I think he will be one of our smarter ones."** Granted an opening mark of 132, the six year old took full advantage by winning the rescheduled EBF Final at Kempton (2m 5f : Good/Soft) by a hard held six and a half lengths. He outclassed his seventeen opponents before sprinting clear on the run-in. Yet to race beyond two miles five, the Grade 2 Persian War Novices' Hurdle at Chepstow (9th October), a race Team Ditcheat have won seven times, is likely to be his first port of call before tackling open company.

The Stayers' Hurdle may be beyond him but it would be no surprise to see the unbeaten **GLYNN** develop into a Graded hurdler over two and a half miles plus this season. A winning Irish pointer when handled by Stuart Crawford, the Winged Love gelding changed hands for £85,000 at the Aintree April Sales last year before joining Nicky Henderson. Restricted to one outing over timber, he won by eleven lengths at Doncaster (2m 3f : Good/Soft) in January. His rider Jerry McGrath was impressed saying afterwards: **"I hope that looked as good as it felt. Glynn gave me an incredible feel. He settled very well, jumped and travelled - I wouldn't be scared to drop him down to two miles. We were expecting a good run and he delivered with flying colours. He isn't the biggest in the world but he's very well put together."** Entered at the Cheltenham Festival, his trainer commented the following month: **"He looked very good at Doncaster, but hasn't come back to that form since. He's had only one run and is only a baby. I'd like to find him a nice little race and finish on a good note and put him away for next year when he'll be a good horse."** Unfortunately, that never materialised and the six year old therefore lacks experience. He is potentially very good though and could be ideal for something like the Relkeel Hurdle at Cheltenham on New Year's Day. Nicky Henderson has won the Grade 2 event on three occasions (Zaynar (2009) & Oscar Whisky (2011 & 2012)).

Given the fact she is unbeaten over three miles (2 from 2) and her Festival form figures are 1F2, **BENIE DES DIEUX** is tailormade for the Stayers' Hurdle. However, the nine year old isn't an ante-post proposition with so many alternative options available to her next spring, including the newly formed mares' chase. A former French champion hurdle winner, she had four Grade 1 wins to her name and looked better than ever when winning the Grade 2 Galmoy Hurdle at Gowran Park (3m : Soft/Heavy) by twenty one lengths in January. **"Benie Des Dieux could be as good or better than any of the mares we've had. She is special. She is more of a three mile mare than a two mile mare,"** remarked Willie Mullins afterwards. Paul Townend (111112) added: **"I never got to ride Annie Power, so this is probably as good a mare as I've ridden. She's a star. She's all class. I was in my comfort zone everywhere. The thing that impressed me most was how quickly she put it to bed when we straightened up. She loves that slower ground."** Denied by half a length in the mares' hurdle at Cheltenham in March behind Honeysuckle, she allowed the winner first run on the hometurn and couldn't reel in Henry De Bromhead's unbeaten daughter of Sulamani. There are more big prizes to be won with the Rich and Susannah Ricci owned mare, especially over three miles.

INDEX

SELECTED HORSE = BOLD   *Owners' Enclosure & Talking Trainers = Italics*

178

179

ONE JUMP AHEAD UPDATES

I shall be producing **5 One Jump Ahead *Updates*** throughout the 2020/21 National Hunt season. Each *Update* comprises information about the horses in *One Jump Ahead*, **Ante-PostAdvice** (recommendations for the major races), **Big-Race Previews, News fromIreland** from one of the most informed Irish experts Declan Phelan and **Significant Sales. Please note, the *Updates* are ONLY AVAILABLE VIA EMAIL (Not Post).**

It is £6 per *Update* (except £10 for the Cheltenham Festival version) or £34 for ALL 5 via **EMAIL**.

Summary of the 2019/2020 *Updates*:

What The Clients Said:

*"As always your One Jump Ahead and Ahead On The Flat books are informative and packed with valuable information. They are a fantastic read and a great guide to the season. A must for all race fans and make an ideal present for racing enthusiasts. Both the books and Updates throughout the season are an excellent source of reference material. In addition, your 'Client Service' continues to be first class in your analysis and in identifying potential winners. This is testament to your expertise, knowledge and extensive contacts in the racing fraternity and all the hard work and research you put in for your clients."***I.G, Edinburgh**

"Thanks once again for an informative and profitable update the combination of One Jump Ahead and the Updates are not only informative and enjoyable but invaluable for National Hunt fans of all levels of punting interest." **R.J.**

"Excellent work as always; I'm a new customer to the Updates this year and have been very impressed with the quality of your work; your enthusiasm and effort is clear from your work." **D.G.**

"This edition must be the best ever as the winners just keep on coming from the start of the current National Hunt Season. You must be the scourge of the bookmaking fraternity and long may it continue. Well done." **A.H.**

"Thought to drop a note and say great work on the names to note from the November Update. I had two good bets on Epatante and Ribble Valley, and tragically missed Tavus! Brilliant work on pointing these out though." **W.H.**

"Well done with Epatante, glad to see you proved right about her. Perfect race for her today and a good shout from you well in advance - 5/1 in the antepost book, most rewarding." **S.H.**

"Wow what a superb ending to the November meeting. Thanks to Top 40 Prospects Israel Champ completed the meeting with a nice hefty profit. Thanks very much." **S.T.**

"Thanks for the Ferny Hollow ante post info all those months ago. Love it when a plan comes together!" **K.W.**

"Just a quick line to say well done with Ferny Hollow in the Cheltenham bumper - having 25/1 in the antepost book has made today a red letter day." **S.H.**

"Have to thank you Mark for highlighting Ferny Hollow. Backed him at 25s a couple of times back Sept/Oct 2019 and its certainly added big time to a wonderful two betting days at Cheltenham. Been with MH Publications for a good few years now and its info like this that highlights why you are so popular." **K.E.**

"What a day mate. Envoi Allen 10/1,Dame de Compagnie 10/1 & Ferny Hollow 25/1 absolutely brilliant THANK YOU." **F.R.**

"Just to say thanks for Ferny Hollow, took 20's a while ago, I owe you a drink." **J.M.**

"Great service mate, I was on Shishkin at 33/1. Keep up good work." **F.R.**

"I have to write congratulating you on the quality and depth of the Cheltenham preview. It's just a fabulous, objective, deeply researched work. I can't wait to subscribe to the flat packages too." **D.M.**

"Thank you for Epatante 20/1 after it won at Newbury earlier in the season. Great work." **A.S.**

"A brilliant ante post tip at 33-1 Mark. A fantastic start to the week. Thank you." **J.S.**

"Just a line to say a great big thank you, you are a genius, I have enjoyed watching the four days racing. Long may you enjoy the results from Cheltenham and the rest of the National hunt season." **B.J.**

"Well what can I say Mark brilliant week of incredible horse racing, and great results for the Update." **P.S.**

"Well Done and thank you, the Cheltenham Update gave great info and a nice winner today with Truckers Lodge taking the Midlands National." **S.S.**

"Thank you once again for Truckers Lodge, amazing information." **B.J.**

"Great information and the winners keep coming Truckers Lodge. Thank you and well done." **K.R.**

"Excellent Update Mark, capped off by Truckers Lodge in the Midlands National.....thank you!" **I.W.**

"Just a few words to thank you for a fantastic Cheltenham Festival. The Update was packed with top class news and information, one thing is for certain the aeroplane certainly flew. To cap it all off Truckers Lodge hacked up in the Midlands grand national on Saturday not a moment's sorry fantastic." **C.Y.**

"Just wanted to thank you for the superb information this NH season. When Shishkin won the Supreme my Festival was a profitable one and the following results just added to that success, then you followed that up with Truckers Lodge in the Midlands National. Thanks again." **D.S.**

"The Cheltenham bulletin was really the best ever. It made for a most enjoyable 4 days. And the jam on the top was Truckers on Saturday; Thank you for your hard work." **C.P.**

"Just wanted to send a big thank you for all the work you have done over the Jumps Season, there were some fabulous highlights and some great recommendations by yourself." **S.P.**

"I look forward to next year's OJA, I was just flicking through this year's edition and your Top 40 Prospects worked out very well once again (I know you don't need me to tell you) and the book as a whole contributed enormously to me having a very successful Cheltenham Festival with my first real crack at taking ante-post seriously. For that I can't thank you enough." **M.H.**

"I bought One Jump Ahead recently and think it is outstanding work. Some of us do not just judge on results but on quality of insight and yours is first class!" **D.M.**

The PADDY POWER MEETING 2019

WINNERS: JATILUWIH (Advised @ 11/2)

Quote: *"**JATILUWIH** was a winner over fences in France before joining Philip Hobbs earlier this year. The five year old is unbeaten in four races over timber since arriving at Minehead and makes his handicap debut here off 137. He beat subsequent winners Falco Blitz (likely to reoppose here) and Espoir De Romay on his British debut at Ludlow in March before following up at Chepstow in April. Returning to action at Sedgefield in October, he streaked clear to win by thirteen lengths under his owner/jockey David Maxwell. He then made it four out of four when conceding fifteen pounds to West Cork (runner-up again since) and Young Bull (won subsequently) before registering a five lengths victory at Wetherby a few weeks later. The Linda's Lad gelding handles any ground and his opening mark may underestimate him."* **ADVISED @ 11/2 WON @ 11/4**

Plus: **BATTLE OF WILLS (100/30),BUZZ (13/8, 1/2), EPATANTE (3/1, 2/1, 2/1),GOSHEN (3 wins), HOMER (100/30), LION TOWER (100/30, 5/4), NEVER DO NOTHING (2/1), RIBBLE VALLEY (13/8), TAVUS (9/2 & 2/1), WOLF PRINCE (9/10, 9/10), ZOFFEE (10/11)**

Quote: *"It will be interesting to see what Gordon Elliott can achieve with **BATTLE OF WILLS** having been acquired for 52,000gns at the Newmarket Horses in Training Sale last month. A three year old son of Lawman, he won three of his eleven races on the Flat for James Tate and is rated 87. A winner over a mile as a two year old, he scored over ten and twelve furlongs at Nottingham and Ripon (both on good ground) respectively earlier this year. Runner-up on good to soft at the latter venue behind the well handicapped Faylaq in June, he disappointed on his final two starts but is likely to improve for his new handler."* **WON on his hurdles debut at Naas (26/1) @ 100/30**

Quote: *"I was hoping Nicky Henderson would elect to run **EPATANTE** in the Greatwood Hurdle at Cheltenham on Sunday but he relies on another couple of J.P.McManus owned mares, namely Countister and Dame De Compagnie. The head of Seven Barrows issued an encouraging report though about the daughter of No Risk At All earlier this month saying: **"This lovely looker didn't show up at Cheltenham but might have been affected by the pre-Festival flu jabs and has grown and strengthened enormously. Training nicely and**

184

will be aimed at smart handicap hurdles." Featured in last season's Top 40 Prospects, the ex-French trained filly looked a class act when winning at Kempton and Exeter before underperforming in the mares' novices' hurdle at the Festival. Sent off 15/8 favourite, she could only finish ninth having made a mistake at halfway. Officially rated 137, I will be amazed if the five year old doesn't prove considerably better than that. Henderson has won the **Gerry Feilden Hurdle at Newbury (30th November)** *on six occasions and Epatante looks tailormade for the 0-155 two miles event. A flat track may always bring out the best in her."* **WON at the Gerry Feilden Hurdle at Newbury by 6 lengths** @ **3/1**

Quote: *"That comment may also apply to the progressive* **GOSHEN**, *who is set to embark on a National Hunt career following three wins on the Flat in 2019. Gary Moore's Authorized gelding is bred for jumping being a half-brother to Willie Mullins' Listed hurdles winner Elimay. Having shown very little in three starts over a mile and nine furlongs as a juvenile last year, he has proved a different proposition since stepped up to middle distances this term. A twelve lengths winner on his handicap debut at Brighton (1m 4f : Good) in June off 64, he followed up by nine lengths under a six pounds penalty at Sandown (1m 6f : Soft) a week later. Given a break, he returned from an absence of 138 days to win by seven lengths at Nottingham (1m 6f : Soft) in late October off 80 (raised eight pounds since). Despite the fact Goshen still looked green at Colwick Park, he galloped his opponents into submission looking a tremendous staying prospect in the process. Purchased with hurdling in mind, one would expect him to make his jumping bow later this month (entered at Fontwell on Sunday (1.30))."* **WON his first three races over hurdles and was clear when falling at the last in the Triumph Hurdle at the Cheltenham Festival.**

Quote: *"John McConnell has made a good impression in recent seasons sending out 11 winners in Ireland this season and he was also responsible for 7 winners from only 19 runners in the UK last winter. Along with owner Derek Kierans, the pair were active at the Newmarket Autumn Sales.* **NEVER DO NOTHING** *was the most expensive having been purchased for 135,000gns. A three year old by Casamento, he won three of his ten starts on the Flat for Andrew Balding and is rated 91. Two of those wins were gained over a mile as a two year old but he also won over twelve furlongs at Goodwood in June. Placed at Ascot on his final two outings, he has only raced on good or faster ground and could be the ideal type for a juvenile hurdle at Musselburgh."* **WON at Musselburgh on his hurdles debut (1/1) by five and a half lengths** @ **2/1**

Quote: *"As discussed earlier, I spoke to Nicky Richards at Carlisle on Monday and the Greystoke based handler added that his potentially high-class novice hurdler* **RIBBLE VALLEY** *is likely to head to Wetherby towards the end of the month (27th November) for another two miles novices' hurdle under a penalty. The Westerner gelding, who won two of his three bumpers last season, made a smooth start his hurdles career when scooting nine lengths clear at Hexham last week. His connections felt he didn't particularly enjoy the heavy ground but was too good for his nine rivals in any case."* **WON at Wetherby by 11 lengths** @ **13/8**

Quote: *"Jedd O'Keeffe has his jumpers in fine fettle with stable star Sam Spinner making it two out of two over fences at Wetherby recently. Micky Hammond's former assistant has teamed up with owners Quantum during the last twelve months and they have invested heavily at the sales. They were at it again at the Tattersalls Horses in Training Sale at Newmarket last month purchasing Kiefer for 210,000gns and* **TAVUS**. *The latter was acquired for 105,000gns and a juvenile hurdle campaign has been mooted. A progressive type on the Flat for Roger Charlton,* the Pour Moi gelding has won three of his last four starts with his official rating climbing from 60 to 78. Successful at Newbury, Ffos Las and Leicester over trips ranging from twelve to fourteen furlongs, he handles both good and heavy ground. He could be a useful recruit to the northern jumping scene." **WON on his hurdles debut at Newcastle (30/11) @ 9/2**

TALKING TRAINERS: BRIAN ELLISON: WINNERS: BARON DE MIDLETON (6/1 & 4/1), DEFINITLY RED (Evens), KEARNEY HILL (20/1, 2/1), SAM'S ADVENTURE (6/1), SNOOKERED (15/8, 6/5), THE DANCING POET (9/4), THE KING OF MAY (9/2), TUPELO MISSISSIPPI (5/2, 4/1)

Quote: **THE DANCING POET**: *"A half-brother to Dance And Dance, who was runner-up in the Royal Hunt Cup. A ten furlongs winner at Chelmsford in August for Ed Vaughan, we bought him at the Newmarket Horses in Training last month with a view to sending him hurdling. We have schooled him and his jumping has been very good. All being well, he will be running in a juvenile hurdle in December."* **WON on his hurdles debut at Catterick (1/1) @ 9/4**

Quote: **THE KING OF MAY**: "He is a very nice horse who won over hurdles in France before we bought him. A decent juvenile hurdler a couple of seasons ago, he missed the whole of the last campaign but returned from a lengthy absence to win on his chasing debut at Carlisle. He has always worked well and jumps for fun. Therefore his victory wasn't a surprise and it looked a strong race, too. While he will stay further, if necessary, he has a lot of speed so we will keep him to two miles for the time being. The handicapper raised him six pounds for his win at Carlisle but I still think he is well handicapped off 131. I think he is a very good horse." **WON at Sedgefield (26/1) @ 9/2**

Quote: **TUPELO MISSISSIPPI:** "A lovely big horse who was beaten a head in his only Irish point for Colin Bowe. We bought him at the Cheltenham May Sale and his owner Phil Martin has told us to take our time with him. He is a grand horse who is working nicely at home and the plan is to start him off in a bumper in the New Year. Only four, I think he is a very nice horse for the future." **WON 2 bumpers at Newcastle @ 5/2 & 4/1**

CHRISTMAS SPECIAL 2019

CHRISTMAS HURDLE: EPATANTE (Advised @ 9/2) WON @ 2/1
WELSH NATIONAL: POTTERS CORNER (Advised @ 9/1) WON @ 8/1

Quote: *"**EPATANTE** is one of three entries trained by Nicky Henderson with the Seven Barrows outfit seeking their eighth win in the race. The daughter of No Risk At All won two of her three APQS Flat races in France, including a Grade 1 event at St-Cloud. Twice a winner over hurdles for Henderson last season, she flopped in the mares' novice hurdle at the Cheltenham Festival only finishing ninth. Given a break (261 days), she was back to her best with a smooth six lengths win in the Gerry Feilden Hurdle at Newbury last month beating a couple of her stablemates off a mark of 137. Raised thirteen pounds since, this represents a big step up in class but the flat track will be ideal (1 from 1 at Kempton) and the five year old remains unexposed. Kribensis (1988), Fidway (1990) and Gran Alba (1991) completed the Gerry Feilden/Christmas Hurdle double in the same season. Feathard Lady (2005) and Verdana Blue (2018) were the last two mares to win this."* **Advised @ 9/2 – WON by 5 lengths @ 2/1**

Quote: *"**POTTERS CORNER** was third in a Grade 2 bumper at Aintree when trained by Paul Morgan in April 2015 (runner-up in an Irish point prior to that). The Indian Danehill gelding has won 3 of his 10 races since joining Christian Williams enjoying his finest hour last spring. The nine year old beat the mare Ms Parfois by three lengths in the Midlands National at Uttoxeter off a mark of 135 (now rated 145). Kept over hurdles this term, he edged out Remastered by a neck at Chepstow this month off 129. Indeed, he has impressive form figures at the track 1131 and revels in heavy/soft ground. His stable have been relatively quiet this campaign with only a handful of winners since July (no winners from 16 runners in the last 14 days). Conditional jockey Jack Tudor rode him last time and he is set to take off seven pounds here, which could be crucial in such gruelling conditions. Best Price: 9/1 (Bet365, Skybet, William Hill)."* **Advised @ 9/1 – WON @ 8/1**

The IRISH ANGLE by Declan PHELAN: WINNERS: BOB OLINGER (6/4), COBBLER'S WAY (9/2), FAROUK D'ALENE (4/6, 7/4), FULLY CHARGED (11/8), OPPOSITES ATTRACT (15/8, 9/4),

Quote: *"**BOB OLINGER**(Sholokhov) privately acquired from the Pat Doyle yard following a smooth debut win at Turtulla, the pointing track beside the town of Thurles: he will be trained by Henry de Bromhead."* **WON by 10 lengths on his Rules debut at Gowran Park (7/3)**

Quote: *"On Sunday29th at Leopardstown it could be profitable to keep on the right side of ex-pointer **COBBLERS WAY** in the 2m 4f maiden hurdle (12.45): over the years this race has placed a premium on stamina and this son of Oscar is blessed in that department: a bumper winner last Christmas and a proper winter horse, he finished a fine second on his hurdles debut at Navan (to Andy Dufresne): although likely to encounter talented rivals representing Mullins/Elliott in this race, I gather he has been trained with this race in mind and will give a good account of himself: ideally he requires this race to be run at a real good consistent gallop and, if so, he may add to the fine record his handler Henry de Bromhead has had in previous renewals of this maiden hurdle."* **WON @ 9/2**

Quote: *"One horse who will be suited by the winter conditions at Limerick is **FULLY CHARGED**: he is expected to line up in the auction maiden hurdle at Limerick on the 28th (1.05): this grey has his quirks but can gallop as he proved at Castletown in April in the pointing code. On his track debut last month at Punchestown, he ran an excellent second to Alpine Cobra (conceding 5lbs). Always prominent, he ran a most creditable race, and the form has been franked as the winner has since bagged second in a Graded novice hurdle. Alfa Mix, the year younger brother to Fully Charged, won a valuable handicap recently at Navan, and his sibling can reward punters this yuletide. This is another race in the auction series of maiden hurdles and consequently it is a contest devoid of your classier sort from the Mullins/Elliott squads. Fully Charged will be prominent from the start and this grey gelding should be capable of running his rivals into the ground and post a cosy win at the 2m 5f trip."* **WON by 22 lengths @ 11/8**

Quote: *"On the 26th of December, DownRoyal kick off their card with a 2m 4f maiden hurdle at 12.00: Column Of Fire and Opposites Attract finished strongly and almost in unison when second and third to Longhouse Poet at Navan and look like winners in waiting for a middle distance maiden hurdle such as this one. In that Navan event they raced off level weights: this time Column Of Fire shoulders a chunky eight pounds penalty for his bumper success and therefore the scales are certainly tipped in favour of the maiden **OPPOSITES ATTRACT**."* **WON by 8 lengths @ 15/8**

WINNERS: BOB AND CO (EVENS, EVENS), KEEP WONDERING (3/1), SHISHKIN (7/4, 1/2, 6/1), WISHING AND HOPING (13/8, 1/2)

Quote: *"Unfortunately, **SHISHKIN** got no further than the second on his first try over hurdles at Newbury this week. However, Nicky Henderson's five year old was strongly fancied and is viewed as one of, if not the best, novice hurdle prospect at Seven Barrows. The winning pointer lacks experience having reportedly been slow to come to hand but, provided he has another couple of runs between now and March and wins handsomely, the Supreme is his most likely port of call in March. Available at 40/1 with Bet365, the Sholokhov gelding is generally 25/1."* **Advised @ 40/1, he won the Sky Bet Supreme Novices' Hurdle @ 6/1**

Quote: *"**KEEP WONDERING** is one of Declan Phelan's Irish Pointers on page 165 of One Jump Ahead and I feel it is only a matter of time before he breaks his duck under Rules. The Scorpion gelding was beaten less than four lengths by Mossy Fen (fourth in a Grade 2 since and rated 132) on his hurdles debut at Aintree (2m 4f) in November (third has won since). Stepping up to two miles seven at Haydock on his next outing, he was given an ordinary ride, hitting the front too soon and tiring on the run-in. Beaten fifteen lengths by Bally Conor, that doesn't do his performance justice because he went through the race like the best horse but got racing much too early. Unfortunately, the rider that day is retained by the owners so any hope of Richard Johnson or Tom O'Brien taking over in the saddle next time is highly unlikely. However, the five year old looks on a fair mark off 120 and Philip Hobbs invariably runs his novices in handicaps, if he feels they are ahead of the assessor. I am therefore hoping Keep Wondering will go down that route next time."* **WON by 10 lengths at Ffos Las (30/1) @ 3/1**

Quote: *"The other staying novice who has impressed this winter and is also unbeaten over hurdles is another former Irish pointer **FURY ROAD**. Featured in the Top 40 Prospects last season, the Stowaway gelding was an eighteen lengths winner on his reappearance at Down Royal (2m 6f) before beating three opponents by upwards of ten lengths in the Grade 3 Monksfield Novice Hurdle at Navan late last month. Gordon Elliott has entered him in the Grade 2 Land Rover Novice Hurdle at Limerick on Friday (27th December), although he will carry a penalty if lining up. That two miles seven event has produced Faugheen, Martello Tower, Penhill and Weapon's Amnesty (all subsequent Festival winners) in recent years – the last three all went on to win the Albert Bartlett NH at Cheltenham. Gigginstown House Stud have won the three miler twice in the past (Weapon's Amnesty (2009) & Very Wood (2014)) and Fury Road could have a big say in the 2020 version. The five year old is top priced 16/1 (Bet365, Paddy Power)."* **ADVISED @ 16/1 for the Albert Bartlett NH – Beaten a neck in 3rd @ 5/1**

FRENCH REVOLUTION – Part II: WINNERS: FLOUEUR (4/1), SOLO (6/4)

Quote: **FLOUEUR**: *"The triple Grand National winning trainer has also taken charge of this potentially exciting novice hurdler. By the Japanese bred stallion Legolas, he began his career with Liz Doyle in Ireland and finished over thirteen lengths third behind Glens Finale and Egality Mans in a bumper at Sligo in late April. He then found himself in France being trained by Mikael Mescam (former trainer of Mick Pastor who is now with Paul Nicholls) and was a six lengths winner on his hurdles debut at Nantes (2m 1f) in early October. The four year old then followed up by winning at Auteuil less than a month later. A nine lengths winner, he beat the Munir/Souede owned Raffles Classic (third over fences since)."* **WON on his Irish debut at Navan (18/1) @ 4/1**

Quote: **SOLO**: *"That comment also applies to this twice raced three year old who has been bought by Johnny de La Hey, of Cyrname fame, and has joined Paul Nicholls. Under the guidance of Guillaume Macaire, the Kapgarde gelding finished three lengths second on his hurdles debut at Auteuil (2m 2f : Very Soft) in October behind Stratagem (see below). He returned to the same venue four weeks later (2m 1f : Heavy) and made no mistake winning by fifteen lengths. Making all under Adrien Fouchet, he jumped well and galloped his rivals into submission. He could develop into a Triumph Hurdle candidate."* **WON the Grade 2 Adonis Hurdle at Kempton (22/2) by 13 lengths on his UK debut @ 6/4**

TALKING TRAINERS: **EVAN WILLIAMS**: WINNERS: **COCONUT SPLASH (4/6), FADO DES BROSSES (11/8), SUPREME ESCAPE (11/4)**

Quote: **SUPREME ESCAPE**: *"Another we purchased at the Cheltenham April Sale having won an Irish point, he is a strong chasing type who has had three runs over hurdles for us. I thought he ran well last time when finishing fourth at Chepstow. The handicapper has left him alone on 106 and he has shown enough to suggest he can win races this season over hurdles before going over fences in time. He wants a trip."* **WON at Doncaster (24/1) over three miles @ 11/4**

FEBRUARY 2020

BETFAIR HURDLE: **CIEL DE NEIGE (Advised @ 16/1 – 2nd beaten three parts of a length @ 13/2**

Quote: *"**CIEL DE NEIGE** could prove to be Mullins' main challenger. Trained in France by Guy Cherel, the five year old has yet to win in six races over hurdles but has only had three runs for his current yard. Fourth at Auteuil behind Pic D'Orhy, he was beaten less than four lengths when third in the Fred Winter Juvenile Hurdle at Cheltenham in March on his first run for Mullins. Rated 132 on that occasion, he was in receipt of half a stone from the winner Band of Outlaws. Back in action at Fairyhouse in December, he stayed on well in fourth behind stablemates Janidil and Buildmeupbuttercup. The Authorized gelding was then unfortunate not to shed his maiden tag at Limerick over Christmas. Beaten a head by Argumental (fourth since), Donal McInerney's mount endured traffic problems at a crucial stage and nearly ran the wrong side of a rail. Despite running on well, he found the winning post coming too soon. Rated 135, he has plenty more to offer and is capable of winning a handicap of this nature. Owner J.P.McManus and Mullins were responsible for Bleu Et Rouge who finished second to Kalashnikov in this in 2018. Novices have won 8 of the last 10 renewals. Best Price: 16/1 (BetVictor, Coral, Ladbrokes, Paddy Power, William Hill)"* **Advised @ 16/1 – 2nd at 13/2**

CHELTENHAM FESTIVAL HANDICAPS PREVIEW: SAINT ROI – WON the County Hurdle @ 11/2

Quote: *"It will be interesting to see if Ireland's champion trainer enters **SAINT ROI** who was an easy winner at Tramore on New Year's Day. Another gelded son of Coastal Path, he has only raced three times over hurdles and has yet to be allocated a rating. Previously trained in France by Guy Cherel, he finished third in a Listed hurdle at Auteuil in September 2018 before being purchased by J.P.McManus. Absent for 448 days, the five year old was bitterly disappointing* on his first run for his new connections when only fifth in a two miles three maiden hurdle at Clonmel in early December having been sent off 1/3 favourite. However, it was a different story last time as he ran out a decisive nine lengths winner having taken up the running soon after the second last. Subsequent Grade 1 winning novice chaser Notebook won the same two miles maiden hurdle twelve months earlier. Mullins commented afterwards: *"He didn't jump the last day and I said to Paul (Townend) to have him nicely warmed up before the race. We worked on him since and it must have worked as he jumped very well. We won't aim too high and could look for a rated novice or something like that. He could be a good novice by the time Punchestown comes around and will jump a fence in time."* So many of Mullins' horses have improved markedly from their seasonal returns and Saint Roi is no different. The Closutton outfit have run the likes of Al Boum Photo, Dolcita and Laurina at Tramore in recent years and they may have sent another decent one there last month. He may be kept to novice company but, if granted a suitable mark, Mullins will be keen to exploit it. Despite winning over the minimum trip last time, he is bred to stay much further coming from the family of a Grade 1 winner in France over three miles seven."* **WON the County Hurdle by four and a half lengths off a mark of 137 @ 11/2**

WINNER: FIRST ACCOUNT (6/5, 4/5)

Quote: *"FIRST ACCOUNT is featured on page 152 of One Jump Ahead in the Handicap Snips section. The six year old has only raced once this season finishing runner-up at Hexham on his chasing debut in November. The Malinas gelding looked all set for victory approaching the last but paid for an over exuberant ride and was headed on the run-in by Lucinda Russell's Saint Freule. Absent since, the Malinas gelding has been transferred to Keith Dalgleish's yard and is definitely handicapped to win races over fences (rated 117) for his new handler. The former pointer will benefit from better ground in the remaining weeks of the season and is one to look out for in a 0-120 handicap chase over two or two and a half miles."* **WON twice @ 6/5 & 4/5**

The CHELTENHAM FESTIVAL 2020

7 WINNERS: SHISHKIN (6/1), ENVOI ALLEN (Advised @ 5/4), DAME DE COMPAGNIE (Advised @ 10/1), FERNY HOLLOW (Advised @ 12/1), SAMCRO (Advised @ 7/1), SAINT ROI (Advised @ 20/1), AL BOUM PHOTO (Advised @ 4/1)

Quote: *"SHISHKIN (Top 40) is another former Irish pointer having won one of his two starts for Virginia Considine. Purchased on behalf of owner Joe Donnelly for £170,000, he was a smooth eight lengths winner of a Kempton bumper for Nicky Henderson last March. An early casualty (fell at the second) on his hurdles debut at Newbury in December, he made amends in no uncertain terms at the same venue the following month with an easy eleven lengths success. Stepped up to two miles three in the Listed Sidney Banks Memorial NH at Huntingdon last month, he barely came off the bridle to beat the 139 rated Shan Blue by the same margin. The Seven Barrows team have won this three times (River Ceiriog (1986), Flown (1992) and Altior (2016) and this Sholokhov gelding looks top-class."* **WON the Sky Bet Supreme Novices' Hurdle @ 6/1**

Quote: *"DAME DE COMPAGNIE is also entered in the Martin Pipe Conditional Jockeys' Handicap on Friday. A French bumper winner and runner-up over hurdles at Auteuil when* trained by Adrien Lacombe, she has won 3 of her 7 races over hurdles in total. Rated 140, she won a Listed mares' novice hurdle over C&D in April 2018 before being off the track for 577 days. Returning to action in the Greatwood Hurdle at Cheltenham in November, she stayed on well in fifth behind Harambe off 132. Stepped up in distance, Nicky Henderson's mare won a handicap hurdle by four and a half lengths over C&D in December. Upped ten pounds since, she has purposely been kept fresh (90 days) and bids to become the first mare to win this. Her record at the track is 5151 with both wins gained on the New course and her form figures over 2m 3f/2m 4f are 211." **Advised @ 10/1, WON the Coral Cup @ 5/1**

Quote: *"FERNY HOLLOW (Top 40) was a fifteen lengths winner of his only point-to-point for Colin Bowe in February last year. Purchased soon afterwards for £300,000, the five year old has only won one of his three starts in bumpers since joining Willie Mullins. Too keen at both Fairyhouse and Leopardstown, the five year old finished runner-up behind Joseph O'Brien trained opponents on each occasion, namely Eric Bloodaxe and Forged In Fire respectively. Fitted with a hood for the first time at Fairyhouse last month, he was held up and settled better under Patrick Mullins and won handsomely. A four and a quarter lengths scorer from On Eagles Wings, it is a relatively quick turnaround (18 days) but his chance will depend on how he settles. With Patrick Mullins expected to partner the favourite Appreciate It, there must be every chance Paul Townend will partner him for the first time in public. His trainer is looking for his tenth win in the race and there is no doubt this gelded son of Westerner has the ability to go close."* **Advised @ 12/1 WON the Grade 1 bumper @ 11/1**

Quote: *"SAMCRO has been much maligned during the last season and a half having only won one of his last seven starts. A top-class novice hurdler a couple of years ago, he won two Grade 1 events, including the Ballymore NH at this meeting. Gordon Elliott could never get him right last winter as he pursued a Champion Hurdle campaign. Sent chasing in the Autumn, he was a seventeen lengths winner at Down Royal (wore a tongue tie) in November. Going well and virtually upsides Fakir D'Oudairies when crashing out at the second last in the Grade 1 Drinmore NC at Fairyhouse next time, he then produced a tame effort last time. Beaten ten lengths by Faugheen at Limerick on Boxing Day, the eight year old found little off the bridle from the second last. Found to have scoped badly afterwards, he has had a wind operation since. His record at Grade 1 level is 11F25F2. Gordon Elliott won this a couple of years ago with Shattered Love but no eight year old has every landed the prize. On his day, the Germany gelding is top-class and it wouldn't be the biggest shock if he bounced back, especially if Davy Russell rides him for the first time in public."* **Advised @ 7/1 WON the Marsh Novices' Chase @ 4/1**

Quote: *"SAINT ROI is included on page 149 of One Jump Ahead and there is every reason to believe the ex-French gelding will prove considerably better than his opening mark of 137. Runner-up on the Flat and placed over hurdles at Auteuil (Listed) when handled by Guy Cherel, the five year old has only had a couple of runs for J.P.McManus and Willie Mullins. Bitterly disappointing on his Irish debut at Clonmel (2m 3f) in December finishing a remote fifth, the Coastal Path gelding was sent off 1/3 favourite. However, he showed his true worth next time when dropped back to two miles at Tramore on New Year's Day. In the same maiden hurdle in which Notebook had defeated Janidil twelve months earlier, he ran out an emphatic nine lengths winner from Arcadian Sunrise (won twice since). His trainer commented afterwards: "He could be a good novice by the time Punchestown comes around." He has plenty more to offer."* **Advised @ 20/1 WON the County Hurdle @ 11/2**

Quote: *"**AL BOUM PHOTO** will become the first horse since Best Mate in 2004 to win successive Cheltenham Gold Cups. The Buck's Boum gelding has won 5 of his 10 races over fences, including his two and a half lengths victory in the race last year. Runner-up behind Kemboy at the Punchestown Festival next time, he warmed up for this in the same Grade 3 chase at Tramore on New Year's Day which he won last season. A six lengths winner, the time was good and the runner-up Acapella Bourgeois has won the Grade 3 Bobbyjo Chase by fifteen lengths since. Still relatively unexposed over three miles plus (5FR12), he gets on well with Paul Townend (151R121) and has purposely been kept fresh since (72 days off). A faller in the RSA Chase a couple of years ago, he warrants his place at the head of the market."* **Advised @ 4/1 WON the Cheltenham Gold Cup @ 100/30**

FESTIVAL PREVIEW ROUND-UPS:

KIM BAILEY: Quote: *"**IMPERIAL AURA** (novices' handicap chase) has done all his preparation with Vinndication and looks fantastic. Runner-up at Cheltenham in January, I think he is better than he showed that day because we had to get a third run into him to qualify for this. He has course experience and goes there a worthy favourite."* **WON @ 4/1**

ANTHONY BROMLEY: Quote*:* *"**CONCERTISTA** (Mares' Novice Hurdle): "Beaten a short head by one of her stablemates in the Mares' Novices' Hurdle last year, she will attempt to go one better on Thursday. Third in a competitive handicap hurdle at Leopardstown last time, she appreciated the drier ground on that occasion. We are hoping conditions will dry out at Cheltenham between now and then."* **WON @ 9/2**

PAUL CARBERRY: Quote: *"The third and final preview I attended was in the shadows of Fir Park, the home of Motherwell Football Club, on Friday. Over 150 flocked into the Club 100 to listen to the views of **PAUL CARBERRY**, Ian Robinson (owner of Gold Cup winner Imperial Commander) and James Griffin (assistant trainer). Carberry, who rode 14 Festival winners, was very keen on **AL BOUM PHOTO** for the Gold Cup having watched him school after racing at Navan last Tuesday. His nap of the meeting is **SAMCRO** in the Marsh Novices' Chase on Thursday. "I rode Samcro in a schooling race before he made his chasing debut at Down Royal in the Autumn. He worked with Battleoverdoyen and Delta Work and beat them by twenty lengths. He felt like an aeroplane. I am hoping Keith (Donoghue) rides him on Thursday because he has done all the work on him. He bled at Limerick last time but, if Gordon (Elliott) can get him back to his best, there is nothing in that field which will be able to live with him."*

RICH RICCI: The HORSE I AM MOST LOOKING FORWARD TO: **MIN. WON the Ryanair Chase @ 2/1**

TALKING TRAINERS: **PAUL NICHOLLS: WINNER: POLITOLOGUE (6/1)**

Quote: **POLITOLOGUE** (Queen Mother Champion Chase (Wednesday)): *"I have backed him at 33/1 for the Champion Chase because I think he is a massive price. He ran an awesome race in it last year finishing second less than two lengths behind Altior. Runner-up behind Defi Du Seuil on his reappearance in the Shloer Chase at Cheltenham in November, he was conceding three pounds to the winner. He then bled when running below par in the Tingle Creek at Sandown and we have purposely kept him fresh since. The softer the ground, the better his chance and, granted such conditions, I am very hopeful he will finish in the first three. He had a racecourse gallop at Wincanton last Thursday and did a fantastic piece of work. He* *is very fit and at his best when fresh, and the fact Un De Sceaux isn't in the line up is a major plus because he can bowl along in front and try and stretch them."* **WON @ 6/1**

DATES FOR THE DIARY:

Saturday 14ᵗʰ March – UTTOXETER – 3.35 Midlands Grand National
"Paul Nicholls has never won the four and a quarter miles event but he plans to run his Welsh National runner-up TRUCKERS LODGE. The eight year old has only raced four times over fences and remains unexposed. Rated 141, the Westerner gelding won at Chepstow in late October before finishing a length and three quarters runner-up at the same track over Christmas off 139. Only a couple of pounds higher, the champion trainer intended running the former Tom George inmate in the Grand National Trial at Haydock in February but he incurred a cut and was forced to miss out. His record on heavy ground is 212 and it is hoped top weight De Rasher Counter stands his ground, otherwise the weights will rise by at least seven pounds. He is currently available at 10/1 with Coral & Ladbrokes." **Advised @ 10/1 WON the Midlands National by 18 lengths @ 6/1**

Tuesday 17ᵗʰ March – DOWN ROYAL
"Dermot McLoughlin is reportedly targeting the mares' bumper at the Northern Ireland track on St Patrick's day with the once raced DELVINO. A five year old by Dylan Thomas, she is a half-sister to Avellino who won three times for the same stable. She shaped with plenty of promise when runner-up behind the more experienced Julies Stowaway, who had finished second twice at Navan and Limerick, with the highly regarded Ballyadam in third. A reproduction of that run will make her difficult to beat." **WON @ 4/5**

It is £6 per Update (except £10 for the Cheltenham Festival version) or £34 for ALL 5 via EMAIL.

Don't forget to read my Diary @
www.mhpublications.co.uk

ONE JUMP AHEAD UPDATES 2020/2021 ORDER FORM (EMAIL ONLY)

AVAILABLE AT £6.00 EACH (£10 Cheltenham) OR £34 FOR ALL 5

- **CHELTENHAM PADDY POWER MEETING 2020**
  (Will be emailed on Thursday 12th November 2020)

- **CHRISTMAS SPECIAL 2020**
  (Will be emailed on Sunday 20th December 2020)

- **FEBRUARY 2021**

- **MARCH 2021 - CHELTENHAM FESTIVAL PREVIEW**
  (Will be emailed on the Sunday before the Festival)

- **APRIL 2021 – AINTREE PREVIEW**
  (Will be emailed on the Tuesday before the Meeting)

Total Cheque / Postal Order value £............ made payable to MARK HOWARD PUBLICATIONS Ltd. Post your order to: MARK HOWARD PUBLICATIONS. 69 FAIRGARTH DRIVE, KIRKBY LONSDALE, CARNFORTH, LANCASHIRE. LA6 2FB.

NAME: ....

ADDRESS: ....

....

....POST CODE: ....

Email Address: ....

If you have not received your *UPDATE* via email 24 hours before the meeting starts, please contact us immediately.

Available to order via **www.mhpublications.co.uk**